Apoca

Movies

Apocalypse Movies

End of the World Cinema

Kim Newman

 St. Martin's Griffin New York

Author's Note

Thanks to *Chambers Twentieth Century Dictionary*, I am well aware of the specific meanings of the terms 'millennium' ('a thousand years: a thousandth anniversary, millenary; the thousand years after the second coming of Christ; [usually ironical] a coming golden age'), 'Judgement Day' ('a day of final judgement on mankind'), 'Apocalypse' ('the last book of the New Testament, otherwise the Revelation of St. John; any book purporting to reveal the future or last things; a revelation or disclosure'), 'Armageddon' ('the great symbolical battlefield of the Apocalypse, scene of the final struggle between the powers of good and evil; a great war or battle of nations; suggested by the famous battlefield of Megiddo, in the plain of Esdraelon') and 'holocaust' ('a sacrifice in which the whole of the victim was burnt; a huge slaughter or destruction of life'), and have tried to be careful in my use of them. The circumstances of the twentieth century have required a constant shift in language and all of these have been co-opted to signify world-ending or -changing catastrophes, of mankind's own making or otherwise. Similar enthusiasm has been demonstrated in the deployment of buzz-adjectives like 'atomic', 'nuclear', 'thermo-nuclear' or even 'nucular'. As Terry Southern realised, the language of Cold War brinkmanship is subtle, blunt, comical and chilling at the same time. Due care and attention have been exercised.

Acknowledgements

As usual, this book would not have been possible without discussion, books and videotapes, ideas, inspiration and comfort provided by a great many people. Thanks are due to: David Barraclough, Anne Billson, Mike Brecher, Randy Broecker, John Brosnan, Eugene Byrne, Pat Cadigan, Gillian Christie, Jeremy Clarke, Meg Davis, The Flying Pig Bookshop, Barry Forshaw, Neil Gaiman, Mick Hamer, Phil Hardy, Antony Harwood, Richard Holliss, Julia Horstmann, David Howe, Stefan Jaworzyn, Alan Jones, Rodney Jones, Stephen Jones, Bob Kelly, Laurence Lerner, Tim Lucas, Norman Mackenzie, Paul McAuley, Maura McHugh, Silja Muller, Adam Newell, Bryan and Julia Newman, Sasha and Jerome Newman, Peter Nicholls, Simon Oliver, Marcelle Perks, Kay Rowley, David J. Schow, Millie Simpson, Jason Slater, Tom Tunney, Katy Wild.

—Kim Newman, December 1998

Published by arrangement with Titan Publishing Group Ltd., 144 Southwark Street, London SE1 0UP, England.

Library of Congress Cataloging-in-Publication Data

Newman, Kim.
  [Millennium movies]
  Apocalypse movies : end of the world cinema / Kim Newman.
    p. cm.
  Includes bibliographical references and index.
  ISBN 0-312-25369-9
  1. Science fiction films—History and criticism. 2. Nuclear warfare in motion
  pictures. 3. Apocalypse in motion pictures. I. Title.
PN1995.9.S26 N49 2000
791.43'658—dc21

                                   99-54618
                                       CIP

First published in Great Britain under the title *Millennium Movies: End of the World Cinema* by Titan Books

First St. Martin's Griffin Edition: February 2000

10 9 8 7 6 5 4 3 2 1

For Marcelle

Certain sombre facts emerge solid, inexorable, like the shapes of mountains from drifting mist. It is established that henceforward whole populations will take part in war, all doing their utmost, all subjected to the fury of the enemy. It is established that nations who believe that their life is at stake will not be restrained from using any means to secure their existence. *It is probable — nay, certain — that among the means which will next time be at their disposal will be agencies and processes of destruction wholesale, unlimited, and, perhaps, once launched, uncontrollable.*

Winston Churchill, 1924, 'Shall We Commit Suicide?'

Contents

Foreword: Beginning with the End

The end of the world? No big deal. By the time I was ten, I'd been through it dozens of times.

Giant, radioactive, skyscraper-eating monsters were not the problem. Goo-faced nuclear mutants were not the problem. The real evil, it seemed to me, even at age ten, was politics — the cause of all those Final Conflicts. In movie after movie, politics and politicians were the real monsters, the ones culpable for atomically flushing the whole planet, thereby enabling all those big bugs and post-apocalypse wastelands. In many a film blaming the Bomb, politicians were the ones whose squabbles caused them to start stabbing big red buttons and upsetting property values worldwide... so it seemed to make more sense to purge the planet of politicians, because they were (and always will be) troublemakers. You can blow off a giant ant's antennae with a tommy gun; shoot an isotope into the neck of the rhedo-saurus and he's pretty much done. Politicians just keep coming at you in waves until you're subsumed by the undertow of their doubletalk and the riptide of their malign intent, to drown an ignoble death in a muddy suck-hole of lies.

In movies, where events are more clear-cut because they need to serve plot purposes, politicos who hasten the End of the World as We Know It rarely survive to fight the Zeppelin-sized iguanas and club-waving throwbacks left in the subsidence of the big mushroom cloud light show. If the planet is spared in one film, it is quite grimly written off in the next; if the atomic after-effects are not global, then they yield monstrosities with which the military (the political enforcement arm) is unable to cope... until a scientist hands a last ditch bit of technological salvation to the nearest cinder block-jawed hero-in-uniform. In fact, Apocalypse never seemed to have any significant consequences for those who fomented it, while the normal folks — groundpounders and common citizens — were the ones who always had to pick up the bill.

Is there an up side to the End? On one hand, it certainly simplifies conflict in a world that has become too complex for most people to sanely bear. (Politically speaking, many films of the Atomic Decade, roughly 1951-61, render their choices down to black and white, subconsciously emphasising the more significant contrast of Red vs White.) On the other hand, nuke movies are a *de facto* demonstration that the treacherous mettle of science will out, playing on the average citizen's latent distrust of technology. In such scenarios, the Bomb catapults us back to a more comforting realm, where the solutions that matter are the province of agrarian, reproductive human true grit, where nobility can prevail in a hard-survival context devoid of grey tones.

Nuclear catastrophes are generally presented as a loss of control rather than an elective — with exceptions like *Fail Safe*, which plays *both* cards and closes with the voluntary and American-mandated white-out wipe-out of New York City. Needless to say, the President of the United States and the Premier of the USSR, along with all their cronies, weather this difficult-but-necessary crisis and keep their skin; the end montage hammers home repeated images of ordinary working stiffs catching an atomic fireball right where the sun doesn't shine. They are unwilling victims quite readily sacrificed by their elected representatives.

For normal human beings, to solve problems is to pave the way for a new set of bigger and more complex problems. As Stephen King discovered when he was writing his epic novel, *The Stand,* to scrag 99% of the human beings on the planet was to cleanse the world of bullshit — but at the immediate cost of progress, and eventual regression, since the human race usually has to relearn how to feed, clothe and shelter itself.

But the World as You Know It changes, now, on a daily basis, every time someone patents new software — granted, not a very thrilling or narrative sort of watershed (and hence not the sort that would form the basis for a good movie), but a world-changer nonetheless.

These observations and other fall-out were blizzarding through my mind before my scheduled meeting. Big studio, big producer, wanting a big

— really goddamned BIG — nuclear terrorism movie. The end of the world endorsed by all those movies made during the Atomic Decade, or Golden Age of Irradiation, didn't seem all that ominous anymore because we'd seen the same stock bomb-test footage too many times. World War Three became *passé* about the time the Berlin Wall fell down and went boom. Today we know that a bunker and a pair of clunky sunglasses won't make you a survivor. The prime directive: if you sight it, you'd better ignite it — don't tease the audience with nukes and not set off at least one — so we made sure to plot devastation times two: one trashcan nuke vaporises a small mountain town and strategically wipes out the government's entire NEST response cell; a more sophisticated device goes off deep in the tunnels of the New York subway system. In between we had gruesome deaths from exposure to plutonium (thereby demonstrating what a hideously toxic substance it is, since most people don't know the details) and a long-term death due to radiation seeded during the very first atomic tests. We covered the moral scale from the individual to the masses, from personal consequences to worldwide ones... mostly for naught, since *The Peacemaker* handily cooled down the notion of an exciting nuclear terrorism movie. For now.

What I secretly wanted to see was an élite government team of specialists devoted to dealing with all the stuff we really wanted to follow after the fall-out. Instead of addressing the grim realities of losing hair by the handful, puking up your own entrails or becoming a walking tumour festival, we might posit a sort of Impossible Missions Force of atomic fabulism. One member could specialise in giant insects, another in revived dinosaurs. An anthroetymologist would be essential for communicating with Morlocks. An ordnance expert would make weapons recommendations for torching pesky aliens who butt in to hijack our real estate while the planet is healing itself. A nuclear physicist could project how each kind of irradiation might effect monsters-to-be; bunny rabbits, after all, are perfectly harmless at normal size and without buzzsaw fangs, but make them as big as an aircraft carrier and they gain definite nuisance potential. One of the best science fiction short stories written with all this foreknowledge at hand is Edward Bryant's 'giANTS' (1979), which gives us the big bugs we all crave, not in spite of the Square Cube Law, but dependent upon it. For those who walked in late: the big bugs of the Atomic Decade — as well as

the big humans and super-sized dinosaurs — are impossible thanks to this simple law of physics, noted in the story, 'if an insect's dimensions are doubled, the strength and area of its breathing passages are increased by a factor of *four*. But the mass is multiplied by eight. After a certain point, and that point isn't very high, the insect can't move or breathe. It collapses under its own mass.'

Some Atomic Decade stinkers are undeniably *surreal,* such as *Reptilicus,* released in 1962 — fall-out from the Decade, if you will. I could understand that Reptilicus was some sort of prehistoric creature (ie completely made up) and that it could regenerate its entire physical structure from a shred of its tail (ie complete sci-fi hogwash), and that, sure enough, it was not only growing but swelling to enormous size (ie tumescent enough to knock down buildings and squash soldiers). What I did not understand, and what I was absolutely knocked out by (and still am), was the fever-dream notion that Reptilicus has the ability to retaliate by *vomiting* on his attackers — bright yellow/green streamers of puke referred to in the movie as 'acid slime' (wow!).

Now, don't misunderstand me; *Reptilicus* is a dreary little fart of a movie with lousy puppet monster effects and cardboard miniatures, zombie acting by a plank-faced cast of Danes, and an idiot script shovelled through

the sausage conveyor of fast-forward production by sci-fi vandal Sid Pink. It is, you might say, a *bad* film. But it contains two ideas that can only be described as deliriously wonderful, if you're predisposed to this type of film — the pre-title sequence, in which a drilling team brings up fresh blood on the nose of its bore, and the aforementioned Reptilicus emesis. Godzilla had shot a kind of death-ray out of his mouth, but lethal monster throwup was an innovation that remained largely untapped in movies until its reappearance, in a different context, in David Cronenberg's version of *The Fly* in 1986.

Most reference books available at the time, and there were precious few, seemed convinced that Reptilicus's deadly barf was radioactive, and why not? Weren't big monsters just sort of... naturally radioactive, the way Oscar Madison says gravy just 'comes when you cook the meat'? None of the primordial genre film studies of the late 1960s and early-to-mid 1970s (ie pre-*Star Wars*) seemed to know, since their authors wrote text largely dependent upon their imprecise memories of seeing the subject movies. Today, right now, the chances are better than ever that you can procure on demand nearly any film discussed in this book, either on a rental shelf near your home, or via some form of mail order. Today, right now, if you need to know the ins and outs of Reptilicus's non-radioactive vomitus, you can actually plug in the movie and find out, probably within twenty-four hours of reading this.

Kim Newman would want you to go that far. I double-checked *Reptilicus* just to ensure Kim would not have to besmirch his own dignity by including it in the book you are holding now.

Should you sally forth and watch any samples of atomic cinema (with this book at hand, one hopes), you may also discover that many of these films were not really made to withstand repeated viewing, let alone serious study. Not only the passage of time, but step-framing and the ability to scan and re-scan video have killed a lot of the magic and made the suspension of disbelief that much more difficult. Yet these movies endure

— the worst of them as camp, the best as both nostalgia and culture. Moreover, you'll find that the tackiest Roger Corman quickie somehow has the mystical ability to outlast many hits or award nominees released the same year.

Once this stuff grabs your imagination, it never totally relinquishes its hold. When I was eight years old, *World Without End* — which you will find in this book — was pretty near to my concept of a perfect movie. It featured a future Earth, a spaceship, faster-than-light travel, time travel, savage mutant primitives with faces like melted wax, a subterranean hive of humans composed of withered, geeky men wearing tights and silver skullcaps and hot, leggy, over-stimulated babes in Vargas drag. Introduce a quartet of rugged American know-it-alls into this problematic future and *voila!* adventure, or something like it. It was one of those movies whose joys are hard to explain, since it happened to fly in while I was young, and my window of input was wide open. It opens with the surety of ritual, with scratchy, orange-tinted, too-obvious stock footage of an atomic blast, followed by a plaster replica of the Earth, rotating grandly in space; add the first to the second and well, that's what atomic cinema is all about. When I saw this film for the first time, on television, I had no idea it was in colour. Once I learned it was in colour, I had no idea it was in CinemaScope (although the opening credits, even on the washed-out pan-and-scan version, specify both CinemaScope and 'print by Technicolor' in nakedly huge titles). Thus, I've had the pleasure of 'rediscovering' it twice as an adult. The punchline came when Kim noted that *World Without End* was, 'for some reason, a lost film in the UK...' thereby empowering me to have even more fun by inflicting one of my childhood faves upon him.

Did I mention that *World Without End* is also a quintessential example of atomic cinema? I'll leave it to Kim to explain further.

But I hope *Apocalypse Movies* can do you the same sort of courtesy, prompting you to discover some films and rediscover others. You may find your imagination seized, and the weight of disbelief not so hard to hoist after all.

David J. Schow,
Hallowe'en 1998

You Are One Day Closer to the End of the World

My earliest television memory is of 'World's End', a *Doctor Who* episode transmitted in November 1964. It was part one of 'The Dalek Invasion of Earth', a serial which revived the pepperpot monsters mainly responsible for the then-new show's instant popularity. The TARDIS materialises in London, beside the familiar Thames. The Doctor, definitively played by William Hartnell, and his companions spend twenty-five minutes furtively exploring the blasted shadow of the optimistic city we knew in the sixties. Battersea Power Station has lost its towers. An official notice warns the public not to dump bodies in the river. Familiar landmarks are bombed-out ruins. Helmeted zombies patrol derelict buildings. In *Science Fiction in the Cinema*, John Baxter notes a subtly unsettling moment: 'Hunting the small group of uncontrolled humans, three automatons pace to the end of a pier, stand silent for a moment, then *at the same moment* turn their heads slowly to face the direction of their quarry. The grainy image and natural location, both reminiscent of news footage, convey a special horror.' A (very) wobbly flying saucer lands in Trafalgar Square, and an extermination-crazy Dalek emerges from the river.

London was still dotted with blitzed wastelands, so the BBC had no difficulty finding desolate locations for the serial. Writer Terry Nation obviously knew many of his adult viewers would remember years when ruthless totalitarians were dropping bombs nightly on the city. Many of my generation wanted to be Daleks when we grew up, and shuffled around in cardboard boxes squawking 'ex-ter-min-ate!' But the images from the show which remain in my memory are of the ruined city; the rest of the serial, when the plot kicks in, isn't nearly as potent, though there are a few all-too-brief and effective bits of early morning location filming with the Daleks trundling over London Bridge. My family lived in London in 1964 and I could easily recognise the rubble-strewn tourist attractions and depressed docklands taken over by the Daleks. If, a year and a half later, the Corporation had aired Peter Watkins's *The War Game* (1966) and exposed me to the more earthbound horrors of all-out nuclear war, I could not have been more horrified, or more fascinated.

The more complicated a civilisation becomes, the more fun it is to imagine the whole works going up in flames. Every culture has a Creation myth and a vision of Apocalypse. Before the cultivation of fiction as an art form, images of mass devastation usually had to be dressed up as religion. In his Revelations, St John the Divine beheld a pale horse, and saw the end of the world as a sub-plot in the last battle between our Redeemer and the Anti-Christ. Among the supporting cast are the Whore of Babylon and the Four Horsemen of the Apocalypse — War, Famine, Pestilence and, with a touch of overkill, Death. With admirable economy, Norse legend combines Creation and Apocalypse in the myth of Ragnarok, at once the story of how the Gods came to make way for the rule of Man and a prophecy of the way the cycle will be completed with our destruction.

Judgement Day and the Twilight of the Gods offer transcendence as well as holocaust, accounting for a strain of exultation which persists even in the gloomiest visions of global disaster. Quite apart from the fact that contemplating the Apocalypse tends to make everyday problems seem trivial, artistic representations of the end of the world cheerfully pander to common fantasies. What if the world we know were destroyed, but you alone (or suitably partnered) survived? The commonest recurring image of the Apocalypse, in literature and film, is the dilapidated and depopulated city. As the survivors tour corpse-littered streets, we are allowed to peer at a world caught unaware by the moment of its extinction. To be the inheritor of worthless riches and an inexhaustible supply of canned food is not perhaps such an unattractive prospect. René Clair's *Paris qui dort* (1923, *The Crazy Ray*) is merely the most benevolent expression of this theme in the cinema. An inventor stops time and the unaffected hero roams around a frozen Paris like a curious spectator in a waxworks.

Left: The Whip Hand, *Otto Waldis*

Unsurprisingly, the first non-divine force seen as a possible threat to humanity's continued existence was Pestilence. The plagues that had ravaged Europe in the middle ages remained a potent memory as late as Mary Shelley's second SF novel, *The Last Man* (1826), in which humanity is wiped out by a virulent disease in 2073. In an early example of the displaced paranoia typical of 1950s monster movies, whereby giant insects or alien invaders are identified with the Soviets, Mrs Shelley's plague comes from Turkey. Genocidal diseases have remained popular with authors who want to return mankind to savagery without the expense of a full-scale war: Jack London's *The Scarlet Plague* (1915), George R. Stewart's *Earth Abides* (1949), Richard Matheson's *I Am Legend* (1954), Chelsea Quinn Yarbro's *Time of the Fourth Horseman* (1976), Stephen King's *The Stand* (1978; extended remix, 1990). In J.J. Connington's *Nordenholt's Million* (1923) and John Christopher's *The Death of Grass* (1956), plant diseases trigger the disaster, but the effects are much the same: a half-wished for descent into dog-eat-dog barbarity and the extermination of all the boring people in the world.

When the Pestilence theme appears in the cinema, it tends to be treated with post-atomic cynicism. Bacteriological weapons are disastrously deployed in films which establish the iconography of a sub-genre with decontamination suits, breached containment facilities, panicky martial law, terrifying disease vector diagrams and towns full of death-struck bodies:

The Whip Hand (1951), *The Satan Bug* (1965), *The Andromeda Strain* (1971), *The Ωmega Man* (1971), *Rage* (1972), *The Crazies* (1973), *The Cassandra Crossing* (1977), *Plague* (1978), *Fukkatsu No Hi* (1980, *Virus*), *Warning Sign* (1988). The sub-genre flowered in the eco-conscious seventies and recurred in the late eighties and nineties as a side-effect of AIDS awareness and Richard Preston's non-fiction best-seller *The Hot Zone* (1994); witness the frequent elaborate and apocalyptic reruns of *The Crazies* like *The Stand* (1994), *Outbreak* (1995) and *Twelve Monkeys* (1995) and trickle-downs like TV's *The Burning Zone* (1996-7) and 'The Pine Bluff Variant' (*The X Files*, 1998).

AIDS itself got a TV biopic in *And the Band Played On* (1993), from Randy Shilts's non-fiction book, which borrows heavily from the fictional Satan bug films. Researchers struggle in laboratory and conference room, as thwarted by budget cuts and medical rivalries as by the virus itself. Even when the government can't be entirely blamed for the disease, it is assumed the proper authorities will deal ineptly or maliciously with the crisis, ruling that large sectors of the population are expendable. In *Return of the Living Dead* (1983), the solution advocated by the army in *The Crazies*, *Lifeforce* (1985) and *Outbreak* is actually put into force — the heroes get word to the outside world that a zombie plague is spreading, and the government calmly has some know-nothing silo functionary push a button that wipes the afflicted town off the map with a nuclear missile.

> The fact that the real history of twentieth-century armaments has kept comfortably abreast of the imagination of the scientific romancers is not their triumph, but rather their tragedy.
> **Brian Stableford, *Scientific Romance in Britain 1890-1950***

The rise of Darwinism brought about a climate of agnosticism which led Victorian scientific romancers to reject the Biblical Apocalypse and dream up a scientifically rationalised End of the World (or, at the very least, Complete and Utter Ruination of Human Civilisation). The secular Apocalypse gave its readers cause to fear not the Wrath of God, but a comet on a collision course with the Earth (Camille Flammarion's *La Fin du monde* [1893-4, *Omega: The Last Days of the World*]; George Griffith's *Olga Romanoff* [1894]; H.G. Wells's 'The Star' [1897], and *In the Days of the*

Comet [1906]; Garrett P. Serviss's *The Second Deluge* [1912]), an uppity species more fit on the evolutionary scale than Man to survive (Wells's 'The Empire of the Ants' [1895]), invaders from another planet (Wells's *The War of the Worlds* [1898]), clouds of poison gas (M.P. Shiel's *The Purple Cloud* [1901]; Doyle's *The Poison Belt* [1913]), invaders from another dimension (Joseph Conrad and Ford Maddox Ford's *The Inheritors* [1901]; William Hope Hodgson's *The House on the Borderland* [1908]), or the fading of the sun (Hodgson's *The Night Land* [1912]).

Alongside these stirring tales of colossal destruction existed a popular genre of 'imaginary war' stories that slaked the same bloodthirsty, fatalist appetites. In the first half of the nineteenth century, British authors understandably imagined a threat from France, in William Burke's *The Armed Briton; or, The Invaders Vanquished* (1806) and the anonymous *The History of the Sudden and Terrible Invasion of England by the French in... May, 1852* (1851). But the form was really popularised by Sir George Tomkyns Chesney in his startling, initially anonymous, pamphlet *The Battle of Dorking: Reminiscences of a Volunteer* (1871), in which an unprepared, complacent Britain is invaded and conquered by an efficient, Bismarck-inspired German army. Chesney, writing after the Franco-Prussian war, was the John Milius of his day, arguing that the British Empire should no longer take its military might for granted, and be eternally prepared to meet foreign aggression. The pamphlet was a remarkable success not for its political content, but for its vision of the home counties at war.

The Battle of Dorking proved a potent, saleable nightmare for an England which hadn't seen a real battle since the Monmouth Rebellion or been threatened with invasion since the Napoleonic Wars. It was widely imitated, and unauthorised sequels appeared: Charles Stone's *What Happened After the Battle of Dorking; or, The Victory of Tunbridge Wells* (1871), M. Moltruhn's *The Other Side at the Battle of Dorking* (1871), Arthur Sketchley's *Mrs Brown at the Battle of Dorking* (1871), Colonel Frederic Nautsch's *The New Battle of Dorking* (1900). There were even more furious rebuttals, along the splenetic lines of *The Battle off Worthing; or Why the Invaders Never Got to Dorking* (1887), by 'A Captain of the Royal Navy'. A topical reissue of the original appeared in Germany in 1940, when Hitler was toying with the idea of Operation Sea Lion, an actual invasion of Britain.

Other nations, too, needed to exercise paranoia and jingoism by imagining themselves invaded by their neighbours, either to fall under unfair onslaughts or bravely rally and see off the perfidious foreigner. Imaginary wars were fought for France (Édouard Dangin's *La Bataille de Berlin en 1875* [1871]; General La Mèche's *La Guerre Franco-Allemande de 1878* [1878]), Germany (Léon Sperber-Niborski's *Krieg mit Russland!* [1881]; *Der rache Krieg zwischen Frankreich und Deutschland* [1887]) and America (Samuel Rockwell Reed's *The War of 1886 Between the United States and Great Britain* [1882]; Samuel Barton's *The Battle of the Swash; and the Capture of Canada* [1888]). Other territories considered revolutions, including Australia (Samuel Albert Rosa's *The Coming Terror; or, The Australian Revolution* [1894]) and Ireland (*Ireland's War! Parnell Victorious* [1882]; *The Battle of Moy; or, How Ireland Gained Her Independence in 1892-1894* [1882]; both anonymous).

The most prolific writer in the field was William LeQueux, who had the Germans rescue Britain from a Franco-Russian invasion in *The Great War in England in 1887* (1894), but recast the Huns in their more traditional role for *The Invasion of 1910* (1906) and the patriotic pot-boilers he continued to write throughout the First World War. The actual conflict did not significantly change LeQueux's politics or literary style, as is evidenced by *German Atrocities* (1914) and *The Zeppelin Destroyer* (1916). For his nastily xenophobic *The Yellow Danger* (1898), M.P. Shiel exploited fears of 'the yellow peril' with a fable in which the white world is swamped by a Sino-Japanese alliance. There were many such stories, as well as a few stodgy satires about the military threat posed by socialists or suffragettes, but most serious scaremongers concentrated on the Germans. Perhaps the best of the genre are Erskine Childers's *The Riddle of the Sands* (1903) and Saki's *When William Came* (1914), both personal attacks on the Kaiser's well-known militarism.

The first half of the twentieth century was so well equipped with wars that imaginary conflicts have tended to disappear, though a few 'alternate history' war games refight battles of World War Two, like Richard Cox's *Sea Lion* (1974) and Kevin Brownlow and Andrew Mollo's film *It Happened Here* (1964). However, the period of peace (in Western Europe, at least) since 1945 encouraged a modest revival of the genre. Michael Moorcock's 'Oswald Bastable' trilogy (*The Warlord of the Air* [1977]; *The*

Land Leviathan [1974]; *The Steel Tsar* [1981]), plays around with elements of the turn-of-the-century imaginary war tale, but takes the development of atomic weapons into account. Moorcock creates alternate worlds with a late Victorian flavour, but overshadows them with the Hiroshima mushroom cloud. The genre was never part of the SF mainstream and in its post-atomic incarnation it has tended to be treated as an adjunct. General Sir John Hackett's *The Third World War: August 1985* (1978) and Whitley Strieber and James Kunetka's *Warday* (1984), which has as many maps and statistics as anything by William LeQueux, are fiction very much in the pattern of *The Battle of Dorking* and its successors.

Chesney and LeQueux, like Hackett and Strieber/Kunetka, emphasise the nearness of their near future settings, and deal strictly in extant weapons and war games-style military accuracy. However, the rapid scientific advances of the late nineteenth century naturally led other writers to more startling extrapolations. Jules Verne describes a submarine warship in *Vingt mille lieues sous les mers* (1870, *Twenty Thousand Leagues Under the Sea*) and a flying fortress in *Robur le conquérant* (1886, *The Clipper of the Clouds*), but puts them at the disposal of individual megalomaniacs like Captain Nemo rather than the governments most likely to build and use such engines of destruction. It was left to George Griffith, in *The Angel of the Revolution* (1893), to combine the imaginary war with Verne-style gadgetry, as a society of rebels develop heavier-than-air flying machines and take over the world. Griffith correctly predicted that the aeroplane would be invented in 1903.

From their beginnings, the movies contributed ambitious, if primitive efforts, with many a silent melodrama envisioning wonderful new inventions used as instruments of war: aeroplanes (*The Pirates of 1920* [1911]; *The Flying Torpedo* [1916]), submarines (*Beneath the Sea* [1915]) or ray projectors (*Pawns of Mars* [1915]; *The Intrigue* [1916]; *The Invisible Ray* [1920]). In the build-up to the Great War, British cinema was full of wind-up futuristic war planes, bullying Junkers abusing Kentish housewives and literal panoramas of destruction: *The Airship Destroyer* (1909, *The Battle in the Clouds*), *England Invaded* (1909), *The Invaders* (1909), *Invasion: Its Possibilities* (1909), *The Aerial Submarine* (1910), *The Aerial Anarchists* (1910), *England's Menace* (1913), *An Englishman's Home* (1913, from George Du Maurier's important 1908 play), *The Great German North*

Above: *Victory and Peace*

Sea Tunnel (1914, reviving century-old fears of a Channel tunnel invasion), *Wake Up!* (1914), *Victory and Peace* (1918). LeQueux's *The Invasion of 1910* became the forty-five minute epic *If England Were Invaded* (1914, *The Raid of 1915*). Across the Atlantic, William Randolph Hearst backed a strange and amazingly racist imaginary war (President Wilson complained about it) in *Patria* (1916), a serial of preparedness propaganda in which America is threatened by an unholy Japanese-Mexican alliance.

'You will conceive a bunch of grapes which are covered by some infinitesimal but noxious bacillus. The gardener desires his grapes to be cleaner. It may be that he needs space to breed some fresh bacillus less noxious than the last. He dips it in the poison and they are gone. Our gardener is, in my opinion, about to dip the solar system; and the human bacillus, the little mortal vibrio which twisted and wriggled upon the outer rind of the earth, will in an instant be sterilised out of existence.'

Professor Challenger, in Conan Doyle's *The Poison Belt*

During the silent era, American movies lagged behind literature, locked by fundamentalists like D.W. Griffith and Cecil B. DeMille into the early Victorian ideas of the Bible belt. Hollywood spectacles were only too pleased to destroy civilisations in religious epics like Griffith's *Intolerance* (1916), DeMille's first bash at *The Ten Commandments* (1923) and Michael Curtiz's *Noah's Ark* (1929), but God-fearing audiences could relish the pagan orgies, crashing temples and smitten multitudes safe in the knowledge that they were too righteous ever to suffer the fate of the Sodomite and Babylonian extras slaughtered *en masse* by megaphone wielding directorial demagogues in riding britches. The main attraction of these films, which became popular all over again in the nuke-conscious fifties, was a combination of the spectacular carnage and spectacularly carnal goings-on that brought down the ire of Jehovah.

Even movie versions of disaster novels tended to inject heavy doses of religion into the destruction. When Abel Gance filmed Flammarion's *Fin du Monde* in 1930, the comet was explicitly depicted as a judgement from God. Gance himself plays Jean Novalic, a would-be messiah who denounces the ribald excesses of humanity in the shadow of doom and gets crucified for his pains. The film (which, like some of Wells's later works, comes perilously near to espousing a fascist new order) contains daring orgy footage that was cut in the export versions. The more moral Americans, reeling under the judgements of the Wall Street Crash, Prohibition and the Depression, replied with a modern flood, Felix E. Feist's *Deluge* (1933). Based on a 1928 novel by S. Fowler Wright, this has New York swept away by a tidal wave to make way for a particularly wet triangular love story. Economy-conscious Hollywood producers took heed of the costly film's commercial failure and vented their urge to smash the world through the rampages of machine-gun-toting mobsters and back-from-the-dead monsters, though spectacular stock footage from *Deluge* was recycled in *SOS Tidal Wave* (1938), *Dick Tracy vs. Crime, Inc.* (1941) and *King of the Rocketmen* (1949).

Above: The
Invisible Ray,
Bela Lugosi,
Boris Karloff

Meanwhile, the Geiger counters were starting to click. Marie Curie — as played by Greer Garson in *Madame Curie* (1943) and Jane Lapotaire in *Marie Curie* (1977) — discovered radium in 1896, and suffered a slow death from radiation poisoning. Her fate, far more than the way new technologies were applied to genocide in World War One, suggested researches into radioactive material could have hideous side-effects. The German *Gold* (1934) involves an early atomic pile and some tinkering with the structure of lead to create precious metal. The same moral lesson about greed was trotted out rather less heavily in range-wars over radioactive elements in *Broadway or Bust* (1924) and *Phantom Empire* (1935). Other tinkerers, like the Curies, learned more practical lessons. Boris Karloff, having discovered 'Radium X' in a meteor, subjects his new element to a bombardment process and turns into a glowing madman who kills at a touch in *The Invisible Ray* (1936), while the equally mad Albert Dekker uses radium deposits to shrink people in *Dr. Cyclops* (1939). These films flirt with the issues of contamination and mutation raised again in the fifties and after. Karloff's glowing touch of death was reprised by many an irradiated monster, including an older Boris in *Die, Monster, Die!* (1965), mutated by another meteor.

Frank R. Stockton has the distinction of being the first author to conceive of an atomic weapon. In *The Great War Syndicate* (1889), he describes a war between Britain and the United States in which two superweapons are put to use — a submarine wrench which pulls the propellers off the battleships, and a cannon 'capable of the total annihilation of matter'. Similar analogues to later super-bombs feature in the films *The War O' Dreams* (1915) and *The Greatest Power* (1917), in which conscience-stricken inventors worry at the terrible uses to which their infernal devices might be put and finally decide the best thing to do is to turn them over to the United States government, who will know best (as a later nuclear figure might exclaim, '*D'oh!*'). A movie serial, *The Great Radium Mystery* (1919), involves an atomic-fuelled supertank. More recognisable ancestors of the atom bomb appear in Robert Cromie's novel *The Crack of Doom* (1895), in which the new weapon completely destroys the Earth, and George Griffith's last novel, *The Lord of Labour* (1911). The most uncannily prophetic vision, however, came as usual from H.G. Wells.

'Ready!' said the steersman.
The gaunt face hardened to grimness, and with both hands the bomb-thrower lifted the big atomic bomb from the box and steadied it against the side. It was a black sphere two feet in diameter. Between its handles was a little celluloid stud, and to this he bent his head until his lips touched it. Then he had to bite in order to let the air in upon the inducive. Sure of its accessibility, he craned his neck over the side of the aeroplane and judged his pace and distance. Then very quickly he bent forward, bit the stud and hoisted the bomb over the side.
'Round,' he whispered inaudibly...
When he could look down again it was like looking down upon the crater of a small volcano. In the open garden before the

Imperial castle a shuddering star of evil splendour spurted and poured up smoke and flame towards him like an accusation. They were too high to distinguish people clearly, or mark the bomb's effect on the building until suddenly the facade tottered and crumbled before the flare as sugar dissolves in water.

H.G. Wells, *The World Set Free*

In *The Visual Encyclopedia of Science Fiction,* Brian Ash comments: '*The World Set Free* (1914) was a remarkable forecast of the use of atomic bombs. It was a genuine science fiction extrapolation from an abstruse scientific paper on infra-atomic energy by the physicist Frederik Soddy in 1909. Wells showed that, following the discovery of infra-atomic power, the Earth throngs with machines worked by atomic energy. Coal and oil become obsolete as fuels, mass unemployment follows, and the world is in turmoil. A global conflict results and before long most of the capital cities of the world are in flames; millions of people die. Here, Wells's vision is extraordinarily accurate, so that he may be forgiven for inventing bombs which do not explode with sudden, cataclysmic violence, but continue emitting furious radiations for a period of seventeen days before dimming to half power and then dimming to half that again in decreasing cycles.'

Wells is the chief prophet of the secular Apocalypse; in addition to inventing SF as a literary genre, he was responsible for creating the conventions still used in fictions of nuclear war before even he conceived of such a thing. When George Pal filmed *The Time Machine* in 1960, he ditched Wells's evolutionary explanation for the degeneration of the human race into the elfin Eloi and the brutish Morlocks in favour of a more immediate, less challenging scenario. Instead of a slow and inevitable decline, the ruined far future is caused by an atomic war in 1966. However, Wells's novel builds up to a vision of the dead Earth that reads like the bleakest possible description of 'nuclear winter', down to the swirling flakes of fall-out.

The darkness grew apace; a cold wind began to blow in freshening gusts from the east, and the showering white flakes in the air increased in number. From the edge of the sea came a ripple and a whisper. Beyond these lifeless sounds the world was silent. Silent? It would be hard to convey the stillness of it. All the sounds of man, the bleating of sheep, the cries of birds, the hum of insects, the stir that makes the background of our lives — all that was over. As the darkness thickened, the eddying flakes grew more abundant, dancing before my eyes; and the cold of the air more intense. At last, one by one, swiftly, one after the other, the white peaks of the distant hills vanished into blackness. The breeze rose to a moaning wind. I saw the black central shadow of the eclipse sweeping towards me. In another moment the pale stars alone were visible. All else was rayless obscurity. The sky was absolutely black.

H.G. Wells, *The Time Machine*

A playful side to Wells delighted in war games. He was clearly fascinated by the imaginary war genre, though unable to take it seriously until 1914. *The War of the Worlds* is, among many other things, a satire of the form, replacing the moustachioed Hun with heat-ray brandishing Martian tripods. His major contribution, *The War in the Air* (1908), is fairly comic, burlesquing LeQueux and Shiel in its description of an invasion of America by the Germans and a Yellow Peril alliance. The farcical beginnings, with a blundering Kipps type stranded aboard a German airship, soon give way to meticulous descriptions of aerial warfare and, finally, a horrific vision of civilisation in ruins. The 'England Under the Martians' section of *The War of the Worlds* introduces survivors who scavenge a life in the London debris, but *The War in the Air* elaborates upon the theme in unpleasant detail. The rat-eating barbarism of Wells's bombed Londoners is echoed in every post-nuke hell from *Mad Max 2* (1981) to *Threads* (1984).

A throwaway sentence in *The War in the Air* mentions that the horrors described are long gone, and that a utopian world state has been established since the fall of civilisation. This theme, of utopia arising from the ruins of a war-smashed world, becomes central to *The World Set Free* and later novels like *The Shape of Things to Come* (1933) and *The Holy Terror* (1939). Wells's descriptions of battle and desolation are more convincing than his hymns to socialist achievement, scientific rationalism and global government. Of the Time Traveller, the Narrator of *The Time Machine* (1895) says, 'He, I know — for the question had been discussed among us long before the Time Machine was made — thought but cheerlessly of the

Advancement of Mankind, and saw in the growing pile of civilisation only a foolish heaping that must inevitably fall back upon and destroy its makers in the end. If that is so, it remains for us to live as though it were not so.' Wells lived long enough to be incensed by the news of the Hiroshima and Nagasaki bombings. His last book, written in 1945, was called *Mind at the End of Its Tether*.

Wells also introduced the post-holocaust world to the cinema. *Things to Come* (1936), the epic collaboration between producer Alexander Korda, director William Cameron Menzies and screenwriter Wells, has long been recognised as a classic SF film, but is too often remembered only by its last third — the section dealing with the technological wonders of the far future. While the sets and special effects of these sequences, not to mention Arthur Bliss's soaring score, remain impressive, the dramatics are particularly clumsy, and Wells is guilty of scientific and cinematic lapses in the absurd conflicts which surround man's first venture into outer space. The first two-thirds of the film, which concern the start of a world-wrecking war and life in the shattered remnants of Everytown (Wells's London), are much more satisfying, and constitute the template for all subsequent post-apocalypse movies.

Like *The Day After* (1983) and *Threads*, *Things to Come* opens in an air of tense normality, with a 1940 Christmas celebration interrupted by the outbreak of war. As in the later films, some characters remain blithely unaware of international tensions and their possible consequences while others make doom-laden speeches. Wells and Menzies tip their hand a little too early — one of the warships lost in the initial engagement is the HMS *Dinosaur* — but segue into a powerful montage of armies marching off, tank warfare, gas attacks and air raids in Everytown. Like many despairing thinkers in the twenties and thirties, Wells was attracted to pacifism but convinced there would be another war (cf the sudden devastating outbreak at the end of Evelyn Waugh's *Vile Bodies* [1930]). However, the conflict in *Things to Come* is depicted not as a necessary crusade against fascism, but a futile and suicidal exercise in destruction which lasts for decades and dwindles from a national struggle into a ragged series of skirmishes between the City People and the Hill People. A new plague, the Wandering Sickness, strikes, and brain-burned zombies struggle over acres of barbed wire.

The central section of the film is set in 1970, and finds the cowed inhabitants of a shattered but still recognisable Everytown under the jackboot of the fur-coated Boss Rudolph (Ralph Richardson), who has risen from the ranks through his ruthless decision to order all Wandering Sickness victims shot on sight. The Boss, who rides in a horse-drawn limousine, is a recognisable ancestor of the Duke of New York (Isaac Hayes, *Escape From New York* [1981]) and the Humungous (Kjell Nilsson, *Mad Max 2*). Instead of Kurt Russell or Mel Gibson, *Things to Come* has Raymond Massey in a black leather flying suit and giant glass helmet as John Cabal, saviour of the wasteland. He descends from the skies as the representative of Wings Over the World, an airborne scientific utopia, and delivers the first draft of the warning the strikingly Cabal-like Klaatu (Michael Rennie) will give at the end of *The Day the Earth Stood Still* (1951) — make peace or die. Most greet Cabal as a hero, the strong leader they really need to help them out of the ruins, but the Boss — who only *seemed* strong — drops dead from an allergic reaction to Massey's 'Peace Gas'. For the first of so many times, a film shows the lowest moment in the curve of history and then gets on with the rebuilding.

She's an Atom
From Manhattan

When you see something that is technically sweet, you go ahead and do it and you argue about what to do about it only after.

J. Robert Oppenheimer

Opposite:
The Beginning
or the End?
Brian Donlevy,
Robert Walker

In one way I feel guilty for all those deaths because... well, they were people with lives to live. But probably some of them, a certain percentage, had done something that deserved punishment, had started wars or harmed others. Maybe I'm a cock-eyed optimist, but... without the idea of splitting the atom to use as a weapon, it might have taken mankind many decades to make of fission and fusion any more than a series of fascinating laboratory experiments.

Bob Lewis, co-pilot of the *Enola Gay*

In *Our Friend the Atom* (1954), Walt Disney's educational film about the discovery and use of atomic power, an animated history book introduces us to the fathers and mother of nuclear fission: Democritus, the Curies, Rutherford, Einstein. Oppenheimer isn't mentioned. By flashing from the splitting of the atom to a lecture on its industrial, medical and agricultural possibilities ('an atomic blast is more than a threat, it is also a regretful waste of heat and energy'), the film quietly ignores the salient fact that the first practical application conceived for the breakthrough was an instrument of wholesale death. At peace, Disney would brook no mention of the late unpleasantness; a decade earlier, in *Victory Through Air Power* (1943), things had been different.

Between Pearl Harbour and Hiroshima, Hollywood helped the American people get used to the idea that dropping bombs was a necessary evil. Disney's *Victory Through Air Power*, a propagandist documentary which includes vividly animated scenes of an American Eagle strangling the Nipponese Octopus, is a publicity job for the theories of Major Alexander de Seversky. He championed strategic as opposed to tactical bombing, which is to say that he was in favour of striking at the enemy's cities and civilian populations rather than armies and military installations (later, he pooh-poohed the effects of the atom bomb, arguing that Hiroshima was only obliterated because it was so shoddily built — if a solid American city were nuked, 'the property damage might have been limited to broken window glass over a wide area'). Given the national outrage over Pearl Harbour and the presentation of the victims of the Nazi blitzes in movies like *Confirm or Deny* (1941) and *Mrs Miniver* (1942), bombing of any kind, let alone strategic bombing, was a hard sell. The practice was too firmly established as one of the enemy's dirty tricks.

However, the Doolittle Raid on Tokyo in April 1942 successfully changed the image. The expedition was primarily a propagandist coup, designed to demonstrate that, a scant four months after the day of infamy, America was back in the war, kicking ass over the enemy's capital. There was a rash of Doolittle films: Delmer Daves's *Destination Tokyo* (1943) has Cary Grant and John Garfield sailing a submarine into Tokyo Harbour to reconnoitre vital pre-raid information; Mervyn LeRoy's *Thirty Seconds Over Tokyo* (1944) finds Spencer Tracy and Van Johnson actually dropping the bombs; and Lewis Milestone's *The Purple Heart* (1944) is about the show trial given downed fliers Dana Andrews and Farley Granger after the incident, and climaxes with their execution for 'war crimes'. In *Looking Away: Hollywood and Vietnam*, Julian Smith writes, 'much of the moral justification for the bombing of Hiroshima and Nagasaki a year later is to be found in these films: it's the enemy's war, he hit us first, he asked for it and he's gonna get it; if we don't do it to him, he'll do it to us.'

Thirty Seconds Over Tokyo directly confronts bleeding hearts in a sequence where Ted Lawson (Van Johnson), the pilot who will lose a leg during the raid and write the book on which the screenplay is based, explains that he does what he does from a passionate commitment to his wife and family, and, by extension, the country which allows him to have such an idyllic home life. 'I don't pretend to like the idea of killing a bunch of people,' he says, 'but it's a case of drop a bomb on them or pretty soon

Left:
Above and
Beyond,
*Robert Taylor
and crew*

they'll be dropping one on Ellen'. This thinking reoccurs almost exactly in *Above and Beyond* (1952), the story of Colonel Paul Tibbetts, the man who dropped the Bomb on Hiroshima. When his wife complains about him bombing children, Tibbetts (Robert Taylor) is infuriated. 'Lucey, don't ever say that to me again. Look, let's clear up one little piece of morality right now — it's not bombs that are horrible. It's war, not just weapons... To lose this war to the gang we're fighting would be the most immoral thing we could do to those kids in there. And don't you forget it.'

It is with such glib moralities that the American war film is happiest, whether in the give-'em-hell-for-Mom's-apple-pie strain of *Thirty Seconds Over Tokyo*, or the equally straightforward war-is-hell-because-Mom's-boys-get-killed branch represented by Lewis Milestone's *All Quiet on the Western Front* (1930). To the men involved, the Manhattan Project was a series of scientific exercises, complicated by the moral dilemmas surrounding the practical application of their findings. In July 1945, sixty atomic scientists presented President Roosevelt with a petition urging that the Bomb not be dropped on Japan until after the enemy had been given a convincing warning and an opportunity for honourable surrender. The subsequent statements and actions of Einstein, Oppenheimer and Julius and Ethel Rosenberg prove that, in varying ways, they found it impossible to live with what they had done. A character in Kurt Vonnegut's *Cat's Cradle* (1963) remarks, 'I was there when they dropped scientific truth on Hiroshima'.

Hollywood can accommodate a dissenting point of view, represented by the well-intentioned but muddle-headed wives of *Thirty Seconds Over Tokyo* and *Above and Beyond*, but only so long as it is instantly squashed by a stirring homily from the likes of Van Johnson or Robert Taylor.

> We were determined to look the beast in the eye... beneath the welder's glasses provided, I wore an extra pair of dark glasses. I smeared my face with suntan lotion... I wore a heavy pair of gloves. Then, through the glasses, I saw a tiny pinpoint of light. I was disappointed. Is this all? Is this what we have worked so hard to develop?
>
> **Edward Teller, of the Trinity test explosion**

In *The Beginning or the End?* (1947), the official biography of the Manhattan Project, the voice of dissent is provided by a young scientist who thinks the Bomb should be used for peace. Finally, he is forced to concede that the most peace-making thing you can do with a bomb is to drop it on as many warlike people as possible. The film is a travesty, partially due to director Norman Taurog and screenwriter Frank Wead working well below their best. Everyone involved appears uncomfortable, not least the actors impersonating famous people standing around a California redwood in the opening scenes. They watch the burial of a time capsule which contains various items, including a print of *The Beginning or the End?*, intended for the edification of the citizens of the twenty-fifth century. 'Our civilisation will have left an enduring record behind it,' announces a narrator. The small crowd wear grim expressions, as if disappointed to learn not *every* print of the film is being buried.

The film proper begins with Hume Cronyn, pretending to be Oppenheimer, addressing himself to posterity. 'For you of the twenty-fifth century, we have recorded our search to unlock the atom. We know the Beginning. Only you of tomorrow — if there is a tomorrow — can know the End.' There follows a plodding recreation of the important events: the first use of an atomic pile at Stagg Field in Chicago; the Trinity test detonation at Alamogordo, New Mexico; the flight of Colonel Tibbetts's plane, the *Enola Gay*, over Japan. The actors playing real people are stiff: Brian Donlevy (General Leslie Groves), Ludwig Stossel (Einstein), Joseph Calleia

(Enrico Fermi), Barry Nelson (Tibbetts), Art Baker (Truman), Godfrey Tearle (Roosevelt). However, the bulk of the film falls to fictional characters, principally Matt (Tom Drake), the idealistic scientist, and Jeff (Robert Walker), an ordinary joe air force officer. The clumsiness of the fact/fiction mixture is established in an early scene, just after Fermi has split the atom. Matt is concerned.

> **Matt:** A chain reaction! If that's so, we can change the world. All the power anyone can use — everywhere!
> **Fermi:** Not so fast. We are blind men reaching into the unknown. Atomic energy can become a terrible weapon of war.
> **Matt:** Look, we've all been educated to believe science should help mankind, not destroy it. All the years of atomic research; must they end up in a bomb?
> **Fermi:** It's inevitable.

Billed as 'the story behind the most Hush-Hush secret of all time', *The Beginning or the End?* is torn between adherence to well-known recent history and the need to make a conventional movie. Furthermore, various individuals and official bodies involved in the Manhattan Project all had the power to tinker with the script. Niels Bohr, for instance, refused to be represented by an actor, and a last-minute change of mind on the part of another real-life scientist meant Agnes Moorehead's role had to be cut from the picture. The military requested many alterations and deletions, including what would have been a classic camp exchange in the cockpit of the *Enola Gay*.

> **Pilot:** Is it true that if you fool around with this stuff [radiation] long enough you don't like girls any more?
> **Jeff:** I hadn't noticed it.

Instead, we get a pompous bit of patriotic smarm.

> **Pilot:** They'll never know what hit them.
> **Jeff:** We've been dropping warning leaflets on them for ten days now. That's ten days more warning than they gave us at Pearl Harbour.

Incidentally, this is a contemptible lie. In *By the Bomb's Early Light*, Paul Boyer reports, 'The American people were... encouraged to believe that the residents of the two doomed cities were given explicit advance warning... the "advance warning" was a clause in the July 26 1945 Potsdam Declaration threatening "prompt and utter destruction" unless the Japanese surrendered unconditionally — words utterly debased by years of wartime propaganda.'

While Jeff remains chipper throughout, and has a wisecracking romance with Groves's secretary (Audrey Totter), Matt is marked for an early death by the fact that he has a beautiful, pregnant wife (Beverly Tyler). Everybody knows that in war films, the young man with a beautiful, pregnant wife can expect to die heroically so that his best buddy can awkwardly break the news to the bereaved family and explain how noble the dear departed was and that his sacrifice was Worth It. Matt exposes himself to a lethal dose of radioactivity at Los Alamos while preventing the Bomb from accidentally going off early (the factual basis for this is the deaths of physicists Harry Daghlian and Louis Slotkin, well *after* V-J day). In a truly ghastly scene, Jeff reads out Matt's final, explanatory letter.

> From the first, I've had my doubts — whether man could ever learn to use this terrifying force for good instead of evil — the dark threat of future atomic war, which can destroy civilisation unless men learn to live together... We stand now where the early savages stood when they ceased running away from the fire. We of an enlightened century can learn to use atomic energy constructively. God has not shown us a new way to destroy ourselves. Atomic energy is the hand He has extended to lift us from the ruins of war and lighten the burden of peace. Ann, you and our boy will see the day when the atoms in a cup of water will heat and light your home... when the power in a pasteboard railway ticket will drive trains across great continents... when the energy in a blade of grass will send planes to distant lands. We have found a path so filled with promise, that when we walk down it we will know everything that went before was the Dark Ages. In the past, man has sought useless war, hunger and pain, has often been vile. Yet... stubbornly he has stumbled out of

chaos, lifted his eyes, and gone on to make a better world. Now in the greatest hour of life on earth, he has faced the secret of the Power of the universe. You, the giver of a new life, must know that what we have unleashed is not The End. Men will learn to use this new knowledge well. They will not fail. For this is the timeless moment when we must prove that human beings are made in the image and likeness of God... or pass forever from the face of the Earth.

Melvin Frank and Norman Panama's *Above and Beyond*, a better film than *The Beginning or the End?*, is still an unsuccessful examination of the momentous event. However, it does get the facts more nearly right: *The Beginning or the End?* has Roosevelt select Hiroshima as a primary target months before the event; *Above and Beyond* reveals that the city was fourth on a list of likely objectives, but the other three were obscured by heavy cloud cover on the day. 'It looks like Hiroshima draws the short straw,' quips a navigator. Like *Strategic Air Command* (1955) and *A Gathering of Eagles* (1963), *Above and Beyond* contrasts the needs of the country with the needs of a neglected wife, finally revealing to the stupid woman that they are one and the same. 'How Much Can A Wife Take?' asks the poster. 'The personal story of pretty Lucey Tibbetts who had the hard luck to fall in love with a hero. This is their story, a tender story... told against the event that changed their lives — and our lives — forever! The Love Story Behind the Multi-Million Secret! It's Real! It's Life! It's Love!'

The film does have the usual moments of unease (Tibbetts: 'I wouldn't think much of myself if I didn't feel uncomfortable.' General: 'Neither would I.') and one unintentionally scary moment when a gung-ho young pilot says of its hero, 'that guy's taken all the fun out of modern warfare', but *Above and Beyond* is mainly, and tediously, devoted to family quarrels. Tibbetts's position is that 'a secret mission is a secret from your wife. A secret from the world'. Hers is 'you're not the man I married. Not any more. You're ambitious. You're heartless'. Lucey (Eleanor Parker) endures the secret training base for a while but takes off when she thinks Paul is spending more time with the *Enola Gay* than her (that he names the plane after his mother, rather than her, is also suggestive). However, when the importance of the mission is revealed, she returns. This, then, is the crucial point, and the horrible irrelevance, of the film. Not only has the Bomb won the war and changed forever man's sense of his permanence on the planet; more importantly, it's brought Robert Taylor and Eleanor Parker back together.

> In some sort of crude sense which no vulgarity, no humour, no overstatement can quite extinguish, the physicists have known sin; and this is a knowledge which they cannot lose.

J. Robert Oppenheimer

Needless to say, neither *The Beginning or the End?* nor *Above and Beyond* goes into the post-blast situation at ground zero lest it taint the hollow clichés of the final letter-reading and marital reunion scenes. Even in the fifties, critics remarked that a few moments of actuality film — such as the stock footage spliced topically onto the end of Gordon Douglas's silly spy movie *First Yank into Tokyo* (1945) — had more impact than all the moral, military and scientific platitudes the movies could come up with. However, a sense of culpability seeped into the popular imagination — Peter Kass's *Time of the Heathen* (1962) and Mark Robson's *Happy Birthday, Wanda June* (1971), from Kurt Vonnegut Jr's 1970 play, feature John Heffernan and William Hickey respectively as shambling hollow men (fictional characters) unable to get over the guilt they feel because they were on the crews that flew the atomic bombing missions.

As the events receded into history, the Manhattan Project and the *Enola Gay* were dramatised several more times, usually for TV miniseries: David Lowell Rich's *Enola Gay: The Men, the Mission, the Atomic Bomb* (1980), scripted by James Poe from the book by Gordon Thomas and Max Morgan-Witts, with Patrick Duffy as Tibbetts, Gregory Harrison as Captain Bill Lewis, Billy Crystal as Lt Jake Beser, Robert Walden as Oppenheimer, Ed Nelson as Truman and Stephen Roberts as Roosevelt; Barry Davis's *Oppenheimer* (1981), scripted by Peter Prince, with Sam Waterston in the title role; the Canadian *The Race For the Bomb* (1987), with Miki Manoljovik and Jean-Paul Muel; Joseph Sargent's *Day One* (1989), scripted by David W. Rintels from Peter Wyden's *Day One: Before Hiroshima and After*, with Brian Dennehy as Groves and David Strathairn as Oppenheimer. Roger Spottiswoode and Koreyoshi Kurahara's *Hiroshima* (1995) ambitiously surrounds the Manhattan Project story with the diplomatic

Above:
Doomwatch

wrangles of the American and Japanese government and the ground zero story of the blasted city. Steve Binder's *Give 'Em Hell, Harry!* (1975), a record of James Whitmore's one-man show about President Truman, includes the decision to give the order to drop the Bomb. Martin Cruz Smith's novel *Stallion Gate* (1986) is a welcome contrast to such solemnities, a spy thriller set against the backdrop of the Manhattan Project.

The TV series *Doomwatch* (1970-72), created by Kit Pedler and Gerry Davis, revolves around the guilt-ridden Dr Spencer Quist (John Paul), one of the concerned Manhattan Project scientists who lobbied Truman to demonstrate rather than deploy the Bomb. After the death by radiation poisoning of his wife, Quist devotes his life to awful warnings against various scientific excesses which mostly seem more relevant now than they did on the show's first screening. Like the similarly-named Professor Quatermass, Quist represents those scientists who have known sin but are determined to make amends and to pursue only beneficial research. The tone of *Doomwatch* is pretty shrill, with shrieking shirts and sideburns for the trendy supporting scientists, but Quist — who doesn't survive the 1999 revival TV movie — is an interesting character and a refreshing alternative to the Edward Teller/Werner von Braun analogues who show up in most post-war mad science movies. Alexander Mackendrick's *The Man in the White Suit* (1951), an allegorical comedy, features a caricature Manhattan Project boffin in genius Alec Guinness. Forced to realise how his apparently pure breakthrough will ruin the lives of millions by devastating an industry, he is still, at the fade-out, so enthused by a sudden insight that he hurries back to the laboratory to perfect the process.

Roland Joffé's *Fat Man and Little Boy* (1989, *Shadow Makers*), co-scripted by Bruce Robinson, covers the same territory as the many television versions. It is effectively a revisionist remake of *The Beginning or the End?*, to the extent of casting John Cusack as another Daghlian-Slotkin stand-in scientist who raises the issues and dies tragically of radiation poisoning while Oppenheimer (Dwight Schultz) and Groves (Paul Newman) clash with each other. Its approach to the story is diametrically opposed to that of the earlier film — the moral everyman audience identification figure is one of the scientists who petitions against the use of the Bomb — but it has as many clunky lines of dialogue ('Jesus, we're trying to tap into the energy that fuels the universe. It's petrifying if I stop to think about it.' 'It's all about ass, isn't it? You either kick it or lick it.' 'Oppenheimer, you ought to stop playing God, because you are not good at it and the position is taken.') and Newman's cartoonish military hawk and Schultz's extremely bland troubled visionary are just as thin as their predecessors. Time is given to political soap sub-plots, like Oppenheimer's relationship with a communist (Natasha Richardson), which means that yet again the awesome affect of the story is eclipsed by movie nonsense love affairs.

> Hiroshima is not a large city. They will bomb other places first.
> By the time it is our turn to be attacked, the war will be over.
> **Mayoral Assistant Maruyama**

It was not until Alain Resnais's *Hiroshima, Mon Amour* (1959), adapted by Marguerite Duras from her own novel, that the people who lived under the *Enola Gay*'s flight path got their lasting testament in Western cinema. Yet, like *Above and Beyond*, the film is about regeneration rather than destruction. Eiji Okada and Emmanuele Riva carry neuroses from their wartime experiences — his is in Hiroshima, hers in Nevers — but their affair enables them to forget, to blossom like the flowers which sprang out of the ashes of atomic devastation just fifteen days after the Bomb was dropped.

It was not realised much abroad at the time, but Resnais was contributing to a well-established cycle of Japanese films that tackled the after-effects of the bombings, usually spotlighting tragically doomed young characters who suffer innocently for the sins of others and seek redemption while succumbing to lingering diseases: Kaneto Shindo's *Genbaku no Ko* (1952, *Children of Hiroshima*), Tomotaka Tasaka's *Nagasaki no Uta wa Wasureji* (1952, *I'll Not Forget the Song of Nagasaki*), Hideo Oba's *Nagasaki no Kane* (1953, *The Bell of Nagasaki*), Hideo Sekigawa's *Hiroshima* (1953), Tadashi Imai's *Junai Monogatari* (1957, *A Story of Pure Love*), Yves Ciampi's *Wasureenu Bojo* (1960, *Typhoon in Nagasaki* — an arthouse rip-off of *Hiroshima, Mon Amour*), Shindo's *Honno* (1966, *Lost Sex*), Koreyoshi Kurahara's *Ai to Shi no Kiroku* (1966, *The Heart of Hiroshima*), Yutaka Oshawa's *Sensei* (1982, *The Teacher*), Kiriro Urayama's *Yumechiyo* (1986), Akira Kurosawa's *Hachigatsu no Kyohshikyoku* (1991, *Rhapsody in August*). Joan Darling's *Hiroshima Maiden* (1988), a TV movie, is the American version, bringing home the reality of the Bomb to America through the character of a survivor (Tamlyn Tomita) who needs plastic surgery.

There was even, daringly, a semi-satire of the Japanese Bomb cycle in Keisuke Kinoshita's *Karumen Junjosu* (1952, *Carmen's Pure Love*), about a grieving mother who blames all the ills of the world on the atom. This perhaps paved the way for less reverent (maybe distasteful) Japanese treatment of the Bomb in Ishiro Honda's *Furankenshutain tai Barugon* (1965, *Frankenstein Conquers the World*) in which the Nazis export the heart of the Frankenstein Monster to Hiroshima during the war and the nuclear blast causes it to regenerate as a giant monster boy, or even the vision of Tokyo destroyed by an apparent nuclear explosion (actually a psychic blast) at the outset of Katsuhiro Otomo's *Akira* (1988). Elliptical, mythologising evocations of the bombings occur in Steven Spielberg's *Empire of the Sun* (1987), from J.G. Ballard's 1984 novel, where the *deus ex machina* blast seems like a Japanese sunrise; and Nicolas Roeg's *Insignificance*

(1985), from the 1982 play by Terry Johnson, featuring an Einstein figure (Michael Emil) suffering from flash-images of the firestorm which finally extend to an extraordinary fantasy of the Monroe figure (Theresa Russell) immolated at ground zero. The long-range cultural fall-out informs Ridley Scott's *Black Rain* (1989), in which a Japanese criminal (stretching a point and justifying the title, which refers to an after-effect of the bomb) declares that the *yakuza* have only come to prominence in the post-holocaust, post-moral climate foisted on Japan by America.

However, outside of John Hersey's journalistic best-seller *Hiroshima* (1946), the story it took decades to confront is the simplest of them all: what it was like for the people at ground zero on the day. *Enola Gay: The Men, the Mission and the Atomic Bomb* keeps cutting embarrassingly to Hiroshima official James Shigeta ignoring all the signs, and TV movies made for the forty-fifth (*Hiroshima: Out of the Ashes* [1990]) and fiftieth (*Hiroshima*) anniversaries give due attention, albeit in somewhat hand-wringing style, to the blasted victims. Rather more effective and quieter are

Masaki Mori's *anime* pair *Hadashi no Gen* (1983, *Barefoot Gen*) and *Hadashi no Gen II* (1986, *Barefoot Gen II*), about a family with young children surviving in the bombed ruins of Hiroshima; Kazuo Kuroki's *Ashita* (1989, *Tomorrow*), dramatising the last day in the lives of a group of Nagasaki residents; and Shohei Imamura's *Kuroi Ame* (1988, *Black Rain*), from Masuji Ibuse's highly-regarded 1966 novel, which follows the decline of a woman (Yoshiko Tanaka) rendered unmarriageable by exposure to fall-out in the wake of Hiroshima.

Peace is Our Profession

The quintessential man of the fifties became the bomber pilot. He was a highly trained technician, a sophisticate who could kill anonymous hundreds without hating them or, indeed feeling anything at all except pleasure for a mission accomplished. Reporters interviewing the men who flew the Hiroshima and Nagasaki missions were pleased to find them 'normal, friendly and well-adjusted.'

Douglas T. Miller and Marion Nowak, *The Fifties: The Way We Really Were*

When the Bomb was really a bomb, the bomber planes which carried it and the bomber pilots who flew them were a considerable part of its mystique. Since Kitty Hawk, America has loved its flying machines and held aviators in awe and respect. The aces of World War One were seen as modern knights, engaging in aerial jousts far above the muddy trenches. By flying the Atlantic, Charles Lindbergh became the hero of a decade. The aviation movie emerged as a Hollywood genre in the late twenties, with William Wellman's *Wings* (1927) and Howard Hughes's *Hells' Angels* (1930). Wellman and Hughes, fliers both, did much to foster the myth that jaunty japesters in biplanes significantly altered the course of the 1914-18 war. In the thirties, planes became involved in civilian heroics for macho epics like John Ford's *Airmail* (1932), Howard Hawks's *Ceiling Zero* (1935), Victor Fleming's *Test Pilot* (1938) and Hawks's *Only Angels Have Wings* (1939). When the Second World War broke out, the cinema got its squadrons in the air for innumerable stirring, patriotic missions. Michael Curtiz's *Dive Bomber* (1941) and Mitchell Leisen's *I Wanted Wings* (1941) managed to take off before Pearl Harbour, while Hawks's *Air Force* (1943), Richard

Right:
The Best
Years of
Our Lives,
*Dana
Andrews*

Wallace's *Bombardier* (1943) and Mervyn LeRoy's *Thirty Seconds Over Tokyo*
speedily got into action to repay the Japanese in kind. William Wyler's *Mrs
Miniver* and King Vidor's *An American Romance* (1944), celebrations respectively of blitzed British pluck and ethnic American industrialism, end
with rank upon rank of gleaming planes taking to the skies to win the war.

After the war was over, the beautiful planes that fly over the Minivers'
bombed church or roll out of Brian Donlevy's armaments plant were
abandoned in fields like the one Dana Andrews visits in Wyler's *The Best
Years of Our Lives* (1946). A soda jerk before the war, Andrews has dis-
played conspicuous bravery and risen through the air force ranks. In his
captain's uniform, he is hailed as a saviour of democracy. Back home, he
finds himself skilled only in jerking soda and dropping bombs on people.
His old sergeant (Fredric March) is now his bank manager; his wartime
wife (Virginia Mayo) has left him for unshaven Steve Cochran; his employ-
ment prospects are minimal. By the time Andrews gets to the airplane
graveyard, we get the feeling that he would have liked the war to continue
indefinitely. Magically shot by cameraman Gregg Toland, the sequence is
unforgettable. Men in overalls strip the planes down for spares. Supposed
to be a swords into ploughshares routine, it seems like a brutal rape of the
finest flower of military technology.

That a yardful of scrapped warplanes can be an effective symbol for the tragic waste of a talented man's future is an indication of the enduring cinematic power and appeal of aviation. The fifties turned out to be Hollywood's most plane-conscious decade. Famous fliers are celebrated in biopics like Gordon Douglas's *The McConnell Story* (1955), John Ford's *The Wings of Eagles* (1957) — a biopic of Frank 'Spig' Wead (John Wayne), screenwriter of *The Beginning or the End?* — and Billy Wilder's *The Spirit of St Louis* (1957); World War Two is turned into instant nostalgia for Sam Wood's *Command Decision* (1949) and Henry King's *Twelve O'Clock High* (1949); Korea is an excuse for Mark Robson's *The Bridges at Toko-Ri* (1954), Douglas Sirk's *Battle Hymn* (1956) and Dick Powell's *The Hunters* (1958); and test pilots feature in Stuart Heisler's *Chain Lightning* (1950), David Lean's *The Sound Barrier* (1952, *Breaking the Sound Barrier*), Robert D. Webb's *On the Threshold of Space* (1956), Mervyn LeRoy's *Toward the Unknown* (1956) and Richard Donner's *X-15* (1961), reappearing as the last heroes of Philip Kaufman's *The Right Stuff* (1983). While later airborne disaster movies depend for their commercial appeal on spectacular crashes, fifties films like William A. Wellman's *The High and the Mighty* (1954), Andrew L. Stone's *Julie* (1956) and Hall Bartlett's *Zero Hour* (1957) climax with against-the-odds forced landings as the unwilling pilots (John Wayne, Doris Day and — surprise, surprise — Dana Andrews, respectively) prove themselves and bring their crippled flying giants safely down to earth.

Though *The Best Years of Our Lives* seems convinced that the age of the plane is over, there are hints of what will come in the next fifteen years. 'We'd better make this a good peace,' pianist Hoagy Carmichael tells amputee Harold Russell, 'because if there's another war, none of us will have a chance.' Barely a year after the Hiroshima and Nagasaki air raids, which lag behind Dresden and Tokyo as the third and fourth most destructive of the war, the concept of a world-destroying nuclear conflict has become current. And with it the notion of the 'good peace', whereby the safety of the world can only be ensured through strength and preparedness. Dana Andrews manages to find a new life with Teresa Wright before the fade-out, but, if two mid-fifties movies are to be credited, his flying career probably isn't over. William Holden in *The Bridges at Toko-Ri* and James Stewart in *Strategic Air Command* feel that they have done their bit by flying in the Big War. In the fifties, all they want to do is settle down with a pretty wife (Grace Kelly, June Allyson) and pursue a rewarding civilian career (the law, baseball). Called out of the reserve for Lesser Wars, they object strongly. Eventually, they come round and do their duty. Holden winds up dead in a Korean ditch, but Stewart turns out to be the man to win the Cold War.

'Though technically we are now at peace,' runs the *Strategic Air Command* press release, 'there hangs over everyone the fear of a surprise attack from without, and here is a picture to build up our confidence in our protective devices and allay some of our uneasy feelings.' Early in the film, the officer who wants to recall Stewart to active duty visits the St Louis Cardinals training field and confronts his civilian opposite number, the ballplayers' fatherly coach. When asked, the officer tells the coach that SAC is 'the air force's global bombing command.' The coach, who probably reads *Life* magazine, is impressed: 'You're the guys who drop the atom bomb?' The officer, momentarily serious, declares, 'We hope we don't have to.' Made with every co-operation the Department of Defence could grant, *Strategic Air Command* is a conservative, frankly propagandist exercise on behalf of the United States' nuclear deterrent, but is as sincere in its desire for perpetual peace as any song by John Lennon or statement from the Greenham Common women.

And yet... there is a seductive quality about the film that is almost sinister. Gary Cooper, as the World War One Brigadier-General who practically invented bombing, gives the hawk's point of view in Otto Preminger's *The Court-Martial of Billy Mitchell* (1955), summing up the twentieth century with 'one day strategic bombing will leave half the world in ruins; I want this country to be in the other half.' However, *Strategic Air Command* has Stewart tell his long-suffering wife they need to make sacrifices because 'there's a kind of war on... we've got to stay ready to fight without fighting.' The earthbound plot of the film mainly concerns the way that Stewart becomes aware of the importance of the work he has been called to and convinces Allyson that she must allow him to commit himself whole-heartedly to it. Stewart and Allyson represent the kindly, conformist, progressive, clean-cut America that SAC is supposed to be protecting. For a while Allyson thinks Stewart is always flying because he loves his planes more than her; but she is eventually assured that he is always flying precisely because of the strength of his love for her.

However, the pictures tell another story. Shot in VistaVision, *Strategic*

Air Command lingers over the smooth, perfectly-proportioned, blue-grey fuselages of its planes as lovingly and pruriently as other films fix their gaze on the bodies of attractive women. (Silvana Pampanini, a minor sex symbol of the fifties, was nick-named The Anatomic Bomb.) Audiences who snicker when Stanley Kubrick depicts a B-52's in-flight fuelling as a kind of sexual intercourse find it difficult to react to the by no means unconscious use of exactly the same symbolism in *Strategic Air Command*. The mechanised eroticism of Anthony Mann's film is overpowering and the script as much as suggests that hanging around such provocative planes makes the men who fly them horny as hell. When Stewart protests at his selection for an important test flight scheduled for the night Allyson is expected to bear their first child, a general brushes aside his objection with 'do you realise that there are fifteen hundred babies born a month to SAC?' In the event, Allyson's daughter is delivered at exactly the same time as Stewart is nursing his bigger baby in for a forced landing. That evening, the pilot is introduced to his firstborn and to his new plane. Forgetting the baby and caressing the B-47, which 'with a crew of three carries the destructive power of the entire B-29 forces used in World War Two', Stewart declares 'she's the most beautiful thing I've ever seen in my life.'

How Have The Mighty Fallen Department: in 1955, *Strategic Air Command* received generally ecstatic reviews and was a major commercial success; in 1978, I was one of the two members of the audience still present at the end of a screening at the University of Sussex. The current critical standing of the film can be gauged from the fact that Norman Mailer cites it as 'a prime example of Shit', and that David Thomson refers to it as 'boringly filled with giant aircraft.' Today, SAC has been subsumed into NORAD, and, like the fighter jocks of *The Right Stuff*, the Jimmy Stewart-style fliers have been replaced by faceless button-pushers. These technocrats, cooped up in their silos and submarines, have not become the subjects of hagiographic films; fighter jocks, relieved of the burden of delivering atomic weapons, remain worthy subjects for macho, technophilic movies — Tony Scott's *Top Gun* (1985) is a reincarnation of Mann's movie, with homoeroticism and pounding rock music thrown into the mix as Tom Cruise rapes the skies in his jet-plane and goes one-on-one with the Soviets in a skirmish that takes the place of all-out war.

After *Strategic Air Command*, the message seemed well and truly delivered. An imitation of sorts, Gordon Douglas's *Bombers B-52* (1957), which parallels Sergeant Karl Malden's problems with a rickety jet and an over-sexed daughter (Natalie Wood), has little to add. However, once General Curtis LeMay, the ferocious head of SAC, got wind of Stanley Kubrick's plans to film Peter George's novel *Two Hours to Doom* (1958, *Red Alert*), in which his men are depicted as homicidal psychotics, he decided it was time for another public relations exercise. Beirne Lay, who had cornered the market in atom bomb scripts with *Above and Beyond* (in which Jim Backus plays an avuncular LeMay) and *Strategic Air Command*, was presumably unavailable. LeMay called in Sy Bartlett who, in addition to being the first American to bomb Berlin, had been Lay's writing partner on *Twelve O'Clock High*, generally rated as the best ever movie about bombing. Bartlett harked back to Henry King's film, in which General Gregory Peck takes over a demoralised and ineffectual Bomber Wing from slacker Gary Merrill and whips it into a fighting-fit credit to the service, and wrote *A Gathering of Eagles*, in which General Rock Hudson takes over a demor-

alised and ineffectual SAC base from slacker Rod Taylor and whips it into a fighting-fit credit to the service.

In *Twelve O'Clock High*, the war adds a certain desperation to Peck's crusade, and a successful bombing raid gives positive proof that his harsh methods do pay off. For *A Gathering of Eagles*, Bartlett and director Delbert Mann need to pep up the peace to add an element of urgency to the story. They seize on SAC's irregular Operational Readiness Inspections (ORI). In the opening scenes, Taylor's motley crew flunk an ORI, but, when the inspection is repeated after Hudson's toughening-up, the planes get into the air at any cost. In *Twelve O'Clock High*, Peck cracks up under the strain and there is some doubt as to whether it really is all worth it; but

A Gathering of Eagles confines its personal drama to a replay of the domestic tiffs of *Above and Beyond* and *Strategic Air Command* as Hudson wins over estranged wife Mary Peach to the SAC cause. As if aware that General Jack D. Ripper would soon be taking over from the *Pillow Talk* man as the typical SAC commander, a *Newsweek* reviewer mentioned that 'without the distinction of Hudson's preternatural charm, it is appallingly clear that only a maniac can run a SAC wing properly.'

Dr. Strangelove or: How I Learned to Stop Worrying and Love the Bomb (1964) and *Fail Safe* (1964) were too much for LeMay. Of course, SAC did not extend these productions the kind of facilities it offered *Strategic Air Command* and *A Gathering of Eagles*, and, at the military's insistence, the films bear half-hearted disclaimers to the effect that the events they depict are, given the stringent safety procedures enforced in the real air force, completely impossible. By now, it was too late for the Bomb. The American cinema's first unpleasant American bomber pilot came in 1962, with Steve McQueen going psycho in Philip Leacock's *The War Lover*, and Slim Pickens, riding an H-bomb like a bucking bronco in *Strangelove*, finally did away with the Jimmy Stewart image. Patriotic war films like Michael Anderson's *The Dam Busters* (1954), in which we are justified in bombing them, gave way to patriotic war films like Guy Hamilton's *Battle of Britain* (1969) and Richard Fleischer and Kinji Fukasuku's *Tora! Tora! Tora!* (1970), in which they are unjustified in bombing us. In Mike Nichols's *Catch-22* (1970), George Roy Hill's *Slaughterhouse Five* (1973) and Vincent Ward's *Map of the Human Heart* (1993), Allied bombings are seen as absurdist atrocities; even Michael Caton-Jones's uncomplicated *Memphis Belle* (1990) concentrates on the sufferings of the overstretched crew of a World War Two B-17.

With a missile-based deterrent, the cinema could afford to reassess the role of the bomber. LeMay's threat to 'bomb North Vietnam back into the Stone Age' was well-publicised. Public opinion turned against those men of the fifties in their grey flannel flying suits who flew their B-52s to protect hearth, home and June Allyson, carrying the Bomb only so they wouldn't have to drop it. To show bomber pilots in a good light, Don Taylor's *The Final Countdown* (1979) has to resort to time travel. The USS *Nimitz*, a nuclear aircraft carrier, is time-warped back to 1941, and Tojo's Pearl Harbour attack force is resurrected as the enemy. Captain Kirk

Douglas agonises more over the ethics of interfering with history than of using the Bomb. The script gets him out of it before an irreversible decision has been made, and audiences the world over didn't give a damn. Even less welcome was John Milius's *Flight of the Intruder* (1990), a Vietnam-set bomber movie which failed even to catch the *Top Gun* anti-commie tailwind and proved an especially thin last hurrah for the men who flew the skies and delivered death.

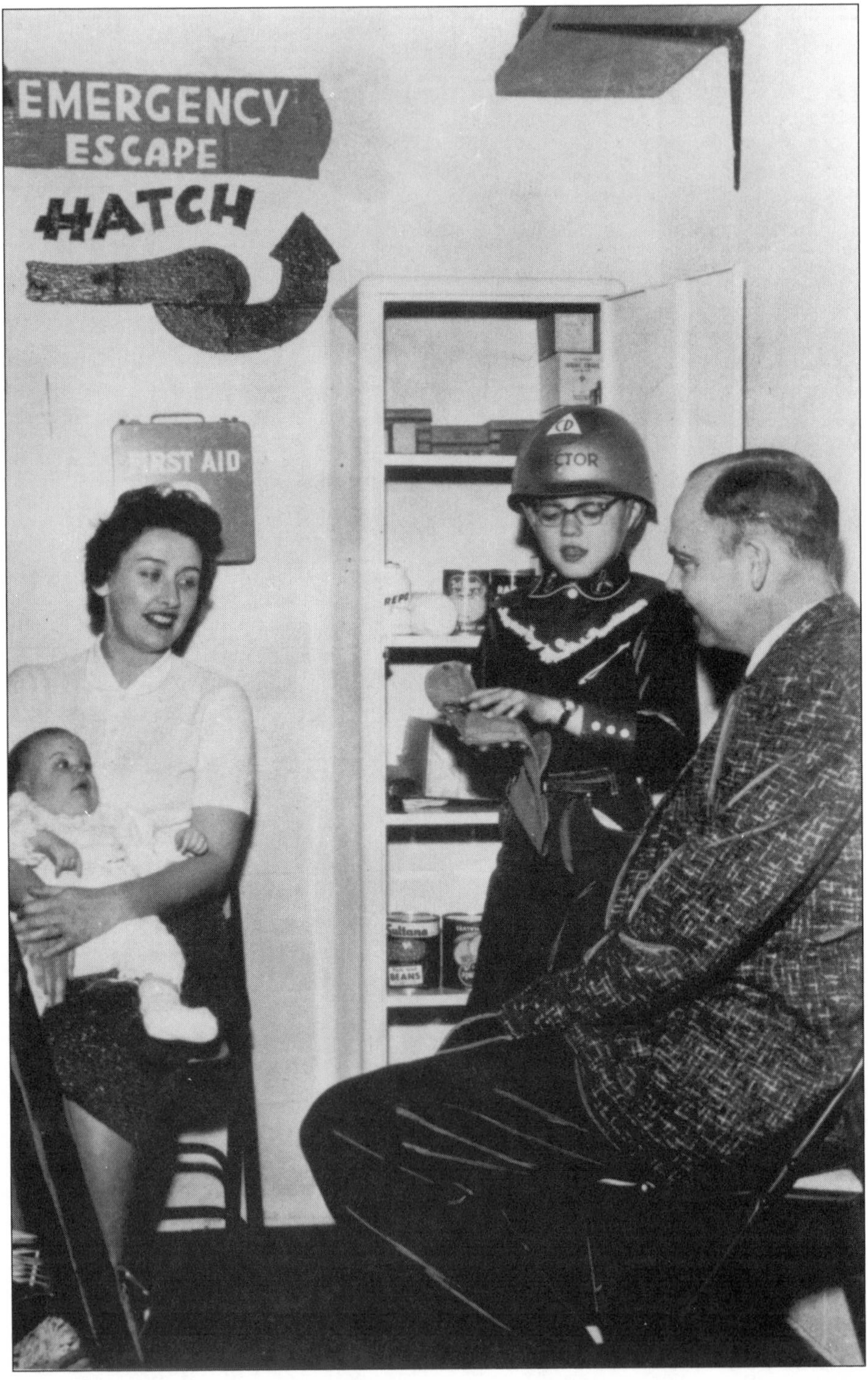
EMERGENCY
ESCAPE
HATCH

The Atomic Decade

The nineteen-fifties... when all we had to worry about were the communists and rock 'n' roll.

Strange Invaders (**1983**)

Opposite:
The Atomic
Cafe

Testing, Testing

In the records of the Atomic Energy Commission (AEC), the Trinity explosion at Alamogordo, New Mexico, is classed as Test Number One. The Hiroshima and Nagasaki missions are listed as Tests Two and Three. In Kevin and Pierce Rafferty and Jayne Loader's *The Atomic Cafe* (1983), a satirical scrapbook of nuke-related snippets from the fifties, Paul Tibbetts can be heard claiming that Hiroshima 'offered a classroom experiment in being able to determine bomb damage'. After the war, testing began in earnest, and a dedicated team of men and women devoted themselves wholeheartedly to the sacred task of irradiating underpopulated and expendable areas of the globe in the name of science and peace.

The movies soon took note of the AEC test programme, not least because film taken during the controlled experiments provided stock footage of mushroom clouds and devastated landscapes that would provide at least forty years' worth of good service for producers without the special effects budget to rig up the kind of fake explosions created in the studio for *The Beginning or the End?* As recently as *Godzilla* (1998), the same old footage (seen in everything from *Savage Mutiny* [1953], through *Attack of the Crab Monsters* [1957], to *Dr. Strangelove*) is trotted out to represent contemporary tests, though the French Mururoa Atoll tests supposedly responsible for Godzilla's mutation were underground detonations, not the Bikini-style surface blasts seen on screen.

Bomb tests were a hot subject in the fifties, and crept into many screenplays. Eugène Lourié's *The Beast From 20,000 Fathoms* (1953), Gordon Douglas's *Them!* (1954), Robert Gordon's *It Came From Beneath the Sea* (1955), Bert I. Gordon's *The Amazing Colossal Man* (1957) and Allan Dwan's *The Most Dangerous Man Alive* (1961) have rampaging monsters of various breeds crop up as side-effects of the tests, while William Cameron Menzies's *Invaders From Mars* (1953) and its semi-remake W. Lee Wilder's *Killers From Space* (1954) have literally alien infiltrators 'taking over' regular Americans in order to subvert the bomb test programme. Marvel Comics' Incredible Hulk, who made his début in 1962, shares his origin (dashing into a test site to save a bystander during a gamma bomb detonation) with the Colossal Man. Guy Green's *SOS Pacific* (1960) has an international cast (Eddie Constantine, Pier Angeli, John Gregson, Richard Attenborough) shipwrecked on a Pacific atoll chosen as an H-Bomb test site. Norman Panama and Melvin Frank's musical *Li'l Abner* (1959), from Al Capp's famous comic strip, finds the American government deciding that Dogpatch, Abner's home town, is the least likely spot in the country to be missed if it happens to get blown off the face of the Earth by a bomb test. Ironically, the Tennessee new town that sprung up around the atomic facilities at Oak Ridge was nicknamed Dogpatch in honour of Capp's mythical nowheresville.

Comedians Mickey Rooney and Jerry Lewis wander onto the Los Alamos Atomic Proving Grounds in Leslie H. Martinson's *The Atomic Kid* (1954) and Norman Taurog's *Living It Up* (1954) respectively; Rooney starts glowing but is otherwise unaffected, while Lewis becomes a national hero when everyone thinks he is dying of radiation poisoning only to become reviled when it turns out that his doctor has made a mistake and the only radioactivity in Lewis's body is due to his luminous watch dial. Rather more upsetting is Kaneto Shindo's *Daigo Fukuryu-Maru* (1959, *Lucky Dragon No. 5*), a fact-based drama about the deaths of a Japanese fishing crew irradiated after a 1954 Pacific H-Bomb test, an incident which also inspired Ishiro Honda's more fanciful if no less bitter *Bijo to Ekatai Ningen* (1958, *The H-Man*). Just a year before the 'Bravo' test, Spencer Gordon Bennet cranked out *Savage Mutiny*, a cheapo programmer which has the distinction of presenting the most distasteful premise. Evil 'foreign agents' plan a propaganda coup around a test detonation on an island off the coast of West Africa by spraying the natives with 'radioactive dust' to suggest Lucky Dragon-style callousness on the part of the West. Then, the baddies lure the islanders back to the blast area 'so the whole world sees how Anglo-Americans use human guinea pigs for their so-called "peaceful" atomic tests'. Jungle Jim (Johnny Weissmuller) and Tamba the irritating chimp save the day; in reality, Anglo-Americans were guilty of almost everything the commie villains of *Savage Mutiny* framed them for.

Split Second (1953), a taut thriller derived in part from *The Petrified Forest* (1936), is perhaps the best of the test movies. Originally shot in 3-D to take advantage of its desert locations, fist-fights and mushroom cloud, the film has escaped convict Sam Hurley (Stephen McNally) and his sidekicks kidnap a group of ordinary citizens and hole up in Lost Hope City, a ghost town next to an A-bomb test tower. The Bomb isn't due to go off until the next morning, so Sam figures that it will be safe to hide out in the danger area for the night. As in all these hostage crisis movies, the worthy and the unworthy alike are tested, and the worthy are found wanting while the unworthy finally reveal hidden virtues. Mrs Garvin (Alexis Smith), a svelte adulteress whose classy outfits brand her as an incipient hysteric, submits to Sam's crude advances and whines throughout for her miserable life. Dorothy (Jan Sterling), the penniless broad who has been a waitress and worse, spurns the heel's slimy advances and settles for the honest reporter hero (Keith Andes).

'You don't think very much of people do you?' the hero asks Sam. 'I was a hero for three years,' replies the psycho, 'watchin' all my pals get their heads blowed off'. In addition to its crazed, cynical World War Two veteran, the film has a just plain crazed World War One veteran (Arthur Hunnicutt) who looks at the gleaming bomb and murmurs 'just think what we coulda' done with a couple of those things at Mons'. Sam's thinking is stuck in 1943 just as surely as the old man's is stuck in 1918. Neither of them show any respect for the destructive power calmly ticking away a hundred yards into the desert. The nuclear device decides to go off an hour early to teach them all a lesson. The unjust are blown out of their getaway car, while the just make it to a nearby abandoned mine and sit out the big bang. As the sobered survivors emerge into the radioactive desert, the doctor (Richard Egan) grimly says, 'Let's take a look at the world of tomorrow'. A mushroom cloud towers into the sky, Lost Hope City isn't even a memory, and Sam is a greasy spot on a rock somewhere.

Now, the finale of *Split Second* seems even more downbeat than it was at the time. The filmmakers didn't know that, by exposing themselves so soon after the detonation, their characters were probably laying the groundwork for fatal doses of radiation-induced bone cancer, leukaemia and congenital cellular disruption. Three years later, RKO, the company that made *Split Second*, sent the film's director Dick Powell and his unit on location to make *The Conqueror* (1956). Set in the Far East, the film was shot amid Utah sand dunes that had been covered with fall-out after a test explosion just like the one in *Split Second*. It has been suggested that the high incidence of cancer-related deaths among the people who worked on *The Conqueror* is due to this exposure. The alleged victims have included John Wayne, Susan Hayward, Agnes Moorehead and Dick Powell.

By the time of Paul Dickson's *Satellite in the Sky* (1956), the cinema was ready to condemn bomb testing on principle, not just because it was liable to create giant ants and human slime monsters. The captain of the first ship in orbit (Kieron Moore) is ordered to take along a 'tritanium bomb', a nuclear device so unpredictable that even loony scientist Donald Wolfit ('How can I possibly take responsibility for everything that *might* happen?') wouldn't risk testing it within the Earth's atmosphere. Wolfit's dangerous fanaticism nearly leads to disaster when the activated bomb sticks to the tail of his rocketship, prompting stowaway reporter Lois Maxwell to lament that 'so much time, money and intelligence is wasted on making bigger and better bombs'. *Satellite in the Sky* is the first of several films (*Beyond the Time Barrier* [1960]; *The Day the Earth Caught Fire* [1962]; *Crack in the World* [1965]) which forecast world-threatening catastrophes unless scientists are prevented from setting off nuclear firecrackers whenever they feel like it: 'Supposing the explosion doesn't dissipate itself in space? This could be the end of the world, for all we know.' In *Keep Watching the Skies!*, Bill Warren exhumes a sinister reaction from the *Hollywood Reporter*: '*Satellite in the Sky* has a pervading philosophy and theme that seem to add up to a plea against the use of atomic bombs for any purpose whatsoever, including tests. Any impressionable and not very well-informed person seeing this *Satellite* could come away with the idea that those advocating atom tests are stupid, irresponsible or even criminally careless.'

Edgar G. Ulmer's *Beyond the Time Barrier* toys with ideas that seem more relevant forty years on, as it apparently discusses the despoliation of the ozone layer. The film's civilisation-wrecking disaster is caused by 'the tons of radioactive dust that have mushroomed up into the ionosphere since the very first A-bomb test... that have remained up there and are slowly destroying the protective screen that has filtered deadly cosmic rays from space since the beginning of time'. This allows for 'a bombardment of radiation from outer space', which inflicts on humanity a 'plague' that causes mutations, baldness, deaf mutism and infertility. It's hard to tell whether it's Ulmer's gloomy personality or sheer carelessness on the part of hack writer Arthur Pierce, but this is one of the most hopeless, miserable, cynical and despairing of all science fiction films, with characters who turn nasty at random and an orgy of rape and violence as the mutants sack the citadel of the civilised. In the frame story, time traveller Robert Clarke is instantly aged by his experience and his awful warning to the present about repeated bomb tests is forgotten in an overly busy wind-up.

In the sixties and after, bomb tests became slightly old hat. Sidney J. Furie's 1965 film of Len Deighton's 1962 novel *The Ipcress File* omits an effective section from the book in which Deighton's British spy hero stumbles around a disorienting and disoriented American Pacific test facility. Testing continued, but literally went underground. Even in the eighties and

nineties, with France, India and Pakistan continuing nuclear weapons test programmes, the movie image of the bomb test is of the 1950s. The prologue of Tobe Hooper's dreary *Spontaneous Combustion* (1990) recreates a newsreel of the period, blithely cheerful about an extremely dangerous experiment, 'explaining' the dangerous psychic powers possessed by its monster hero (Brad Dourif). A more striking left-over from the first phase of the atomic age is the deserted ruin of an 'atomic city', mock-suburban homes still littered with test dummies, in Dominic Serna's *Kalifornia* (1993), which serves as a backdrop for the activities of a group of emblematic, violence-obsessed contemporary Americans.

Eugene Corr's *Desert Bloom* (1986) and Tony Richardson's *Blue Sky* (1994) — both influenced by the 'duck and cover' style of *The Atomic Cafe*

— are double-edged nostalgia movies, recreating a recent past when the characters could plausibly be more concerned with troubled family situations than with the fall-out of tests that take place around the fringes of the plot. In *Desert Bloom*, a Nevada family in the early 1950s come together at dawn, after sundry trials, to watch a mushroom cloud rise from the proving grounds; while Jessica Lange of *Blue Sky*, an emotionally unstable army wife, is forced to get a grip when the authorities try to cover up the accidental irradiation of her husband (Tommy Lee Jones). Philip Ridley's *The Reflecting Skin* (1990) also includes a contaminated soldier (Viggo Mortensen) in its collection of Americana, reviving the sparkly look of the decade but working hard at suggesting underlying corruption. Lee Tamahori's *Mulholland Falls* (1996) takes a conspiracy movie approach, with hard-boiled cops investigating a murder and a cover-up but blundering into a huge desert crater and realising atomic bigwig John Malkovich has essentially been given a licence to kill.

More direct and angry is Michael Pattinson and Bruce Myles's Australian *Ground Zero* (1987), set in the present, with Colin Friels searching for film his newsreel cameraman father shot that reveals how British A-bomb tests in the outback sprinkled fall-out on Aborigines. The film opens with an irradiated plane, buried since 1953 and exhumed by decontamination-suited zombies, bringing the sins of the past back to the present. It should come as no surprise that Friels's crusade to bring out the truth is opposed by creepy government types who want the story suppressed. Peter Markle's made-for-TV movie *Nightbreaker* (1989, *Advance to Ground Zero*) is a similar, slightly more earnest, issue effort. A doctor, played by Emilio Estevez in the fifties scenes and Martin Sheen in the present-day sequences, exposes the American army's callous and deliberate exposure of its servicemen to radiation just to see what would happen to them.

Sheltermania

When the Major emerged from his casts, a metamorphosis had occurred: He was no longer bold and brash. In fact, the first project he undertook was to renovate the basement family room into a bomb shelter as a surprise for Mother's birthday. We kids were delighted. I took my girl friends down there to play house; and we confronted such ethical issues as whether or not to let old Mr Thornberg next door share our shelter when the bomb dropped, or whether to slam the door in his miserly face, as he did to us on Halloween nights.

Lisa Alther, *Kinflicks*

In Terrell O. Morse's *Unknown World* (1951), the Society to Save Civilisation, a band of concerned scientists, declares that 'modern civilisation could be brought by atomic fission to dust and ruins... this could mean not only the end of our own civilisation but of the very possibility of future civilisations'. Led by bleeding heart Dr Jeremiah Morley (Victor Kilian), the assembled geniuses invent a tunnelling machine and mount an expedition deep into the Earth. In the event of a surface-destroying war, Morley hopes the human race can take refuge in specially constructed cavern cities. Devil-may-care playboy Wright Thompson Jr (Bruce Kellogg) finances the trip on the condition he be allowed to come along. 'You don't like my kind of guy, do you?' he asks Dr Joan Lindsey (Marilyn Nash), an 'ardent feminist' whose starched disposition suggests she isn't too keen on anybody's kind of guy. Before the picture is over, the scientists have learned their lesson and ordinary joe Thompson is proved right.

As they go deeper, the explorers get more depressed. 'People have dignity only in relation to many other people,' moans Joan. 'Alone, a man is as useless as that rock over there.' The caverns are found, but their peculiar atmosphere makes everyone feel listless — the air renders all mammals sterile. His vision of an underground colony ruined, Morley despairs: 'Why go back to a world bent on self-destruction?' But the ardent feminist's heart has melted and she cheerfully accompanies Thompson back to the surface where 'the universe is still in harmony'. Popping out of a volcano, the heroine comments, 'I feel like I'll live forever'.

Limply acted and resolutely unexciting, *Unknown World* is a dreary little film, but interesting as an early example of anti-survivalism. Made before the shelter fever of the fifties had really got started, it seems all the more redundant because its judgements on the burrowers are off-beam. The wrong-headed Morley is a gloomy Oppenheimer figure, epitome of defeatism, whereas the 'civil defence' survival craze was actually championed by Edward Teller, a right-wing patriot far more likely to appeal to regular blokes like Wright Thompson than pinko weirdies like Joan Lindsey. In the finale, Joan is no longer a doomwatcher, but we are not told to what she will henceforth devote her energy. Does she enlist in the AEC and help build up America's deterrent? Does she start a campaign for nuclear arms controls? Or does she have Thompson's babies and try not to worry her pretty little head about men's business?

> Fall-out shelters have been used in a number of ways in fiction: as a high-pressure environment for the blossoming of love affairs, as a refuge for religious cultists, as emotional pressure cookers provoking violent conflict, and even as time-travel machines. Indeed they have usually served every purpose except that for which real shelters are ostensibly designed: the protection of their inhabitants from blast and radiation. Whatever their perspective, all but a handful of authors writing about shelters view them as metaphors for racial suicide, a symbol of the self-destructing nature of nuclear weapons, which make us our own prisoners of war.

> **Paul Brians, *Nuclear Holocausts: Atomic War in Fiction, 1895-1984***

The removal of entire populations to subterranean strongholds, which seems to be the agenda of *Unknown World*, was one of the least likely of many impractical schemes proposed in the 1950s and sixties for 'civil defence'. As with Ronald Reagan's Strategic Defence Initiative of the eighties, the civil defence stratagems of the Eisenhower-Kennedy era were an irrational response to an insoluble problem — having invented and used the bomb as an offensive weapon, America *must* be able to protect its own citizenry and way of life from the bombs of other powers. It was seriously suggested that cities should be redeveloped horizontally rather than vertically to disperse the population and essential services, making them impossible to wipe out entirely with one ground zero blast. In this sense, the expansionist, freeway-strangled Los Angeles we see a-borning in Robert Zemeckis's *Who Framed Roger Rabbit* (1988) and Jack Nicholson's *The Two Jakes* (1990), both of which feature significant explosions, is the first truly post-atomic city.

During an endless series of practice evacuations and 'duck and cover' drills, the truth finally sank in that, as a British army pamphlet put it, the only real defence against the atom bomb was 'not to be there when it goes off'. It was in this climate that the bomb shelter became an American institution. Novels set in shelters for government personnel (Mordecai Roshwald's *Level 7* [1959]) or made available to the ordinary people (Robert Moore Williams's *The Day They H-bombed Los Angeles* [1961]) tended to the elegiac or the cynical — Roshwald depicts the shelter as delaying but not halting the deadly seepage of radiation, and Williams finally reveals that the H-bomb has been dropped by the American Government as a last-ditch defence against body-snatched zombies in the thrall of 'a mutated protein molecule'. Dr Strangelove himself advocates the emergency relocation of the nation's top political, military and scientific brass to the bottom of 'our deepest mineshafts', along with a harem of attractive young women to assist in aggressive procreation and repopulation, while Joseph Losey's *The Damned* (1961) has the most ruthless of all shelter programmes, forcing a group of children to live underground in a radioactive environment even before the Bomb drops.

The real shelter controversy sprang up from the concept of individual or family units, which a whole cowboy industry tried to persuade the paranoid suburbanites of the fifties were as essential to any sitcom perfect home as a pool in the backyard, a finned car in the garage or aluminium siding on the house. Thankfully, the various doubts about the nuke-worthiness of such structures were never actually tested, though it is certain that six weeks drinking distilled water, eating canned food and playing Scrabble was unlikely to be much help in living through a nuclear winter. However, the many magazine articles which gave lists of the supplies essential for any well-stocked shelter did spotlight the most divisive and disturbing aspect of this early flowering of what came to be known as survivalism. Most of the well-prepared, buttoned-down men intended to keep guns in their shelter to defend them against lesser-prepared, irradiated neighbours who might try to force themselves in. The fable of 'The Grasshopper and the Ant' was much cited as justification, and few suggested Americans might react like blitzed Londoners, helping each other out and defying the bombers. There was even theological debate as to whether it was Christian or not to prepare for such an eventuality, and the populations of certain rural areas were known to have made discreet preparations to resist the flood-tides of horribly afflicted city folk who would be expected to swarm into the countryside in the event of World War Three. This, of course, begged the question as to who the Enemy might be; it seemed that those best-prepared to survive were more committed to resisting their fellow Americans than any communists.

The movies took the shelter fad a lot less seriously than everyone else. Well-prepared characters in the cinema are total maniacs — like Glenn Anders in Orson Welles's *Lady From Shanghai* (1948), who plans an insurance fraud so that he can retreat to the South Seas, and Sonny Tufts in Lew Landers's *Run for the Hills* (1953), who goes broke living in a cave to escape the holocaust. In 'The Photographer' (*Mission: Impossible*, 1967), the Impossible Mission Force team fool American traitor Anthony Zerbe — nestled in his own shelter — into believing war has come by setting up a diorama of devastation around his periscope. Owning a bomb shelter is almost as embarrassing as driving an Edsel in such knowing retro efforts as Larry Cohen's *Full Moon High* (1981) and Joe Dante's *Matinee* (1993). In Paul Bartel's *Shelf Life* (1992), a family retreats into their shelter in 1963, certain that the JFK assassination is the first shot of World War Three, and stay underground for thirty years, convinced that the world outside is an ashen wasteland. A rare example of characters actually living through a real war in a shelter is Albert Pyun's *Radioactive Dreams* (1986), which prefigures *Shelf Life* in suggesting the kind of distorted private world cooped-up survivors raised in a shelter might create.

The most rigorous examination of the shelter mentality is Akira Kurosawa's powerful but inconclusive *Ikimono no Kiroku* (1955, *Living in Fear/Record of a Living Being*). Kiichi Nakajima (Toshiro Mifune), wealthy head of a Japanese industrial family, has wasted several million yen on a fall-out shelter that latest scientific journals suggest will be useless. Convinced that South America is the only place likely to survive World War Three, Nakajima tries to sell up and relocate his family empire, including mistresses, illegitimate offspring and trusted retainers, to Brazil. His dependents get together and take him before a family court to have him declared semi-competent. 'Your worry is the worry of all Japanese,' says one of the court. A judge (Takashi Shimura) begins to wonder just how crazy or sane Nakajima really is. Though it presents all the moral and practical arguments for and against its hero's schemes, *Ikimono no Kiroku* never reaches a verdict. The crumbling of traditional Japanese values and the threat of the Bomb are appreciable motives, but Nakajima's actions, prompted by newspaper articles and overheard conversations, are capricious whims. The film is a tragedy; its strong central figure is destroyed by internal and external forces that cannot be reconciled. Nakajima's attempted flight to Brazil is as much to resist the Westernised notions which are undercutting his patriarchal authority as it is to evade nuclear holocaust. Afraid the family is bound to Japan by its material wealth, Nakajima burns down his foundry. Confined to an asylum, he is thrown into a blind panic by the rising sun which he takes for the first flash of the next war.

In 1961, with the Berlin crisis on-going, President John F. Kennedy accused Nikita Khruschev of 'atomic blackmail' and put the weight of his administration behind a civil defence drive whose international purpose was to demonstrate to the Soviets that America was willing and able to survive a nuclear exchange. In retrospect, this seems like a cynical power play in the rapid escalation of missile-pointing that would climax in Cuba, but at the time, the effect on ordinary Americans — who, in being counselled to build personal fall-out shelters, had in effect been told that in the event of a nuclear war they were on their own and that their survival was their own responsibility — was undeniable. Perhaps the single most effective fictional reaction to this climate of terror was 'The Shelter', an episode of *The Twilight Zone* broadcast in September 1961. In one of Rod Serling's simple but effective little morality stories, we see a happy suburban scene crumble when it is announced that missiles are on the way and Doc Stockton (Larry Gates) hurries his wife and child into the shelter he alone in the street has troubled to build. In a virtual replay of the paranoid spasms of 'The Monsters Are Due on Maple Street' (1960), the suburban, middle-class 'average Americans' become a terrified and terrifying mob, begging and pleading with Doc to be allowed to share the shelter they have previously sneered at, and then using force to batter their way in, to plunder the limited resources set aside for Doc's family. Of course, it turns out to be a false alarm, but the neighbourhood is as shattered as it would have been by war. As the shocked, sobered neighbours disperse, Serling concludes 'no moral, no message, no prophetic tract, just a simple statement of fact: for civilisation to survive, the human race must remain civilised. Tonight's very small exercise in logic from *The Twilight Zone*'. Two weeks after 'The Shelter' was broadcast, ex-President Eisenhower (perhaps with intent to score points off Kennedy) gave a speech against home shelters, declaring that he would not wish to survive if his family were to die.

The defining crisis of this era was the Soviet-American face-off over the siting of Russian missiles in Cuba, ninety minutes away from the US coast ('just as if we suddenly began to put a major number of [missiles] in Turkey,' complained Kennedy; 'well, we *did*, Mr President,' an aide reminded him). The attitudes of this era are expertly evoked in *Matinee*, which does its best to provide a light-hearted assessment of the importance of mythical terrors to a terrified world. Set in Key West, Florida, during the US Naval blockade of Cuba, Joe Dante's film has horror movie producer Lawrence Woolsey (John Goodman), a cigar-wielding huckster, arrive in town for a special preview of his latest epic, *Mant!*, 'in Atomo-Vision and Rumble-Rama'. Theatre manager (Robert Picardo), who listens constantly to the CONELRAD emergency channel via an ear-plug and has a 'We'll Bury You' Khrushchev poster in his office, is a prissy fanatic who has made plans to survive in his vault-like basement shelter, with his goldfish and a pump-action shotgun. 'There's no phone,' muses a teenage girl who chances upon the shelter, only to think it through for herself and shudder.

A general in *Mant!* (Kevin McCarthy) declares 'you don't build weapons to wheel 'em down the street in parades' as he prepares to bomb Chicago to get rid of a mutated giant ant-man, and the kids who attend Woolsey's preview are all infected in one way or another by the panic, from the younger brother who watches TV news all day to the beatnik girl (Lisa Jakub) who resists taking part in a duck-and-cover drill with 'they tell you to put your hands behind your neck and they keep building bombs'. When the Rumble-Rama effect makes the manager think the war has come, Jakub and the young hero (Simon Fenton) are trapped inside but the manager is left outside, sobbing. Though the shelter manufacturers have adver-

1962: The possible end of civilisation as we know it.
And for Lawrence Woolsey, business is booming!

tised that the structure is impregnable, it only takes a few moments to crowbar it open. Yet another crisis comes when the theatre's overloaded balcony is on the point of collapse but 'Atomo-Vision' — a William Castle-style process whereby it seems that the wall of the cinema has been blown out by an explosion and a vivid orange mushroom cloud is seen rising from the horizon beyond — clears the house. The ending, of course, is upbeat, as the crisis is resolved (in real life, the Russians withdrew their missiles and Kennedy quietly pulled his own weapons out of Turkey) and Woolsey departs in the certainty of a hit, but there's something ominous in the triumphalism of the last image — an American naval helicopter blotting out the screen as the soundtrack excerpts 'The Lion Sleeps Tonight'.

Atom Spies

Prior to the shooting of *Notorious*, Ben Hecht and I went over to the California Institute of Technology at Pasadena to meet Dr Millikan, at that time one of the leading scientists in America. We were shown into his offices and there in a corner was a bust of Einstein. Very impressive. The first question we asked him was: 'Dr Millikan, how large would an atom bomb be?' He looked at us and said, 'you want to have yourselves arrested and me arrested as well?' Then he spent an hour telling us how impossible our idea was, and he concluded that if only they could harness hydrogen, then there would be something. He thought that he had succeeded in convincing us that we were barking up the wrong tree, but I learned later that afterward the FBI had me under surveillance for three months.

Alfred Hitchcock, in *Hitchcock*

The history of atomic espionage began in World War Two, as Germany and the Allies were competing to construct the first generation of nuclear weapons. Shortly after Hiroshima, a number of movies on the subject appeared. Lew Landers's *Shadow of Terror* (1945), a formula cheapie about an inventor persecuted by Nazi spies, included some mushroom cloud footage spliced in at the last minute in order to cash in on the news from Los Alamos and points East; Henry Hathaway's *The House on 92nd Street* (1945, originally to be called *Now It Can be Told*) has FBI agents expose quivering Gene Lockhart as the traitor leaking Manhattan Project secrets to Nazi transvestite Signe Hasso; Fritz Lang's *Cloak and Dagger* (1946) finds nuclear physicist Gary Cooper undercover in Italy to check up on some pitchblende and a missing genius only to wind up in the thick of an Axis A-bomb scheme. Paul L. Stein's *Lisbon Story* (1946) and Lawrence Huntington's *Night Boat to Dublin* (1946) deal with the rescue of friendly atomic scientists from the Nazis; Alfred Hitchcock's *Notorious* (1946) has Ingrid Bergman and Cary Grant infiltrating a fascist group in Brazil, discovering uranium-filled bottles in Claude Rains's wine cellar. In later years, Anthony Mann's *The Heroes of Telemark* (1965) features scientist Kirk Douglas and partisan Richard Harris blowing up a German heavy water plant in Norway, while Peter Carter's *A Man Called Intrepid* (1979) and Sheldon Larry's *92 Grosvenor Street* (1985), resurrect the rescue-the-physicist-from-occupied-Europe plot.

In these films, the Bomb is never more than an impressive-sounding, newsworthy peg for an exciting storyline. Hitchcock, who coined the term 'MacGuffin' to describe such narrative conveniences, reveals that the atomic angle of the *Notorious* script caused problems. 'I introduce the MacGuffin,' he told François Truffaut, 'four or five samples of uranium concealed in wine bottles. The producer said, "What in the name of goodness is that?" I said, "This is uranium; it's the thing they are going to make an atom bomb with". And he asked, "What atom bomb?" This was in 1944, a year before Hiroshima. I had only one clue. A writer friend of mine had told me that scientists were working on a secret project some place in New Mexico. It was so secret that once they went into the plant, they never emerged again. I was also aware that the Germans were conducting experiments with heavy water in Norway. So these clues brought me to the uranium MacGuffin. The producer was sceptical, and he felt it was absurd to use the idea of an atom bomb as the basis for our story. I told him it wasn't the basis for the story, but only the MacGuffin, and I explained that there was no need to attach too much importance to it. Finally, I said, "Look, if you don't like uranium, let's make it industrial diamonds, which the Germans need to cut their tools with." And I pointed out that if it had not been a wartime story, we could have hinged our plot on the theft of diamonds, that the gimmick was unimportant'.

Sam Fuller's *Pickup on South Street* (1953) has a patriotic policeman (Murvyn Vye) rail against a pickpocket (Richard Widmark) who has ref-

Above: Cloak and Dagger, Gary Cooper, Lilli Palmer, Vladimir Sokoloff

used to help him track down a communist spy ring, saying, 'you're no better than the traitors who gave Stalin the A-bomb!' Atomic espionage films of the Cold War place more weight on their MacGuffins than their World War Two predecessors. After all, Hitler never did get hold of the Bomb; but, thanks allegedly to leaked secrets, the Russians did become a nuclear power. World War Two atom spy films have the occasional humanist platitude ('God have mercy on us if we haven't the sense to keep the world at peace,' concludes Cooper in *Cloak and Dagger*), but anti-commie paranoia films are full of hysterical Americanism and bloodthirsty red-baiting. Fuller and Widmark followed up *Pickup on South Street* with *Hell and High Water* (1954), in which a group of American mercenaries investigate a Chinese communist scheme to build atomic missiles in the Arctic.

The execution of the Rosenbergs (filmed *à clef* in Sidney Lumet's *Daniel* [1983]) focused pro- and anti-McCarthy debate on the atomic issue, and suggested that nuclear researchers were in the front line of the Cold War. Gordon Douglas's *Walk a Crooked Mile* (1948), Jerry Hopper's *The*

Atomic City (1952), Russell Rouse's *The Thief* (1952), Seymour Friedman's *I'll Get You* (1953), Lewis Allen's *A Bullet for Joey* (1955), Ken Hughes's *Timeslip* (1956), Henri-Georges Clouzot's *Les Espions* (1957, *The Spies*), Alan Bromly's *Follow That Horse* (1960), Mark Robson's *The Prize* (1963), Montgomery Tully's *The Defector* (1963), Marcel Ophuls's *Feu à volonté* (1965), Raoul Lévy's *L'Espion* (1966, *The Defector*) and Alfred Hitchcock's *Torn Curtain* (1966) treat atomic experts as an internationally negotiable currency. In Robert Aldrich's *World for Ransom* (1954), nuclear physicist Arthur Shields, 'one of the four men in the world who knows how to set off the H-bomb', muses that his discipline used to be an academic backwater, shortly before he is kidnapped and offered for sale to the highest bidder. There was even a ludicrous Soviet exercise in propaganda, Abram Room's *Sieriebristaya Pyl* (1953, *Silver Dust*), set in a grossly caricatured capitalist America overrun by robber barons, war-mongers and gangsters, featuring an evil American scientist who tests his radioactive dust on expendable human subjects.

Espionage films tend to deal with isolated characters, under intense pressure and in an alien environment. For the spy, or the innocent person caught up in the world of the spy, paranoia is less a mental complaint than a useful and necessary world view. The atom spy movies of the fifties present a universe that is out of joint. *D.O.A.* (1949) has notary Edmond O'Brien witness an illegal iridium transfer and unknowingly become a marked man. In a nightmarish jazz club, he is slipped a poisoned drink. A visit to the doctor convinces him that he has less than a week in which to live and track down his killer. Directed by Rudolph Maté, *D.O.A.* drops suggestive hints (the iridium MacGuffin, the luminescent poison) of an atomic angle for its hero's plight, but buries the issue in shadows and brutal violence. The Bomb is merely one of several factors — the threat of communist or fascist subversion, post-war traumas, criminal conspiracies, existential angst — that make the *film noir* hero's life into a psychological minefield, but as the Cold War intensified, it became more important.

The masterpiece of nuclear *noir* is Robert Aldrich's *Kiss Me Deadly* (1955), a subversive reading of Mickey Spillane's 1953 thick-ear novel, in which the world is so off balance that the credits roll backwards. Private eye Mike Hammer (Ralph Meeker) is no Bogart-style knight in a trenchcoat, but a sleazy, sadistic bum motivated mainly by lust and avarice. One night,

Hammer picks up Christine (Cloris Leachman), a neurotic hitchhiker naked but for a raincoat. She slips him a few desperate clues, including a scrap of Christina Rossetti ('remember me'), and they are driven off the road by bad guys. She is tortured to death and he obsessively investigates, going from one shady, frightened character to the next. The loner is persecuted by the police/FBI and the communists/Mafia but he continues to beat and blunder his way through the mystery. 'They are the Nameless Ones,' observes Velda (Maxine Cooper), Hammer's secretary, of the unseen enemy, 'who will kill for the Great Whatsit'. Hammer figures that a MacGuffin which everyone makes such a fuss over must be worth a hell of a lot, and stays on the case in the hope of raking in the big bucks.

Right: Kiss Me Deadly, *Gaby Rodgers*

One of the terrified witnesses approached early in the film has disfiguring keloids on his face, but Hammer doesn't get the message. When he peeks into the black box hidden in a locker at an exclusive club, he is momentarily blinded and receives second degree wrist burns. At last, Pat Murphy (Wesley Addy), the only cop in town who can stand being in a room with him, tries to impress the shamus with the importance of the Great Whatsit. 'I'm going to name a few words... meaningless words... just letters jumbled together... but they're unimportant. Try to understand what they mean. Manhattan Project. Los Alamos. Trinity.' Hammer understands, but that doesn't stop him heading for the beach house where arch villain Dr Soberin (Albert Dekker) is holding Velda prisoner.

The private eye turns up just in time to see Gabrielle (Gaby Rodgers), Soberin's moll, close the case for him by shooting the evil doctor. She wants to cash in on what's in the black box, and starts wrestling with the locks. Soberin tries to explain that the box contains not cash, drugs or negotiable bonds, but highly unstable fissionable material. However, he is too intellectual to get the message over. 'The head of the Medusa, that's what's in the box, and whoever looks on her face will be turned not into stone but brimstone and ashes.' Gabrielle misses the classical reference, and a mushroom cloud rises from the Californian beach front. In the words of Hammer's best friend (Nick Dennis), '3-D pow!... Va-va-voom!'

Mutants and Monsters

Sci-fi has always been fascinated with the Other, and critics of popular culture have been quick to point out that the Other is always other than itself, which is to say, the pods and blobs are 'symbols' standing in for something else. Ever since Susan Sontag pointed to the fact that the Other in 50s sci-fi was often linked to radiation, it has been customary to equate the Other with the Bomb. John and Jane Doe might think they're being attacked by elephantine aphids run riot in their garden, but we know better. The hypothetical film informs us that a tactical nuclear weapon has been set off at the desert test site just ten miles away from the Doe residence; one step ahead, we realise that it is radiation that has caused the ravenous aphids to double in size every ten minutes, and jumping to conclusions, we decide that *The Attack of the Giant Aphids* is really about the arms race, and that John and Jane are down with a severe case of nuclear anxiety. But films like this are not primarily worried about the Bomb; they loved the Bomb, or at least the technology that made it possible. The Does may not be as dumb as we thought, and to understand what these films did worry about, all we have to do is look at what's before our very eyes; it's aphids after all, nature run amok.

Peter Biskind, *Seeing is Believing: How Hollywood Taught Us to Stop Worrying and Love the Fifties*

Opposite:
The Thing From Another World, *James Arness*

Science fiction films of the fifties, the period when nuke-awareness was at its height, are full of monsters. And the monsters tend to be radioactive. Peter Biskind, quoted above, tries to reduce the monster movies of the fifties to expressions of the oldest theme in the horror cannon, nature run amok, but monsters are rarely as simple as they at first seem. *The Thing From Another World* (1951), the first monster of the fifties, is a vegetable vampire from outer space who looks like Boris Karloff in a boiler suit. As played by James Arness, the Thing is Dracula, the Frankenstein Monster, the Enemy Invader and Nature Run Amok in one catch-all package. The Bomb is never actually mentioned in the Howard Hawks/Christian Nyby film, but there is a possibly significant moment when an explosive intended to free a flying saucer from the Arctic ice proves much more destructive than the soldiers who set it off expect it to be. With its means of getting back to Another World blown to bits, the Thing might reasonably see itself as the victim of a pre-emptive first strike from the human race, and thus be rather more justified in killing everyone it runs into than the film suggests.

The Thing From Another World ends famously with the American military/scientific (with the emphasis on the former) team triumphant over the 'intellectual carrot', and Scotty (Douglas Spencer), the wise-cracking reporter, turning serious as he delivers the fade-out speech to the rest of the English-speaking world: 'I bring you a warning... tell the world... tell this to everybody wherever they are... watch the skies! Keep watching the skies!' Among other things, this prompts the audience to remember just what that good ol' American base in the middle of the Arctic is there for. It's part of the Distant Early Warning system, watching the skies with radar should the Soviets ever mount a bomber attack. The Russians are further implicated by the fact that the only sympathiser the Thing finds on this world is a cold, unemotional scientist with a beard and a fur hat. Nature may be running amok in The Thing, but the suggestion is that the rampant vegetation has friends in the Kremlin. The film may not be about the arms race, but the Cold War certainly forms a potent subtext for the SF thrills of man against monster.

The first real atomic monster movie is Samuel Newfield's *The Lost Continent* (1951), a very cheap item from Lippert, the company that had produced *Rocketship X-M* (1950), the first real atomic Awful Warning movie. Its historic status aside, *The Lost Continent* is a minor film and the radioactive elements almost completely arbitrary. Major Cesar Romero leads an expedition to the South Seas in search of a downed, nuclear-powered rocket. It turns up on an island where dinosaurs have been 'kept alive by uranium deposits.' The magic mineral pulled the experimental missile from the skies and can probably be blamed for the green tinting of all the lost continent scenes. Radiation is a funny thing, we are told in these films, it has strange powers. In fact, it can do anything convenient for the plot.

This kind of radiation causes Douglas Fairbanks Jr's duck to lay uranium eggs in Val Guest's *Mr Drake's Duck* (1950), makes Mickey Rooney glow in *The Atomic Kid*, puts Peter Arne seven and a half seconds into the future in *Timeslip*, creates geniuses or zombies in John Gilling's *The Gamma People* (1956), shrinks Grant Williams in Jack Arnold's *The Incredible Shrinking Man* (1957), grows Glenn Langan in Bert I. Gordon's *The Amazing Colossal Man*, revives a murderous native as a walking tree in Dan Milner's *From Hell It Came* (1957), makes Japanese gangsters sentient slime in Ishiro Honda's *Bijo to Ekatai Ningen*, turns Ron Randell to steel in Allan Dwan's *The Most Dangerous Man Alive* and makes Tor Johnson into Coleman Francis's *The Beast of Yucca Flats* (1961). In 1962, Stan Lee could get away with having Peter Parker, The Amazing Spider-Man, develop his super-powers after being bitten by a radioactive spider; and Marvel's mutant group The Uncanny X-Men, who followed by a year, were originally 'children of the atom', the superfreak offspring of those exposed to radioactivity during the Manhattan Project.

For all its scientific double-talk, *The Lost Continent* is as much of a throwback as its man-in-a-suit tyrannosaurus. It is an imitation of the greatest nature run amok film of all, *King Kong* (1933). In 1952, a re-released *Kong* earned four times as much as it had done during its original Depression run. This success encouraged Warner Brothers to launch the atomic monster cycle, first by distributing the independently-made *The Beast From 20,000 Fathoms*, then by producing *Them!*. In *Beast*, a dinosaur frozen for millennia in the same ice that had held the Thing is thawed by an Arctic bomb test. As a result, the 'rhedosaurus' not only has the people-eating and building-smashing habits of *King Kong* but is also highly radioactive. Soldiers tracking it by spilled blood sicken and die of a nuke-related plague. In *Them!*, New Mexico bomb testing has caused successive generations of ants to get bigger — a rare instance (along with *World Without End* [1956]) of a script which seems to understand that genetic mutation means effects showing up in the offspring of the irradiated rather than assuming radiation has magical transformative properties. By the time the film starts, the insects are twenty feet long and need *lebensraum*. Like *King Kong*, the films find their monsters in isolated and under-

populated regions, then bring them to a city for the finale. The Beast heads for its ancient breeding grounds in New York; the ants take their last stand in the Los Angeles storm drains.

Despite its awkward puppet creatures, *Them!* is by far the more successful of the two films. While *Beast* is content to ape the *King Kong* plot and fill in the non-monster scenes with aimless chatter, *Them!* effectively presents itself as a documentary-style thriller along the lines of *The House on 92nd Street*, *The Naked City* (1948) or *Panic in the Streets* (1950). Well directed by Gordon Douglas, the film is strongly cast, nicely written and, given the central absurdity of the giant ants, sensibly plotted. Steve Rubin wrote in *Cinefantastique* that the film's power 'lies in its ability to deliver a subtle but crucial message of the hazards of the nuclear age.' Ted Sherdeman, the film's writer and original producer, saw *Them!* as an opportunity to deal with his own atomic anxieties. 'I was a Lieutenant Colonel then,' he said of the Hiroshima bombing, 'and when I heard the news I just went over to the curb and started throwing up.' Dr Medford (Edmund Gwenn), the humanist scientist, has a few grim lines about the Biblical prophecy that 'the Beasts will rule the Earth'. There is also no question but that the bombs tested by

Our Side are responsible for the menace, but in its endorsement of the official line *Them!* is hardly ambiguous.

As soon as the New Mexico police discover the ants' first victim was an FBI man on vacation, the Bureau is called in. Their plaster of Paris impressions of mysterious footprints and the presence of large amounts of formic acid in the corpse lead to the summoning of a pair of experts from the US Department of Agriculture. Cop James Whitmore, G-Man James Arness, elderly bug specialist Gwenn and pretty bug specialist Joan Weldon are the heart of the team, but they can call upon the entire resources of the country's law enforcement agencies, military might and scientific establishments. These are not quaking victims of atomic paranoia, but the level-headed nine-to-fivers who weighed up the consequences and decided to drop the Bomb in the first place. Like the semi-documentaries on which it is patterned, *Them!* is a hymn to the government. In the exciting finish, the military swing briskly into action in defence of the city and the monsters are convincingly taken out with superior firepower. Joe Public is ignored as the experts get on with their jobs. Before the battle, a Tannoy announces 'your personal safety and the safety of the entire city will depend on your full co-operation with the military authorities.'

Them! drops the touchy issue of the Bomb itself in order to reaffirm the worth of the society that made it possible, though it ends with Gwenn pondering the question of what further mutations might be thrown up by all the nuclear tests subsequent to the one that created the ants. *The Beast From 20,000 Fathoms*, however, displays a fearful circularity — the rhedosaurus is accidentally revived by the atom bomb, but it is also deliberately killed with an injected isotope. In a satisfying finale, Paul Christian and sharpshooter Lee Van Cleef face up to the Beast in the flaming ruins of Coney Island and shoot a radioactive device into the creature's neck. Ray Harryhausen's splendid special effects creation thrashes to its death with Geiger counters still clicking. *Gojira* (1954, *Godzilla, King of Monsters*), *It Came From Beneath the Sea* and *Behemoth the Sea Monster* (1959, *The Giant Behemoth*) also feature primordial monsters awakened by underwater bomb tests who are done away with thanks to the judicial application of a handy ultimate weapon. The message here is that science and the military can contain any monstrosity they might inadvertently unleash. The safety precautions work.

After *The Beast From 20,000 Fathoms* and *Them!*, the Bomb and its side-effects became central to monster movies. Somehow, the atomic angle became bankable. The titles alone are testimony: *Atom Man vs Superman* (1950), *U-238 and the Witch Doctor* (1953, a cut-down of the serial *Jungle Drums of Africa*), *The Creature with the Atom Brain* (1955), *Atomic Rulers of the World* (1956, originally *Kotetsu no Kyojin*), *The H-Man* (originally *Bijo no Ekatai Ningen*), *The Atomic Submarine* (1959), *Atom Age Vampire* (1960, actually an Italian film, *Seddok, l'erede di Satana*), *The Atomic Brain* (1963, *Monstrosity*), *The Fiend With the Atomic Brain* (1972, *Blood of Ghastly Horror*). *Man-Made Monster* (1941) was re-released as *The Atomic Monster*, *Bride of the Monster* (1955) was originally *Bride of the Atom*, the British *Time-slip* became *The Atomic Man* in America and a feature-length version of the 1936 *Flash Gordon* serial was retitled *Atomic Spaceship*. Just as later films would put 'sex' or 'blood' in their titles, these movies capitalise on atomic buzz-words to lure in a nuke-conscious audience. Sometimes, the deception was deliberate — Kurt Neumann's *The Fly* (1958), a film about a matter transmitter that deals in atoms but not atomics, was misleadingly advertised as 'the first time Atomic Mutation on humans has been shown on screen.'

The sublime terror that accompanies the epochal failure of society and individual men and women has not, especially in the case of the 1950s creature film, been represented in holy enough language. The characters in most of these efforts are flat caricatures who bathetically spout maudlin clichés, mouth scientific mumbo-jumbo, and scream hysterically for far too long in the direction of monstrously large reptiles. These gross efforts, pathetic claptrap, answer the most significant question of the 20th century with tacky special effects, papier-mâché sets, and idiotic plots. How can lumbering dinosaurs spewing atomic fire, giant carnivorous plants, and implacable mutant insects approach the fiery chaos that engulfed Japan? The force that killed too many in a hellish firestorm, the force that poisoned thousands more with pestilent radiation, the force powerful enough to etch the shadows of unknowing pedestrians into the cement is not a fit subject for cheap Hollywood productions. We needed a responsible contemporary of Bosch or Goya and not Samuel Z. Arkoff or Roger Corman to render, in proper proportions, our deadliest spectacle.

Jonathan Lake Crane, *Terror and Everyday Life: Singular Moments in the History of the Horror Film*

Aside from occasional class acts like *The Thing From Another World, The Day the Earth Stood Still, Forbidden Planet* (1956), *Invasion of the Body Snatchers* (1956) or Jack Arnold's remarkable series for Universal, SF in the fifties was strictly a B genre. However, it would be an error to assume that the low-grade atomic paranoia movies constitute a coherent expression of a single point of view. Even among the quickest of the quickies, there exists a surprising spectrum of attitudes to the atomic society. These films fall roughly into two separate groups — those produced by the B units of major studios to support their own A features, and those made by independent producers for grindhouse and drive-in double bills. In the former camp we have Columbia's *It Came From Beneath the Sea*, Universal's *The Deadly Mantis* (1957) and United Artists's *The Monster That Challenged the World* (1957); while the latter is represented by the likes of *The Amazing Colossal Man* and Roger Corman's *Attack of the Crab Monsters*, both released through American International.

On the whole, the major studios have better special effects and thus are more confident in staging scenes of mass devastation (though the Deadly Mantis's attack on Washington is every bit as feeble and unconvincing as the Colossal Man's rampage in Las Vegas). They can afford to rely on the fairly expansive formula of *The Beast From 20,000 Fathoms* and *Them!*, building up to a battle between monster and military. Not uncoincidentally, the major studio films cited above were made with the co-operation of the Department of Defence; independent producers almost never received loans of men and *materiel* from the armed forces. The indies are forced to use claustrophobic settings and fewer characters, and do without heavy artillery. Sometimes this means that the monsters have to be weedy enough to be killed off with a blowtorch (*It Conquered the World* [1956]) or hot rod headlights (*Invasion of the Saucer Men* [1957]), but occasionally budgetary restrictions lend a doomy feeling of helplessness to the struggle.

At the major studios, quick-thinking military men of action are valued more than the muddle-headed men of science. In Robert Gordon's *It Came From Beneath the Sea*, the love triangle is resolved when Dr Donald Curtis steps aside so that navy man Kenneth Tobey can get Faith Domergue to give up the laboratory for the kitchen. Which shouldn't be too hard, since all she does while the boys are discussing the giant octopus that threatens San Francisco is make coffee and look beautiful. Arnold Laven's *The Monster That Challenged the World* is more interesting in its military/scientific polarity. Prehistoric eggs long dormant in an inland sea are hatched into giant mollusc creatures when nuclear waste is dumped. The fault is squarely with civilian eggheads (atomic power), but the victims who get fried and/or eaten are down-to-earth Navy fliers. Lieutenant Commander Tim Holt romances base secretary Audrey Dalton, a widow whose little girl likes to play in the laboratory. A nascent scientist, the kid learns her lesson when her tampering with the thermostat awakens the last of the killer snails. Holt saves everyone, the equation between reckless science and childish blundering has been made, and we realise white-coats need uniforms to bail them out when they foul up.

In *It Came From Beneath the Sea*, Tobey reprimands a hesitant comrade with 'you're not afraid of a little radiation, are ya?' The major studios were unable to exclude the atomic angle from their films, but tended to play it down. Only in the independently-produced, studio-released *The*

Beast From 20,000 Fathoms do we get to see the test that revives the monster; in *Them!* and *It Came From Beneath the Sea* the big bangs take place off-screen before the action. Nathan Juran's *The Deadly Mantis* opens with twenty minutes of stock footage from air force shorts (*Guardians All, One Plane — One Bomb, SFP308*) and a narration that informs us of the great job being done for the free world by SAC and the DEW line. The giant praying mantis isn't woken by the Bomb, but by an erupting volcano. The military spot the big bug as it flies south and are ready for it by the time it reaches the States. *The Deadly Mantis* is a symbol for the Bomb all right, only the Bomb it symbolises belongs to Someone Else.

The independent films are less afraid to make allegations. In *The Amazing Colossal Man*, we see Colonel Glenn Langan disobey orders and rush into the site of a 'plutonium bomb' test in order to rescue the pilot of a crashed plane. Exposed to the blast, he has all his skin and bodily hair burned off. *Attack of the Crab Monsters* concerns a scientific team sent to a Pacific Island to assess the effects of fall-out from H-bomb tests on the flora and fauna. Both films deal with innocent victims of ill-advised tests and feature conscience-stricken Oppenheimer-type scientists trying to solve the problem in a test tube while the army is out blowing things up. The major studios present simple soldier heroes who act by the book and never question orders, but the independents are actively anti-military. 'What sins could a man commit in a single life time that he should deserve this?' asks the misanthropic, confused, doubting Colossal Man, flashing back to hand-to-hand dirtiness in Korea. *The Amazing Colossal Man* isn't a very good film, but it fits the anxious/paranoid view of the fifties better than self-confident exercises like *The Deadly Mantis*. Gordon brought the Colossal Man back in *War of the Colossal Beast* (1958, *The Terror Strikes*) and starred another radioactive giant in *The Cyclops* (1957). Since he used wonder drugs to make people and animals big in *Beginning of the End* (1957), *Village of the Giants* (1965) and *Food of the Gods* (1976), shrunk people with light rays in *Attack of the Puppet People* (1958, *Six Inches Tall*) and never bothered to explain the gigantism of *The Spider* (1958, *Earth Versus the Spider*), he was obviously more interested in the effect than the cause.

Attack of the Crab Monsters, despite its ludicrous villains, is a decent, chilling little film. Though the monsters look especially ridiculous in stills, they are slightly more effective in the film itself, which is dimly-lit enough

to disguise the shortcomings of the giant crab outfits. Its military charac-ters get killed early, leaving the problem to be solved by a group of multi-national scientists. One by one, they are murdered and decapitated, and the island crumbles until it is little more than an atoll. Whereas major stu-dio monsters tend to be mindless destruction machines, the independents favour intelligent, even articulate, mutations. The Colossal Man rants end-lessly about his personal problems; the Crab Monsters absorb the contents of the brains they eat, and get smarter with each kill. Like the creature in Corman's *The Day the World Ended* (1956) and the invulnerable gangster in *The Most Dangerous Man Alive*, the Crab Monsters are functional muta-tions, more fit than man to survive a radiation-polluted environment. In this, films were following science fiction magazines, where, as Paul Brians points out in *Nuclear Holocausts: Atomic War in Fiction 1895-1984*, 'the most common side effect of radiation is not blindness, hemophilia or limblessness; it is the ability to read minds.'

The majors were unwilling or unable to deal with their atomic monsters in anything but the most cut-and-dried, official-line-toeing terms. The doubts of *The Amazing Colossal Man* or the dreads of *Attack of the Crab Monsters* are nowhere to be found. Jack Arnold, a liberal whose films were made within the studio system, touches only tangentially on nuclear issues. However, Arnold's *The Incredible Shrinking Man*, inspiration of course for *The Amazing Colossal Man*, is an atomic mutation movie. Grant Williams's yacht drifts through a radioactive dust cloud and he begins to shrink. The origin of the cloud is barely considered, and the film is concerned mainly with the physical and psychological plight of a man growing too small for his white-collar life. Screenwriter Richard Matheson, who later worked with Roger Corman on his Edgar Allan Poe films, adapted his novel *The Shrinking Man* (1956) and ended his script with an echo of Corman's benevolent mutation theme by having Williams enter a subatomic world of wonders and make peace with the universe. Arnold and Matheson have a more generous vision than Bert I. Gordon; the Amazing Colossal Man is gunned down on Boulder Dam, but the Incredible Shrinking Man finds transcendence in a microscopic landscape.

Outside America, the concerns were subtly (sometimes not so subtly) different. Japan's Toho Studios were so impressed with *The Beast From 20,000 Fathoms* that they assigned Ishiro Honda to direct an unofficial remake, *Gojira*. The film was a big hit in Japan, and got exported to the rest of the world as *Godzilla, King of Monsters*, with new scenes involving Raymond Burr as an American reporter spliced into the old footage. *Gojira* is a film from the nation that had the Bomb dropped on them, and it shows. We identify with King Kong and to some extent share his desire to trash New York, but the devastation of Tokyo in *Gojira* is agonising. The film opens in the burning ruins of the city, and flashes back to the lead-up story. *Gojira* is a rare monster movie to go into the nasty details of the catastrophe: hordes of injured refugees, thronging field hospitals, churches full of widows and orphans. The monster is not only completely unsympathetic, but also a far more explicit symbol for the Bomb than any of its American counterparts. The creature has fiery radioactive breath, and its spines glow ominously whenever it exterminates anything.

Gojira is, at one remove, about the physical after-effects of the Bomb (a chilling little scene, not in the export version, has a doctor diagnose that a perky little girl with radiation poisoning is inescapably doomed), but it also tries to discuss the moral dilemma surrounding its use. Godzilla is an enemy as unreasonable and implacable as any dictator, and conventional weapons are useless against it. The film's hero, an embittered scientist, has invented an unlikely-sounding ultimate weapon, the Oxygen Destroyer. With the Oxygen Destroyer, Godzilla could be defeated, but the scientist wants to suppress his invention for the good of humanity. In an American film, the tension would rise from the race-against-time development of the monster-destroying weapon, which would then be used speedily and with no qualms (cf *Earth vs the Flying Saucers* [1956]). Much of the last third of *Gojira* is taken up with the scientist agonising over the ethics of unleashing such a terrible force. In a typically Japanese heroic gesture, he finally deploys the Oxygen Destroyer against the monster, turning it instantly into a skeleton, then commits suicide so that his deadly knowledge will be lost forever.

The film was a sensational success, in Japan and abroad, and led to the thriving and popular *Kaiju Eiga* genre of giant monster movies. Godzilla was swiftly brought back for Motoyoshi Oda's *Gojira no Gyakushu* (1955, *Gigantis the Fire Monster*), a quickie sequel which introduced not the oxygen-destroyed skeleton in Tokyo Bay but a relative, who proceeded to stomp through a series of encounters with rival monsters up to 1975, then vanished until Koji Hashimoto's *Gojira* (1984, *Godzilla 1985*) resurrected the original beast and inaugurated its own cycle, which wound up in 1995 to make way for Roland Emmerich's Americanised *Godzilla* (1998). Less impressive as an effects-created creature than Harryhausen's rhedosaurus, Godzilla — a lumbering stuntman in a suit, dragging a tail across fabulously detailed miniature sets — became a far more lasting icon of the unleashed atom, though he gradually reformed under the influence of the children who formed the core of his adoring audience.

The first Japanese monster movies were sombre, black and white efforts, with few of the wisecracks found in contemporary American films. However, the tone of the films soon changed. In Honda's *Sora no Dai-Kaiju Radon* (1956, *Rodan*), a pair of revived pterodactyls make sonic booms that are as destructive as A-bomb blasts, but they don't mean any harm and, when one is killed, the mate commits grief-stricken suicide by flying into a volcano. *Rodan* is sentimental in pretty-pretty colours, while *Gojira* is grim in black and white. In later *Kaiju Eiga* films, the scenes of mass destruction

are visually appealing and almost cheerful. The most charmingly surreal of the run is Honda's *Mosura* (1961, *Mothra*), which features a giant moth revived by nuclear testing in the Pacific and also caricatures America as the aggressive Republic of Roliscia, but features such fantastical devices as tiny twin singing princesses to give it a fairytale feel. In subsequent films, the monsters reformed and became sympathetic, protecting the Earth from alien invaders, befriending small children and paternally encouraging young love.

Godzilla began a series of monster bouts with Honda's *Kingu Kongu tai Gojira* (1963, *King Kong vs Godzilla*) and *Mosura tai Gojira* (1964, *Godzilla vs the Thing*), then began his rehabilitation by teaming with former enemy Mothra and Rodan against a triple-threat from outer space in Honda's *Ghidorah Sandai Kaiju Chikyu Saidai no Kessen* (1964, *Ghidrah the Three-Headed Monster*). *Mosura tai Gojira* is the last of the original series to pay much attention to Godzilla's nuclear origins, visiting the formerly paradisic island home of Mothra, where a Japanese reporter (Akira Takarada) muses 'it's like the end of the world here... this island alone is good reason to end nuclear testing', and it has a streak of melancholy to go with its colourful and destructive battle scenes. Not coincidentally, it was also the last film to cast Godzilla as a bad guy; once the giant reptile was on our side, his radioactivity wore off or went unmentioned, and his fire-breathing trick was just another attribute of his dragon-like hero status rather than a mark of mutation.

In his increasingly silly, occasionally endearing way, Godzilla took on Ghidrah again (Honda's *Kaiju Daisenso* [1965, *Monster Zero*] and *Kaiju Soshingeki* [1968, *Destroy All Monsters*]), battled a giant lobster (Jun Fukuda's *Gojira, Ebirah, Mosura: Nankai no Dai Ketto* [1966, *Ebirah, Horror of the Deep*]), learned parental responsibility (Fukuda's *Kaiju Shima no Kessen: Gojira no Musuko* [1967, *Son of Godzilla*]), appeared in the *Play It Again, Sam* fantasies of a bullied child (Honda's *Oru Kaiju Daishingeki* [1969, *Godzilla's Revenge*]), tackled a creature who embodies pollution in a brief return to seriousness (Yoshimitsu Benno's *Gojira tai Hedora* [1971, *Godzilla vs the Smog Monster*]) and dealt with ridiculous-looking creatures (eg Gigan, a fat metallic parrot with a buzzsaw in its stomach for breaking up wrestling holds) under the control of alien invaders (Fukuda's *Chikyu Kogeki Meirei: Gojira tai Gaigan* [1972, *Godzilla vs Gigan*], *Gojira tai Megaro* [1973, *Godzilla vs Megalon*] and *Gojira tai Mekagojira* [1974, *Godzilla vs the Bionic Monster*], and Honda's *Mekagojira no Gyakushu* [1975, *Monsters From an Unknown Planet/Terror of Mechagodzilla*]).

Godzilla's change of heart was influenced by the success of a series from Toho's great rival, Daiei Studios. Noriaki Yuasa's *Daikaiju Gamera* (1965, *Gammera the Invincible*) introduced Gamera, a giant turtle who divides his time between rescuing children and tearing chunks out of more ferocious, malevolent monsters. There were Japanese monster movies which didn't imitate the city-stomping Godzilla and Gamera films, often featuring bizarre human mutations created by scientific experiment or mishap. The stalwart Ishiro Honda alone was responsible for the human blob gangster of *Bijo to Ekatai Ningen*, the self-explanatory *Gasu Ningen dai Ichigo* (1960, *The Human Vapor*) and the shipwrecked yacht party who transform into colourful fungus creatures in *Matango* (1963, *Matango — Fungus of Terror/Attack of the Mushroom People*). In competition with these oddities were the teleporting electro-man of Jun Fukuda's *The Secret of the Telegian* (1960) and Peter Dyneley as the man who splits into two monsters in George Breakston and Kenneth Crane's American-Japanese co-production *The Split* (1961, *The Manster*). However, the G-force was irresistible and many imitators weighed into the fray, affording the spectacle of sumo wrestlers in uncomfortable suits grappling among decreasingly impressive miniature sets: Honda's *Uchu Daikaiju Dogora* (1964, *Dagora the Space Monster*), Haruyasu Noguchi's *Daikyoju Gappa* (1967, *Gappa the Triphibian Monster*), Kazui Nihonmatsu's *Uchu Daikaiju Guilala* (1967, *The X From Outer Space*), Honda's *Kessen Nankai no Daikaiju* (1970, *Yog — Monster From Space*).

In the fifties, Britain was failing to come to terms with its increasing irrelevance to the global superpower confrontation. British atomic monster movies are therefore much more nervous than their American inspirations. Leslie Norman's *X the Unknown* (1956) and Arthur Crabtree's *Fiend Without a Face* (1958) seem to be pro-militarist movies along the lines of *Them!* but are far less self-confident. In *X the Unknown*, the army confronts a ravenous radioactive blob from the bowels of the Earth in Scotland; while *Fiend* (set in a home counties version of Manitoba) exonerates a military atomic installation and blames the brain-eating monsters on a local mad scientist. The scripts are woodenly heroic, with stolid soldiers and dedicated military scientists handling problems bravely, but the visuals tell another story. *X the Unknown* opens with a bored army unit using Geiger counters on a desolate beach, and an edgy, black and white gloom is cast over the entire film. Sympathetic characters (including children) are gruesomely eaten and the government men who face the crisis are high-handed time-servers. *Fiend Without a Face* undercuts its endorsement of the army with an amazingly graphic final shoot-out as the brain creatures are splattered to death. As in many British films of the time, the authorities are presented as remote and unsympathetic. Joseph Losey, who was to have made *X the Unknown* for Hammer, returned to the company with *The Damned*, the most vicious indictment imaginable of official policy in the face of the possibility of nuclear holocaust.

The atomic mutation cycle began to lose momentum in the late fifties. The majors dropped the genre first, then the independents began to cool off. Eugene Lourié, director of *The Beast From 20,000 Fathoms*, went to Britain to do yet another remake, *Behemoth the Sea Monster*. Two years later, he did the story again as *Gorgo* (1961), but cut the nuke angle completely. Meanwhile, Fred F. Sears's *The Werewolf* (1956), Gene Fowler's *I Was a Teenage Werewolf* (1957) and Herbert L. Strock's *Blood of Dracula* (1958, *Blood Is My Heritage*) combined radiation with more traditional movie monstrousness. During this cycle, even Baron Frankenstein (Boris Karloff) needed to employ an atomic pile, in Howard W. Koch's *Frankenstein 1970* (1958). In these films, mad scientists turn innocents into monsters in order to create a hardier human being able to survive in a tougher, post-holocaust world. Here, the soldier/scientist opposition is downplayed in favour of generation gap stories in which elderly scientists are intent on ruling the lives of happy-go-lucky teenagers who only want their inalienable right to drag-race, neck and listen to rock 'n' roll.

After the first burst of mutant movies, when any self-respecting monster had to be radioactive, the sub-genre's half-life dwindled. The task of keeping the form ticking over was left to a trickle of mostly ridiculous and self-explanatory obscurities like Kenneth G. Crane's *Monster From Green Hell* (1958; giant wasps in Africa), Bernard L. Kowalski's *Attack of the Giant Leeches* (1960, *Demons of the Swamp*), Robert Hutton's *The Slime People* (1963; more scaly than slimy), Del Tenney's *The Horror of Party Beach* (1964; underwater fish-human zombies), Lawrence Huntington's

The Vulture (1967; Akim Tamiroff with wings and clawed feet), Harry Essex's *Octaman* (1971; yes, a man with an octopus for a head), Stephen Traxler's *Slithis* (1978, *Spawn of the Slithis*), Douglas Camfield's TV serial *The Nightmare Man* (1981; a Soviet pilot fused with his crashed atomic warplane) and Greydon Clark's *The Uninvited* (1987; a cute cat escaped from a nuclear lab, who periodically transforms into a killer puppet).

Beach blanket boppers in their bikinis and ball-huggers are being menaced by monsters that were created when drums of radioactive waste leaked. But not to worry; though a few girls get carved up, all comes right in the end in time for one last wiener roast before school starts again. These things happen only rarely because directors, writers and producers want them to happen; they happen on their own. The producers of *The Horror of Party Beach*, for example, were two Connecticut drive-in owners who saw a chance to turn a quick buck in the low-budget horror-movie game. The fact that they created a film which foresaw a problem that would become very real ten years down the road was only an accident... but an accident, like Three Mile Island, that perhaps had to happen sooner or later... The producers of *The Horror of Party Beach* never sat down, I'm sure (just as I'm sure the producers of *The China Syndrome* did), and said to each other: 'Look — we're going to warn the people of America about the dangers of nuclear reactors, and we will sugar coat the pill of this vital message with an entertaining story line.' No, the line of discussion would have been more apt to go like this: because our target audience is young, we'll feature young people, and because our target audience is interested in sex, we'll site it on a sun-and-surf type beach, which allows us to show all the flesh the censors will allow. And because our target audience like grue, we'll give them gross monsters. But because any horror film has got to at least pay lip service to credibility, there had to be some reason for these monsters to suddenly come out of the ocean and start doing all these antisocial things. What the producers decided upon was nuclear waste, leaking from those dumped canisters. I'm sure it was one of the least important points in their preproduction discussions, and for that very reason it becomes very important.

Stephen King, *Danse Macabre*

By the late sixties, the stragglers of the radioactive mutant film were confined to a few out-of-touch countries like South Korea (Kiduck Kim's *Dai Koesu Yongkari* [1967, *Yongary — Monster From the Deep*]) and the Philippines (Gerardo de Leon's *Brides of Blood* [1968]). In George A. Romero's seminal horror film *Night of the Living Dead* (1968), the dead come back to life and start eating the living. We are reminded of the radioactive parasites that got the corpses walking in Edward L. Cahn's *Invisible Invaders* (1959), but when the situation is 'explained' as the result of radiation from a crashed space probe, it's supposed to be a joke. The film is an assault on our complacency and its events are so horrifying that the actual reason for the violence — obscured further in Romero's follow-ups *Dawn of the Dead* (1979, *Zombies*) and *Day of the Dead* (1984) — is simply irrelevant.

All monster movies have subtexts; if *Them!* is about the Bomb, then *Night of the Living Dead* is about Vietnam. In the seventies, films like George McCowan's *Frogs* (1972) and Peter Sasdy's *Doomwatch* (1972) are about pollution. In the eighties, there was a mini-trend of toxic waste monster movies (John Bud Cardos's *Mutant* [1984]; Graham Baker's *Impulse* [1984]; Michael Herz and Samuel Weil's *The Toxic Avenger* [1984]), and Douglas Cheek's *C.H.U.D.* (1984) mixes toxic with nuclear waste and comes up with radioactive cannibal mutants wandering the New York sewers. Troma, following up their Toxic Avenger, got into the nuclear business with a run of ghastly wannabe comedies illustrating the dire consequences of storing radioactive waste in a high school: *Class of Nuke 'Em High* (1986), *Class of Nuke 'Em High, Part II: Subhumanoid Meltdown* (1991), *Class of Nuke 'Em High III: The Good, the Bad and the Subhumanoid* (1992). Troma's anything-for-offence approach, which includes the rampages of Tromie the Giant Nuclear Squirrel, is curiously self-defeating — by straining to make the kind of cult kitsch the makers of *The Horror of Party Beach* came up with without effort, they create very thin, bad-tasting beer indeed, and the foregrounding of an anti-nuke sub-text only serves to make it utterly meaningless.

The rehabilitation of Godzilla in films like *Gojira tai Hedora* parallels the recession in nuclear anxiety during *détente*. However, Koji Hashimoto's *Gojira*, a remake-cum-revisionary-sequel, sets aside all the series since the original and tries to get serious again, indicting (in the Japanese version, at least) both the Soviets and the Americans as the Japanese government resists pressure to deploy nuclear weapons against the revived monster. This led to a revival of the *Kaiju Eiga*, re-introducing Ghidorah, Mothra and the rest of the gang, and refining Godzilla's origin story. In Kazuki Omori's *Gojira tai Kingu Ghidora* (1991, *Godzilla vs King Ghidorah*), we learn that Godzilla was originally an 'ordinary' dinosaur, a prehistoric survival friendly to Japanese troops in the Pacific during World War Two, and that it mutated into the familiar creature thanks to bomb tests. Time travellers from the future, out to forestall Japan's economic dominance, try to tinker with the past and unmake the monster, but it seems that the post-1945 nuclear world will inevitably create the Godzilla it needs. The new series also included Kazuki Omori's *Gojira tai Beolante* (1989, *Godzilla vs Biollante*), Takao Okawara's *Gojira tai Mosura* (1992, *Godzilla vs Mothra*) and *Gojira tai Mechagojira* (1993, *Godzilla vs Mechagodzilla*) and Kenshou Yamashita's *Gojira tai Supeesu Gojira* (1994, *Godzilla vs Space Godzilla*), then climaxed with pleasing circularity by bringing back original heroine Momoko Kochi and the Oxygen Destroyer, incarnated as a monster in Takao Okawara's *Gojira tai Desutoroia* (1995, *Godzilla vs Destroyer*) and the supposedly final death of the original Godzilla.

With Godzilla reaching the end of his second screen series in the mid-nineties, Daiei took the opportunity to get back in the *Kaiju Eiga* game by reviving their own monster, giving him a new origin myth and pitting him against the bird-creatures of Noriaki Yuasa's *Gamera tai Gyaos* (1967, *Gamera vs Gaos*) in Shusuke Kaneko's *Gamera Daikaiju Kuchu Kessen* (1997, *Gamera the Guardian of the Universe*). Successful enough to relaunch the series, this back-to-basics Japanese monster movie is among the best of its genre. Kaneko takes the absurd epic with a refreshingly straight face, making some sequences actually moving or frightening as well as exciting on a smash-'em-up level. Gamera himself remains more than a tad ridiculous, especially when using jet exhausts to turn his shell into a species of flying saucer (we are told the monster is 'not the product of evolution', which explains a lot). The silly design of the original is modified, but Gamera is still stuck with ridiculous aspects like a set of impractical tusks, though the quality of the miniature work as cities are devastated and monsters tangle with each other is exemplary.

In a familiar plot structure, the film opens with various omens and sightings, sends off experts to puzzle together the mystery while the monsters go from glimpsed attacks to all-out war, culminating in a big showdown between the good guy creature and the avian embodiment of flesh-eating evil. As in the 1990s Godzilla films, a young girl is psychically linked to Gamera, adding a rooting interest in that she sympathetically shares the wounds inflicted on him by the especially vicious Gyaos monsters. The script has a few adult touches — the ornithologist heroine learns of her mentor's fate when she finds his glasses in a lump of Gyaos excrement — but goes out of its way not to throw in the pseudo-American razzmatazz of the resurgent Toho films. The heroes are models of Japanese virtue, dutiful and polite; the big moral quandary faced by the authorities is again whether Japan has the right to launch a military attack even in defence (and the army chooses to attack the wrong monster). We are even shown how monster attacks affect Tokyo's public transport system and the value of the yen (it plummets). Though the film opens with a ship carrying plutonium waste encountering the Gyaos, these monsters are — like Mothra — more mystic in origin, and it turns out that Gamera, who is disguised as an island when we first meet him, was genetically engineered by a lost civilisation for the purpose of defending the world against any monsters that might come along of their own accord or be created by man's hubris.

Roland Emmerich's American *Godzilla* amusingly replaces the anti-American bias of the Japanese films with an indictment of the perfidious French, whose Pacific tests have not awakened a dinosaur but mutated an iguana (as in Mark Jacobson's odd literary novel *Gojiro*, 1991) into a stream-lined, lantern-jawed beast which heads for New York in a *de facto* remake of *The Beast From 20,000 Fathoms*. The lazy comic edge of the Hollywood *Godzilla* obscures its reversal of the militarism of Emmerich's *Independence Day* (1996) — as much damage is caused to the city by the bungled application of American firepower as by the monster. At one point, heat-seeking missiles are fired at a cold-blooded beast. It is perhaps a symptom of the changes of anxiety about the nuclear threat that *Godzilla* even lets its ostensible villains off lightly. Jean Reno, the French covert operative in charge of covering up the fiasco, is heroic and sympathetic, while the army are clod-hopping rather than callous. This monster is just another big animal (nature run amok, again), suggesting a world more worried about nuclear tests because of their impact on the environment than because they might be a preliminary for war.

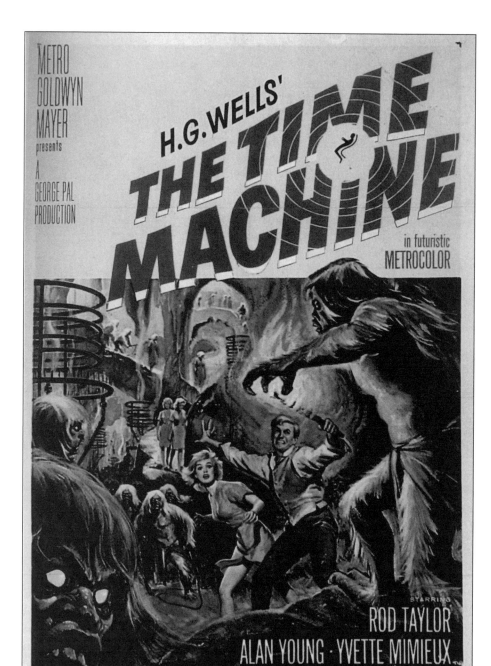

Norms vs
Mutates

What you are about to see may never happen... but to this anxious age in which we live, it presents a fearsome warning... our story begins with... THE END!

The Day the World Ended

While nuclear anxiety, atomic mutation and mass devastation were common themes in fifties cinema, films that dared to depict the world as it might be after an all-out nuclear war were comparatively rare. *Five* (1951) is the first of the few. Though released by Columbia, the film came from a non-Hollywood vacuum even further away from the movie mainstream than the poverty row outfits who had nervously touched on atomic issues in quickies like *Rocketship X-M* and *Unknown World*. Written, produced, designed and directed by one man band Arch Oboler, *Five* is an expansion of his radio play *The Word*. Oboler had made his name with the innovative radio show *Lights Out* (1934-47), and his films never quite shook off the talkiness necessary for the purely aural medium. Enacted by unknowns whose strained emotionalism matches Oboler's purple patches, *Five* has a historical place as the film which staked out the post-nuclear wasteland as a particular province of the cinema.

'A story about the day after tomorrow', *Five* opens with a montage of scare headlines, the already familiar mushroom cloud footage and a Biblical pronouncement ('the deadly wind passeth over it and it is gone... and the place thereof shall know it no more!'). The bleak little story, which prefigures *Night of the Living Dead* in its outline and attitude, has an ill-matched group of survivors whittled down by radiation sickness, murder and poetic justice to a more manageable Two. The ultimate survivors are Michael (William Phipps), an understandably embittered idealist ('you and I are in a dead world and I'm glad it's dead! Cheap little honky-tonk of a world!'), and Roseanne (Susan Douglas), a pretty young widow suited to the task of being Eve for a new human race ('remember how important box-tops used to be?'). The expendable Three are Eric (James Anderson), a neo-fascist mountaineer and non-specific foreigner who was on top of Everest during the hostilities; Charles (Charles Lampkin), a shuffling black doorman who gets killed by Eric as an example of extreme prejudice; and Barnstaple (Earl Lee), a white collar worker who cracks under the strain and keeps protesting that he's only on vacation.

Oboler's survivors are as emblematic a cross-section of society as ever got together during a movie disaster, and the contrivances required to bring them from as far afield as Tibet and the Empire State Building to a Frank Lloyd Wright house in California put a severe strain on the solemn credibility of the script. In some confrontation scenes, Oboler seems to think that nuclear war isn't bad enough and subsumes the horrors of the unleashed atom into a general diatribe against man's inhumanity to man or other failings ('the blessing of our age, the American canning industry... it reduced your taste to baked beans and hash'). When it shuts up, by virtue of being the first film to get to ground zero, *Five* has memorable moments. A foraging expedition to a town littered with skeletons makes powerful use of real locations and, though absurd, is the first of many such explorations. The painstaking, back-breaking work necessary to raise the pathetic patch of irradiated corn upon which the future of the human race depends is conveyed in a potent montage that sets up the unforgettable moment when the villain, whose rottenness is about on the level of a capitalist in a Soviet silent movie, casually swerves his fast car through the field.

'As long as things keep growing,' we are told, 'everything will be all right.' In the first of many such endings, Michael and Roseanne wander off in search of the Future. An epilogue quotes Revelations, 'and I saw a new Heaven and a new Earth... and there shall be no more death... no more sorrow... no more tears... Behold! I make all things new!' To which critic Robert Hatch replied in *The New Republic*, 'what we fear from the next war is famine and disease and bestiality; tyranny and the loss of whatever human dignity we have inherited from past generations. To suppose that the atom will bring quick death for millions and a bright, clean world for a bright, clean boy and girl to repopulate is to tell a fairy story to the soft-minded.' However, the *Five* fade-out is not quite the happy prospect we expect: Roseanne, a rare visibly pregnant women in a fifties film, loses her baby and becomes comatose with despair. The final sign of hope is not new human life, but the heroine's decision to help the hero raise corn.

Another representative sample of the American people is assembled for Alfred E. Green's *Invasion USA* (1952). The mysterious 'forecaster' Mr Ohman (Dan O'Herlihy) sits in a New York bar, swirling a huge brandy and eavesdropping as a bunch of complacent citizens debate 'the universal draft — army, labour, factories, everything'. Industrialist Robert Bice, owner of a ploughshare factory, has recently rebutted a government suggestion that he convert it to sword production. Congressman Wade Crosby is against the administration's aggressive armaments policy. Rancher Erik Blythe just wants to get back to his crops. And reporter Gerald Mohr is too busy falling in love with nurse Peggie Castle to care about any threat to his country. They all agree stockpiling weapons and maintaining a huge standing army is a waste of time, money and manpower. Mr Ohman nods sagely and smiles enigmatically. Then the television broadcast is interrupted. The Enemy has invaded Alaska.

Certain that 'this is it, the final game of the World Series and we're the home team', everyone rushes out of the bar, guiltily determined to give their all to the war effort. As they get killed, they barely have enough time to reflect that none of this would be happening if they hadn't been such peaceniks. *Invasion USA* is a short film but manages to cram in a lot of implausibilities. Acres of World War Two and natural disaster footage is spliced in almost at random. The Enemy dresses its troops in American uniforms because a) it's a sneaky commie trick and b) producer Albert Zugsmith is thus able to use stock footage of American soldiers and pass it off as the other side. A sinister (Jewish-looking?) factory employee (Aram Katcher) turns out to be a fifth columnist. Atom bombs are dropped on airports and, in a quite impressive scene that was a first in 1952, New York City. All the drinkers, including the hero and heroine, get killed (Castle self-defenestrates in order to avoid being raped by a Red), but they wake up back in the bar. Ohman has hypnotised them in order to teach an important lesson. Their attitudes permanently changed, they dash off to buy Cold War bonds. According to the poster, Hedda Hopper thought *Invasion USA* 'will scare the pants off you!'

In *Science Fiction in the Cinema*, John Baxter has a few kind words for the film: 'one remembers the ennui of the bar, the flaccid discussion of conscription and world tension. Later, people line up at a desk to hear war news of distant areas and a disinterested official tells families that their homes have been wiped out by a bomb, or occupied and burnt to the ground. The hypnosis device is specious, but as a mirror of its time, *Invasion USA* is a fascinating fossil.' Bill Warren, in *Keep Watching the Skies!*, is less charitable to Green and Zugsmith: 'the masses of the people in the United States tend to be rather paranoid in general; a corrupt picture like *Invasion USA* only plays on the worst fears and magnifies the tendency towards such paranoia. It's a film that could have been made by Senator Joe McCarthy himself. Though the enemy troops are not quite specified, they do start their invasion with Alaska, which is mere miles from the Soviet Union; Russian MiGs are shown; and some of the stock footage used is printed reversed left-to-right, so the letters are backward. This was to make them look Cyrillic, and, therefore, Russian. The *American Mercury*, then the self-appointed mouthpiece of the anti-communist, anti-un-American fanatics, is shown in the film. The message of *Invasion USA* isn't just that we should consider the possibility that another war (and one with the communist nations in particular) will take place, but that we should actively prepare for one to the point of providing armaments and, in the case of newscasters, actually foment the "inevitable" conflict.'

Captive Women (1952), a story of tribal warfare in what is left of New York in the year 3000, is more significant than it sounds. Written and produced by Aubrey Wisberg and Jack Pollexfen, who had just had a minor hit with Edgar G. Ulmer's *The Man From Planet X* (1951), directed by former editor Stuart Gilmore, and generally tinkered with by Howard Hughes (who came up with the bondage-flavoured title) and Albert Zugsmith of *Invasion USA* fame, *Captive Women* is the first of the Norms vs Mutates movies. While *Five* is the ancestor of a strain of fairly serious nuclear war films dealing with the immediate after-effects of the Bomb (*On the Beach* [1959]; *The War Game*; *The Day After*; *Testament* [1983]; *Threads*), *Captive Women*, set a few safe centuries after the major unpleasantness, establishes the conventions for the post-holocaust action/adventure film (*Teenage Caveman* [1958]; *Planet of the Apes* [1968]; *The Ultimate Warrior* [1975];

Mad Max 2; *Radioactive Dreams*). In *Captive Women*, the Norms and Mutates end their squabbles and band together to fight off the evil Upriver People, who are invading Manhattan Island through the Hudson Tunnel in search of available women. A not-terribly-hideous Mutate (Ron Randell) falls for a hubba-hubba Norm girl (Margaret Field), and we are assured that their descendants will be the perfect specimens required to lift the human race out of savagery.

The Norms and the Mutates kept up their feud until the eighties. In Edward Bernds's *World Without End*, Edgar G. Ulmer's *Beyond the Time Barrier*, George Pal's *The Time Machine*, Ib Melchior's *The Time Travelers* (1964), Gordon Flemyng's *Dr. Who and the Daleks* (1965), David L. Hewitt's *Journey to the Center of Time* (1967), Henning Schellerup's *The Time Machine* (1978), Paul Donovan's *DefCon 4* (1984) and the *Planet of the Apes* series, pre-holocaust heroes are projected into a blasted future. Invariably, the heroes side with the Norms, who are trying to build civilisation and tend to wear white togas, against the Mutates, who are into barbarism in a big way and frequently have more or fewer eyes than usual. H.G. Wells, whose Norms, the Eloi, were as useless and doomed as his Mutates, the Morlocks, would have recognised the cosy simplifications of these movies, all of which rip off his plot, for the twaddle they are. He would also doubtless not have been too keen on the casting of two-fisted Rod Taylor (who had been through it all in *World Without End*) as his dispassionate Time Traveller. *World Without End* is typical of the batch: twentieth century astronauts arrive in a future where humanity has dwindled into overcivilised but listless underground-dwellers, a decorative assembly of Vargas girls and tribally savage cyclops in furs. Though a treacherous villain thinks it's a bad idea, our heroes reunite humanity by reinventing the bazooka and overthrowing the Mutate leader.

The wasteland of *Beyond the Time Barrier*, which the time traveller assumes to be due to atomic warfare, is actually the upshot of a plague (indirectly caused by nuclear testing), but it's hard to tell the difference. The nuke aspects of the cycle are opportunist, providing an excuse only for a few matte shots of shattered skyscrapers and the spontaneous appearance of any monster the producer might have left over from his last film. The imaginative vision of the Norms vs Mutates movie is limited to a warmed-up leftover of the Settlers vs Indians Western. Pure-bred, Aryan-looking

Good Guys are threatened by horrible, malformed, gene pool-polluting Bad Guys, but are saved by a macho intruder from our world who chips in with some good old scientific know-how and a few strong right hooks. The hero finds an unmarked, beautiful, frequently mute, Norm to settle down with. It is probably not coincidental that these films sprang up when Westerns (*Broken Arrow* [1950]; *Apache* [1954]; *Run of the Arrow* [1957]) were reassessing their treatment of real Indians. Norman Spinrad's novel *The Iron Dream* (1972), is an explicit attack on the latent fascism of Norms vs Mutates stories, with a Hitlerian hero who proposes a Final Solution to the Mutant Problem.

> I'm very much interested in the concept of nuclear holocaust. I think the possibility for it happening is there. Personally, I don't think it's going to occur, but I think that, through film, we should keep on cautioning and warning people that it might.
>
> **Roger Corman**

The Day the World Ended, the first of producer-director Roger Corman's cautionary nuclear tales, is a trashy, vital synthesis of the parable pretentiousness of *Five* and monster movie commercialism. After TD Day (Total Destruction Day, to the uninitiated), yet another group of survivors hole up in an unaffected valley, arguing among themselves. Retreater Maddison (Paul Birch) has stocked up with bottled water and canned food, and made sure that his house is sited between lead-filled mountains. He had planned to survive with daughter Louise (Lori Nelson) and her handsome fiancé, but the boyfriend was in town when the Bomb fell and has been mutating into a three-eyed, four-armed, horned and fanged Mutant (played by monster-maker Paul Blaisdell). With the logical candidate out of the way, there is a great deal of debate about who should play Adam to Louise's Eve. The people's choice is Rick (Richard Denning), a handsome geologist who soon gets over the shock of World War Three ('I think I'm beginning to want to live again,' he tells the girl. 'It's taken seven weeks and you'), but stiff competition is put up by Tony Lamont (Mike 'Touch' Connors), a flashy hood who waves his revolver around, sneers a lot and makes post-holocaust conversational gambits like, 'you got a pretty good taste in sports shirts, mister.'

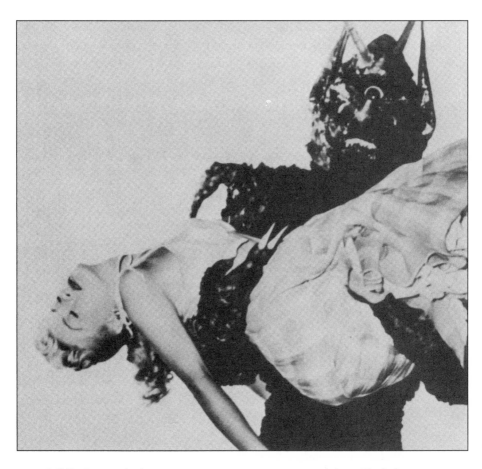

Above: The
Day the World
Ended, *Lori
Nelson, Paul
Blaisdell*

While Corman's characters are even more stereotyped than Oboler's
(there's also a gun-moll with a heart of gold and a crusty prospector who
talks to his mule), their cliché dialogue is pithier and the B picture cast
chew on it with more conviction. Confined by the budget to the happy
valley, the film drops unnerving hints of a misty, mutated outside world
where hordes of monsters are battling for supremacy. *The Day the World
Ended* is the first film to have its characters mutate for reasons more complicated than the need to get a monster in the film; the rubbery creatures
are adapting to a poisoned environment. In the end, everyone except Rick
and Louise is killed; non-radioactive rains come and the mutant melts
away in the shower like the Wicked Witch of the West. 'Man created but
God destroyed,' says Louise as the mutant sizzles. 'He brought the rain and

the fresh air.' The dying Maddison, succumbing happily to radiation poisoning, has heard a voice on the radio. 'There are others out there,' he tells the happy couple. 'There's a future out there — for you. You've got to go and find it.' As Rick and Louise leave the valley, the end title reads THE BEGINNING.

Having noticed that the Norms vs Mutates movies are also little more than post-holocaust variations on cavemen films like *One Million B.C.* (1940), Corman took dinosaur footage from the Hal Roach picture and cut it into his next nuke warning. He called the film *Prehistoric World,* but American International Pictures released it as *Teenage Caveman* and a shocked British distributor retitled it *Out of the Darkness.* A rebellious young hunter (Robert Vaughn) breaks the taboos imposed by the tribal elders ('the Law... is old, and age is not always truth') and ventures into the Forbidden Lands, where the fearsome God That Gives Death With Its Touch turns out to be an old man in a tatty decontamination suit. As in Colin Finbow's *Dark Enemy* (1984) and Antonio Margheriti's *Il mondo di Yor* (1983, *Yor, The Hunter From the Future* — the export title gives away the twist), Corman's apparently prehistoric setting is revealed to be the aftermath of an atomic war, though it is ambiguous as to whether we are in the immediate future or a forgotten past. An atomic war has wiped out a civilisation and all that remains are meaningless, half-understood rituals. It is the first of the cinema's few attempts at creating the kind of logical, post-nuclear society featured in novels like Walter M. Miller Jr's *A Canticle for Leibowitz* (1960) and Russell Hoban's *Riddley Walker* (1980).

'I've always thought of it as a missed opportunity,' said Corman of *Teenage Caveman.* 'With a few more days and a little bit more money we could have made a genuinely good film instead of a pretty good one.' The script is hectoring ('have you ever wondered, father, what is beyond the burning plain, beyond the river, perhaps beyond the great green forest?') and the performances are makeshift, particularly from Darrah Marshall (a former Miss Teenage America) as the Girl and Frank De Kova as a glowering, silent movie villain. However, the reversal, which admittedly would have been rejected as overly obvious by any SF magazine of the fifties, is strong enough to make the film oddly unforgettable. There is also an interesting undertone to the conclusion: we are supposed to sympathise with Vaughn as he kicks against the elders, but it is implied that the progress

that comes when youth questions the Law inevitably leads to more warfare and yet another catastrophic collapse.

The Last Woman on Earth (1960), Corman's final nuclear holocaust movie, is the most minimalist end-of-the-world movie ever made. Shot in VistaScope and garish EastmanColor, the film manages to make Puerto Rican locations look like poverty row studio mock-ups. There are only three speaking characters, most of the action takes place out of doors and civilisation is wiped out without so much as a snippet of stock footage. While sneering crook Harold Gurn (Anthony Carbone), his wife Evelyn (Betsy Jones-Moreland) and their tarnished idealist lawyer Martin (Edward Wain, actually screenwriter Robert Towne) are scuba diving, something burns up all the oxygen in the atmosphere and everyone asphyxiates. No firestorms, no radioactive ruins, no toppled cities, no charred corpses. We don't even see the victims falling over. The survivors figure the phenomenon must be due to 'a bigger and better bomb' and get through the global catastrophe by breathing bottled air. The tropical foliage soon photosynthesises the atmosphere back to a breathable normal.

Naturally, a triangle develops, and the film turns into a game of odd-one-out, with each of the characters in turn excluded from the relationship between the other two. (Coincidentally, Roman Polanski, for whom Towne would write *Chinatown* [1974], uses an extremely similar plot in *Noz W Wodzie* [1962, *Knife in the Water*]). Harold is all for getting the old world back together, while Martin wants to set up a freer, less neurotic society, and Evelyn's shifting loyalties signal the course of the argument. The finale takes place in a church, with Martin dying on the altar. 'I killed him,' gasps Harold, who had earlier bashed the lawyer with a rock. 'Will we never learn?' 'He didn't think so,' comments the Last Woman on Earth. Stiffly acted and economically directed, the film is the least coherent and most interesting of the post-holocaust morality plays. Existing in the nexus between exploitation and art, *The Last Woman on Earth* survives its cheapskate production and haphazard scripting by conveying a real sense of a world changing. Most post-nuclear movies see the same old story starting over, but this one believes the society we are left with after the Bomb will be radically different. Even the zombie performances can be read as the natural result of a trauma that has left the characters in a Marienbad kind of trance.

> This was an interesting movie because we never actually had a finished script to work with. Bob Towne was the writer. I think it was his first script ever. We were going to Puerto Rico to shoot this back to back with *Battle of Blood Island* (1960). Bob didn't have the script finished in time, though. Our budget was so low I couldn't afford to bring him along as a writer so I decided to make him the juvenile lead because I did have it in the budget to take my actors along. We wrote the script as we filmed. Essentially, there never was a script. We just got pages day by day. We never knew one day what we were going to do next. We still managed to shoot it in two weeks. A lot of people see these films today and ask me if I knew I was being existential. No. I was primarily aware that I was in trouble. I was shooting with hardly any money and less time.
>
> **Roger Corman, *The Films of Roger Corman: Brilliance on a Budget***

Like many Corman productions, *The Last Woman on Earth* was made to cash in on a more important but less interesting movie, Ranald MacDougall's *The World, the Flesh and the Devil* (1959). Adapted loosely from M.P. Shiel's 1901 novel *The Purple Cloud*, the film has humanity all but exterminated in a war fought with radioactive gas. Buildings are left intact, but people are instantly vaporised — one wonders if the inventors of the neutron bomb were trying to mimic the effect. Ralph (Harry Belafonte), a black miner, lives through the calamity trapped in an under-ground shaft. He digs his way out and takes up residence in a deserted Manhattan where he gets to play Robinson Crusoe. He meets Sarah (Inger Stevens), a cheery ingenue who tactlessly reminds him, during a quarrel, that she's 'free, white and twenty-one.' The World and the Flesh are soon intruded upon by the Devil, Ben (Mel Ferrer), a bigot who thinks he should claim Sarah as his woman and that Ralph should shine their shoes. The macho brawling turns into World War Four and the men snipe at each other amid the concrete canyons. The final shoot-out takes place in front of the UN building, where the survivors are overcome by conscience. They sort out their racial and sexual differences, and invent a new kind of fam-ily unit. The film is choked by the strained significance that blights *Five*, but it does have the best depopulated city sequences.

Commercially, *The World, the Flesh and the Devil* was eclipsed by *On the Beach*. In the sixties, the post-nuke cheapie all but died out as the major studios scraped up the budgetary clout to get their atomic acts together. There were a few stragglers, including Barry Mahon's *Rocket Attack, U.S.A.* (1959), a spy thriller which ends with the Soviets nuking New York; and Larry Buchanan's *In the Year 2889* (1965), a static, rotten remake of *The Day the World Ended*. Fredric Gedette's *This Is Not a Test* (1962), the *Twilight Zone*-ish story of a random group of travellers caught on the road when war breaks out, prefigures *Night of the Living Dead* in its argument about whether to run for a mine or try to survive cooped up in the back of a truck. It also manages, in its grotty, panicky way, to suggest the futility of by-the-book survivalism represented by a state trooper who kills a pet poodle to save air in an impromptu shelter, and winds up banging on the doors to be let in as the big blast comes. It would not be until the early eighties, with the flood of films unleashed by the international success of the *Mad Max* movies, that the Norms and the Mutates really got going again.

The Shadow
of Doom

The Cold War produced an atmosphere of anxiety and para-noia: anxiety mainly caused by the ever-present possibility of atomic war between the two super-powers and the resulting global destruction; paranoia caused by the fear of communist subversion, an invasion from within by people who looked like ordinary Americans but who were actually the pawns of an alien power. As a result of these fears most SF films of the 1950s reflect a number of basic themes: the atomic bomb and its after-effects; the effects of atomic radiation; alien invasion and possession by aliens; and world destruction.

John Brosnan, *Future Tense: The Cinema of Science Fiction*

Opposite:
The Day of
the Triffids,
Janette Scott

Bombs in Space

Destination Moon (1950), the film that kick-started the fifties SF cycle, has its expedition backed by a combination of private enterprise and the mili-tary who claim the moon 'in the name of the peoples of the United States and the Earth.' The film is so in love with its gleaming, atomic-powered rocketry, and so bored with the stiff characters included as concessions to mass appeal, that many people misremember the movie and assume the trip to the moon is made solely as a scientific exercise. In cinematic terms, the rewards for such a journey are mostly aesthetic; as in Georges Méliès's charming *Le Voyage dans la lune* (1902), where a chorus line from the *Folies Bergère* assists the blast-off, and the lunar missile lodges itself in the eye of the man in the moon. In fact, an early briefing scene in *Destination Moon* explains it is vital to American interests that military bases be established before an unidentified, missile-hoarding nation gets there.

By the sixties, the space race and the missile gap were inextricably linked as political issues. America's against-the-odds emergence as a front-runner in both contests was central to President Kennedy's messianic image. The Russians had the Bomb, then they had Sputnik; many Americans were terrified at the prospect of spooning under a commie moon. Ironically, Russia's initial success in space was due to inferior technology — their bombs were bulkier, and so rockets designed to deliver them had to be able to get a greater yield in the air. The prophetic nature of *Destination Moon* is confirmed by Philip Kaufman's *The Right Stuff*, which is cynical where the earlier film is patriotic, but also suggests a Cold War motivation for the first manned space flights. Like *Destination Moon*, *The Right Stuff* balances the earthly motivation for the mission against the beauty, bravery and technological wonder of the achievement.

In Roy Ward Baker's *Quatermass and the Pit* (1967), from Nigel Kneale's 1959 TV serial, Professor Bernard Quatermass (Andrew Keir) has to argue with his military and political masters against the co-opting of his moon project exclusively for 'defence' purposes — though, in Val Guest's *Quatermass 2* (1957), from the 1955 serial, an earlier incarnation of the Professor (Brian Donlevy) uses a faulty atomic rocket as a missile against potential alien invaders. Kneale's Professor, who made his TV début in *The Quatermass Experiment* (1953, filmed by Guest in 1955), is unusual as a boffin whose attitude to his rocket project, which admittedly wavers between his various outings, is often at odds with those of his government sponsors. Whether Kneale's kindly Brit or Hammer's bullish Yank, Quatermass refuses to serve any cause but science and humankind, though he is certainly — like Alec Guinness in *The Man in the White Suit* — confronted often with the human costs of his almost fanatical devotion to pure science. Paul Dickson's *Satellite in the Sky* is another British attempt to question why space exploration should come under military rather than scientific command — accepted as a matter of course by the likes of *World Without End* — but it was not until the Reaganite Strategic Defence Initiative (SDI) debate of the eighties that this became a hot topic.

While producer George Pal and director Irving Pichel were making *Destination Moon*, in colour and with meticulous special effects, distributor Robert L. Lippert decided to beat them into theatres by having Kurt Neumann write, produce and direct a cheaper, mostly black and white

lunar voyage. *Rocketship X-M*, whose remit includes investigating the possibility that 'an unassailable base could be established on the moon and control world peace', is knocked off course and crash-lands on a red tinted Mars. The crew find 'immense deposits of pitchblende' and a ruined city in a radioactive desert, then realise that a once-glorious Martian civilisation has destroyed itself, going from 'atomic age to stone age' through warfare. After a skirmish with the pathetic mutant savages who are all that's left of the planet's former rulers, the X-M takes off. The ending is surprisingly downbeat for the fifties: even the crew members who survive Mars are killed trying to get back to Earth. Morris Ankrum, head of the project, scribbles down a few calculations and starts work on the R-X-M 2.

Rocketship X-M is the first film to depict a world destroyed by nuclear war. It may not add up to more than a few paintings of the smashed city, tinted location shots of the Mojave Desert and scrawny extras in bald wigs, but it's still an effective low budget vision of the unthinkable. The film's scream of terror comes not from the heroine but from a blind savage, confronted by Earthmen who are alien invaders to her. 'What a lesson here for our world,' muses scientist John Emery, 'one war, thousands of years of civilisation wiped out.' The movie prefigures the desolate, post-holocaust landscapes of many subsequent films, but also the terracentric, anti-intellectual attitudes of much SF cinema. Like the Metalunans of *This Island Earth* (1955) and the Krel of *Forbidden Planet*, the *Rocketship X-M* Martians pay the price for becoming too intelligent, ignoring the simple pleasures of American mankind, and flirting with notions of social control and hive mind militarism similar to those practised by Certain Foreign Powers. The film's romantic sub-plot has a coldly glamorous foreign egghead (Osa Massen) warm up to he-man pilot Lloyd Bridges, learning she has spent too much time on rocket fuel formulae and not enough on womanly pursuits. 'I suppose you think that women should only cook and sew and bear children?' she teases Bridges, only for him to snap, 'isn't that enough?' By the end of the film, she has changed her mind and is hugging him as they burn up on re-entry.

In the popular imagination of the early fifties, there was little difference between Hitler and Stalin; between the Third Reich and the Socialist Utopia. Actors who had made a speciality of playing villainous Nazis easily made the transition to villainous Reds, and thrillers like William Cameron Menzies's *The Whip Hand* feature ex-Nazis currently working for Russia as bad guys. When an evil extra-terrestrial society is shown, it combines the worst features of fascism and communism. And, of course, totalitarian aliens are always fighting atomic wars. The Metalunans of *This Island Earth* kidnap nuclear scientists from our world and force them to contribute to their pointless, mutually destructive war with the Zahgons. The images of war in Joseph M. Newman's film (many contributed by the uncredited Jack Arnold) are more affecting than those of *Rocketship X-M*. A shattered planetary crust barely shields a futuristic but crumbling city, continual air raids rumble and flash in the background, highly advanced technology gives way to brute force. The Metalunans, with their high foreheads and white hair, are so manifestly unlike us (and like Nazis or communists) that we are allowed to feel superior. *This Island Earth* reinforces the notion that it couldn't happen here, and if it did it wouldn't be our fault. Exeter (Jeff Morrow), Metalunan equivalent of a Good German or a Russian Dissident, is in charge of the alien brain drain on Earth. He comes to appreciate Mozart and grey flannel suits as exemplars of the right, the true, the *only* workable way of life. He sacrifices himself to save the hero and heroine, but the rest of his society is so wrapped up in making war that they don't mind mutating into insectoid horrors.

The Monitor (Douglas Spencer), dictator of Metaluna, when he is at last sure of the planet's doom, suggests that his people should emigrate *en masse* to the Earth. The idea that once the aliens have nuked each other into the rubble they'll want to get their claws into a fresh, green, unspoiled planet like ours is recurrent. Roger Corman's *Not of This Earth* (1957) features a lone invader (Paul Birch) in a conservative suit and dark glasses, teleported from somewhere called Davanna. His race is dying thanks to 'centuries of atomic warfare', and they want our blood to replace their poisoned bodily fluids. The invaders of Ishiro Honda's *Chikyu Boeigun* (1957, *The Mysterians*) are slightly more reasonable, if rather more extreme in their demonstration of military might. Nuclear war has made their women infertile and they want six of ours to help repopulate the planet. To persuade us, they unleash a giant rampaging robot aardvark, and then come out of their saucer a-blastin' with a colourful array of super-destructive weaponry. In both cases, the Earth is seen as totally justified in telling the aliens to go back to their nuked planets and stew in their own fall-out.

The presence of galactic troublemakers like the Metalunans, the Davannans and the Mysterians provides a justification for the existence of the Bomb as a deterrent. If the Nazis had had atomic weapons, they'd have used them without conscience. An elementary lesson in preparedness and controlled aggression is taught in Gordon Flemyng's *Dr. Who and the Daleks*, from Terry Nation's serial 'The Mutants' (*Doctor Who*, 1963-4). The dotty scientist (Peter Cushing) and his companions travel to Skaro, a planet all but destroyed by a 'neutronic war'. In a petrified forest, they discover the good guy survivors, the Thals, who are pale, very wet, well-spoken pacifists with a now-unfortunate tendency to look like Julian Clary; in the metal city live the bad guy survivors, the Daleks, who are fascist mutants in trundling metal suits with a philosophy of 'exterminate and conquer'. The Thals meekly accept their lot. 'We are a peaceful people,' says the head man, 'we see no reason to kill others. The last war destroyed almost everything on this planet. We do not want another.' Such defeatism gets the Doctor's dander up and, by suggesting the chief's girlfriend be turned over to the Daleks 'for experimentation', he convinces the Thals that there are 'some things worth fighting for.'

Right:
Dr. Who and
the Daleks,
Peter Cushing,
Roy Castle,
Jennie Linden,
Roberta Tovey

In a later TV serial, 'Genesis of the Daleks' (1975), Nation revised the history of the War on Skaro, making it an amalgam of the worst aspects of the twentieth century's real and imagined world wars: trench warfare, gas attacks, fascist secret police, woolly-headed military planners, ranting teenage generals, slave labourers dying as they assemble the unshielded radioactive elements of nuclear-capability V-weapons, genegineered freaks tooled for survival, irresponsible scientists who serve whichever regime funds their research, mutants lost in no man's land, ruined economies and ecologies, even ugly décor. Davros (Michael Wisher), the cyborg creator of the Daleks, is a bizarre mix of Werner von Braun, Dr Mengele, Oppenheimer and the planners of Joseph Losey's *The Damned*, his commitment to mercilessness ironically paying off as his perfected new species exterminate him. This impressively grim vision for what was essentially children's television sobers even Tom Baker's clownish Time Lord, and did not go down well with Mary Whitehouse, but its all-encompassing condemnation of war tends to muddle the original attack on specific weapons and Nation — as in all his work — seems torn between war-hating pacifism and the need to be militant in the face of fascism. *Doctor Who* wavered in ideology throughout its long run, with the Doctor arguing against the unconsidered deployment of genocidal weaponry (the 'Z-Bomb' of 'The Tenth Planet' [1966]) or condemning the wholesale massacre of alien species ('Doctor Who and the Silurians' [1970]) but often whipping together Manhattan Project-esque superweaponry to eradicate a threat to whichever side (usually human) he has chosen to support in a conflict that, as the Time Lords repeatedly tell him, ought to be none of his business ('The Ice Warriors' [1967]; 'Image of the Fendahl' [1977]; 'Silver Nemesis' [1988]).

Only in *Rocketship X-M* is the example of a nuclear war on another planet used as an explicit warning to the people of Earth. Other explorations of the theme are designed to reflect well on our planet, or at least the Western half of it. *This Island Earth* congratulates the human race on not indulging in full-scale nuclear war. *Dr. Who and the Daleks* suggests that peace and love are fine as ideals, but need to be backed up with heavy firepower — like Richard Marquand's *Return of the Jedi* (1983), the film cops out in the finale by having the primitive heroes overcome the super-technological villains by battering their domes in with sticks and stones. Since George Lucas's *Star Wars* (1977), planet-destroying weapons have become commonplace in the cinema. David Lynch's *Dune* (1984), released during a period of intense debate about the earthly purpose of nuclear weapons, features the most casual use of atomics in the cinema, as a minor help to the good guys during the final shoot-'em-up. Roland Emmerich's *Stargate* (1994) assumes a mission through a warp-gate to an unknown world will require a nuclear device as part of the standard equipment. It is entirely apt that Ronald Reagan should have appropriated Lucas's title for his fantasy satellite weapons system. *Star Wars* and its successors — most recently, albeit with an ironic edge, Paul Verhoeven's *Starship Troopers* (1997), from Robert A. Heinlein's 1959 novel — invisibly conspired to make the strategic use of atomic weapons acceptable in the cinema.

Byron Haskin's *From the Earth to the Moon* (1958), derived loosely from Jules Verne's *De la terre à la lune* (1865), is one of a cluster of fictions — including Richard Fleischer's *20,000 Leagues Under the Sea* (1954), Karel Zeman's Verne-derived *Vynález Zkáky* (1958, *An Invention of Destruction*), George Pal's *Atlantis, the Lost Continent* (1961), Umberto Scarpelli's *Il gigante di Metropolis* (1962, *The Giant of Metropolis*), Russell Mulcahy's *The Shadow* (1994) and Ronald Clark's novel *Queen Victoria's Bomb* (1967) — to assume atomic power was discovered in the past, and the secret lost. This talky, boring picture has the distinction of being the most confused, hawkish and maudlin of the bombs-in-space movies. Armaments manufacturer Victor Barbicane (Joseph Cotten) hopes to get his business through the slump caused by the end of the Civil War through demonstrating 'Power X', an explosive process 'so deadly, so powerful, that if placed in the wrong hands... could mean the destruction of the entire world'. When his original plan to fire a Power X shell at the moon is nixed by President Grant (Morris Ankrum in a beard) as likely to provoke international outrage, Barbicane falls back on his second choice, using his Power X shell to *visit* the moon.

The film's 'villain' is Stuyvesant Nicholls (George Sanders), a Southerner horrified that 'governments which furiously slew thousands on the field of battle can now look forward to the slaughter of millions, nay tens of millions.' Barbicane is an early advocate of deterrent, with a uniquely capitalist twist — when he explains that a Power X shell 'fired from the smallest country in the world... could explode over the capital of any country which threatened them', a munitions manufacturer associate muses 'every government would have to have one, sold by one of us.' Barbicane and Nicholls are Teller and Oppenheimer figures, and spend the perfunctory space voyage arguing with each other about the applications and dangers of Power X. The peacenik is also a scurvy saboteur and so the secret is lost when both of them crash into the moon, though Nicholls admits at the last that Barbicane is right to think that 'with the whole world in possession of Power X, then there would have been no next war.' In a silly punchline, the fate of the expedition inspires Jules Verne (Carl Esmond) to pick up a pen.

Alien Invasions

For the most part, *War of the Worlds* (1953) is that rarity, a defeatist SF film. One of the few movies to take advantage of the pulp magazine concept of a mass invasion from outer space, it uses interplanetary conflict as an excuse for presenting a vision of the global consequences of high-tech warfare. The Martians arrive in meteorites and cruise over the world's cities in lovely, manta-shaped flying machines, projecting death rays from cobraneck antennae. In an initial attack that must count as the sneakiest since Pearl Harbour, they blast three innocent citizens who approach a meteor hoping to make friendly contact. One fellow even suggests 'welcome to

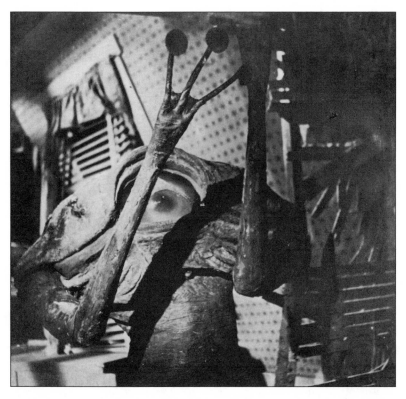

Left:
War of
the Worlds

California' as a suitable greeting to beings from another world. The heat ray vaporises these jovial everymen instantly, leaving Hiroshima-like blast shadows on the ground. The Martians' perfidy is confirmed when, during a battle with Earth's armies, they casually wipe out a priest who tries to make peace with them by reciting the Twenty-third Psalm. Having shocked us with these individual atrocities, the film proceeds to depict the complete and utter defeat of the human race and the levelling of the planet's major cities.

Of course, *War of the Worlds* is trying to be a scary movie, and its images are calculated to strike terror into the hearts of mid-western audiences. Before Vietnam, American audiences (at least in the North) were unused to the sight of their armed forces losing a war. Films had been made about the Alamo, Little Big Horn and the fall of the Philippines, but these lost battles were merely set-backs for a country which would inevitably come out on top; eventual victory is always assured. In *War of the Worlds*, the Martians win. Producer George Pal and director Byron Haskin make their invaders even more unstoppable than those in H.G. Wells's 1898 novel. Wells's Martians at least lose a few machines during their take-over of the world, but the film's aliens aren't even scratched by the mightiest weapons we can come up with. The horror increases as each conventional strategy is tried and fails. We know all is really lost when, after brief official heart-searching, America decides to use the Bomb. The fifties' two most streamlined and unwieldy symbols of technological achievement are combined when an atomic device is loaded onto the Flying Wing. The Martians, surrounded by an impenetrable force field, ignore the Bomb. After this near sacrilege, the human race has nothing left to do but panic or pray. Finally, the aliens are destroyed, not through any human agency, but by germs. The narrator assures us that the triumphant bacteria were put on Earth by God.

War of the Worlds is an inflated version of the Cold War hysteria that had been behind smaller invasions like the one in *The Thing From Another World*. While it is probably going too far to identify the Martians exclusively with the Russians, it is noticeable that the montage of the world's cities under alien rule excludes any shots of Moscow in ruins (mention is made, however, of the heroic struggles of the Chinese). Supposedly serious treatments of nuclear war, from *Five* to *Threads*, are forced by good taste and their sense of social/political responsibility to stay away from the kind of colourful holocaust Haskin relishes in *War of the Worlds*. The Martian war machines are as sleek and beautiful as the planes of *Strategic Air Command* and the destruction wrought by the heat rays, expertly created by the special effects men, is as exhilarating as it is frightening. The film's SF elements divorce it sufficiently from reality to allow for an almost erotic apocalypse. With its pretty colours, flashing lights and unearthly zapping noises, *War of the Worlds* discovers the pornography of the Bomb.

Because it relies so heavily on expensive effects, *War of the Worlds* is the least imitated of all great SF films. Sherman Rose's *Target Earth* (1954) tries to do it on the cheap, with a few survivors in an evacuated city harassed by a single cardboard robot that supposedly represents a horde of Venusian invaders. Phil Tucker's even cheaper *Robot Monster* (1953) takes place *after* almost all of humanity has been wiped out by a single alien invader, a gorilla in a space-helmet. Cost-conscious onslaughts are also mounted in Edward L. Cahn's *Invisible Invaders* (1959), in which unseen but radioactive beings reanimate pasty-faced dead extras to overwhelm civilisation, and Terence Fisher's *The Earth Dies Screaming* (1964), which has a few robots and a few more zombies menace a few survivors in eerily empty home counties locations. Fred F. Sears's *Earth vs the Flying Saucers* and Ishiro Honda's *Chikyu Boeigun* borrow the basic format of a large scale invasion from outer space, and re-use much of the imagery (*Earth vs the Flying Saucers* literally re-uses some *War of the Worlds* explosions), but stay away from the downbeat plot. It took thirty years for effects spectacles to become common enough for the material to be tapped again: Roland Emmerich's *Independence Day* is essentially a remake — it retains the moment when the Bomb is laughed off by the aliens — while Tim Burton's *Mars Attacks!* (1996) is a bizarro parody.

These films pile on the megatonnage as the aliens make their first strikes, but concentrate on the heroic, against-the-clock efforts of the scientists who develop super-weapons (often relying on sound rather than visual effects) to repel the invaders. *Deus ex machina* bugs aren't dramatic or heroic enough a solution to these problems: *Target Earth*'s Whit Bissell discovers an oscillating frequency which splinters Venusian robot cathode tubes (!), Hugh Marlowe invents a sonic gun that disables Ray Harryhausen's Flying Saucers, Robert Hutton and John Agar work out that 'high-pitched sound waves' not only kill the Invisible Invaders but render them visible as well, and in *Chikyu Boeigun* the Japanese devise an energy tank that effectively counters the Mysterians' array of death machines. Will Smith and Jeff Goldblum in *ID4* (as the poster insists we call it) deliver a computer virus to the master saucer and Lukas Haas discovers that Burton's big-brained Martian baddies are vulnerable to amplified Slim Whitman songs. Often, these projects are seen as the next step in weaponry, rendering nuclear weapons obsolete — in *Target Earth*, the cheap and safe sound weapon is invented just before the authorities are about to turn 'atomic artillery' against 'one of our own cities', a strategy actually employed (cheaply) against a golem in London in *It!* (1966).

World War Two remains the central metaphor of most mass invasions — the Daleks of Gordon Flemyng's *Daleks' Invasion Earth 2150 A.D.* (1966), from Terry Nation's serial 'The Dalek Invasion of Earth' (*Doctor Who*, 1964), and the Visitors of Kenneth Johnson's *V* (1983) are fascist aliens —

and the movies borrow heavily from the resistance-and-collaboration clichés developed during the War. The battles of *War of the Worlds*, *Earth vs the Flying Saucers*, *Invisible Invaders* and *Daleks' Invasion Earth 2150 A.D.* are modelled on blitzkriegs past, often to the inclusion of forties newsreel footage. A sign of some imaginative progress is Stuart Orme's *The Puppet Masters* (1994), from Robert A. Heinlein's 1951 novel, in which an alien invasion is greeted with strategies patterned on those of the Cold War, even to the extent of nuclear sabre-rattling, as an enemy actually does try to take over America through subversion and the fifth column just like McCarthy said they would. Made after the Cold War, *ID4* tentatively tries to come up with villains not modelled on the Nazis or the Reds; its aliens are environmentally despoiling capitalists who strip-mine and abandon entire planets.

Though free with the unthinkable (global nuclear devastation), invasion films tend to be deterrent-conscious. Once the Martians, the Saucer Men and the Mysterians have learned that they can't pick on Earthlings, they have no choice but to retreat to their dying worlds and sulk. The emphasis on the secret research team who come up with an ultimate weapon with which to defeat the enemy is obviously a hangover from the Manhattan Project. Even *Chikyu Boeigun*, unlike Honda's *Gojira*, endorses the unhesitating use of the new weapon against the enemy. Considerably less gung-ho are Andrei Tarkovsky's *Stalker* (1979), James Cameron's *The Abyss* (1989) and 'Trial By Fire' (*The Outer Limits*, 1996), in which willingness to deploy nuclear weapons against ambiguous alien visitors is a sign of Earthly (and specifically American) paranoid insanity. *Mars Attacks!*, irreverent about everything other films take seriously, reverts to a parodic rerun of Wells's original ending; after our military, scientific and political resources prove to be pathetically useless, the simplest creatures on Earth — a lonely teenager, a game grandmother, a washed-up boxer, plus Tom Jones and Slim Whitman — see off the invaders.

The high concept of *Independence Day*, the most commercially successful of the mass invasion movies, is to crossbreed *War of the Worlds* with *Earthquake* (1974). By delivering unprecedented spectacle and disaster, the film reaped an enormous box-office take. Mile-wide flying saucers appear in the skies over the world's major cities (with the emphasis, of course, on Los Angeles, New York and Washington) and, after a tense countdown as only cable TV engineer Jeff Goldblum intuits what might happen, huge

rays blast said metropoli into smoking rubble. President Bill Pullman, an ex-fighter pilot struggling with a wimp image, fights back, but impenetrable alien force fields mean our planes get knocked out of the skies. All hope is not lost, however — hotshot pilot Will Smith, big brain Goldblum, big heart Pullman and sundry 'representative' human beings get together at the secret base where America has hidden the alien ship that crashed at Roswell in the 1940s. Avowed atheists start praying, many-clawed aliens sneer at our pathetic resistance and once-UFO-abducted goon Randy Quaid looks forward to payback, while the plucky survivors come up with a hare-brained plan to save the world 'that just might work'.

The finale strains hard as overworked effects men try to come up with a climax which tops the holocausts of the first two acts. What the film doesn't manage is to make our inevitable victory over the aliens as convincing as their initial crushing of the Earth. Falling back on such unlikelinesses as Smith being able to work the controls of a spaceship designed for a species with eight-foot tentacles, the compatibility of our computer

Above:
Independence Day

software with a machine from a different star system and everyone in the world doing what the American President says is good for them at the same time, the wind-up is dumb but infallibly uplifting. With a kind of reverential America-first patriotism only a German director, fresh off the equally silly *Stargate*, could take seriously, *ID4* segues from SF/disaster hybrid into religio-nationalist epic on a scale not seen in Hollywood since the heyday of Cecil B. DeMille. It violates the so-called First Rule — that you can't make a good film without a good script. It comes close to being a great film, and it not only has a truly atrocious script (favourite line: 'they'll never let you fly the space shuttle if you marry a stripper') but a deadening dose of religiosity (Yiddische poppa Judd Hirsch sadly escapes alien death rays) and an even more crippling orgy of red-white-and-blue pride. The likeable, second rank all-star cast try hard — Brent Spiner gets the Man of the Match award as a comical scientist — but there's little that can be done with characters like the Stalwart General (Robert Loggia), the Gutsy First Lady (Mary McDonnell) and the Screaming Queen Who Calls His Mother (Harvey Fierstein). What you get for your money is not depth but breadth, and that's where *Independence Day* delivers.

From the eerie opening scenes as the unshifting sands of the moon are disturbed by the presence of the alien mothership to the astonishing images of Armageddon from outer space — fireballs erupting through entire cities, hundreds of flying cars in flames, hordes of extras scythed down like wheat — Emmerich delivers all that 1950s films (*Earth vs the Flying Saucers*) and 1980s TV series (*V*) had to leave offscreen. Like *2001: A Space Odyssey* (1968), *Star Wars* and *Jurassic Park* (1992), it ups the special effects stakes (if not always in quality, then certainly in quantity) and gets close to putting on screen the images conjured up in readers' minds by epic-scale written science fiction. Early on, it exterminates memories of the feelgood UFOs of *Close Encounters of the Third Kind* (1977) as an attempt to communicate with the aliens is greeted with a raygun blast, but the Spielberg film it borrows most from is *1941* (1979), with ordinary Americans panicked by rumours of war but finally joining together in a celebration of Hollywood's love of mass devastation and massive counter-attacks, with Quaid even reprising John Belushi's cracked flyboy act.

The American box office disappointment of *Mars Attacks!* in the wake of the blockbusting success of *Independence Day* answers the long-standing question of how Stanley Kubrick's nightmare comedy *Dr. Strangelove* might have fared if it had opened *after* rather than before Sidney Lumet's similarly-themed Cold War flashpoint movie *Fail Safe*. In the sixties, the hit was the hip, cynical, satirical take on nuclear Armageddon and the flop was the square, solemn, serious version, in which everyone acts with stifling nobility and reason. By the mid-nineties, attitudes had reversed — the mass audience was more prepared for a B movie hymn to the American Spirit of Endurance than a *MAD* Magazine grotesque vision of a country deservedly laid waste by bug-eyed monsters. There are as many similarities between *Mars Attacks!* and *ID4* as there are between *Strangelove* and *Fail Safe*; indeed, all four films have their crisis confronting presidents, conflicting military and scientific advisors, big White House sets, aerial actions and exploded cities. One or two moments even play like canny parody, though are presumably coincidental — Burton replaces *ID4*'s momentous detonation of Washington landmarks with a hilarious scene as a flying saucer nudges a monument so it leans this way and then that in an effort to topple it perfectly onto a pack of Boy Scouts. While the Earthlings of *ID4* are awed and impressed by the appearance of the alien ships, the venal fools and knaves of *Mars Attacks!* barely take any notice, being too caught up in crassly petty endeavours from real estate deals to re-election campaigns. The most subtle, most astonishing element of Burton's savage satire is that his President Dale (Jack Nicholson) chooses to greet the Martian Ambassador with a windy paraphrase of Rodney King's famous 'why can't we just get along' speech. Typically, the invader then personally kills the President with a detachable hand that turns into an alien flag that unfurls to mark the conquest of Earth.

Nicholson also takes the secondary role of a Vegas hustler (suggesting that President and con man are two sides of the same coin, perhaps), and does surprisingly well in both parts, successfully toning down his natural flamboyance to play the most powerful stooge in the world. There is even room for a tiny shrug of humour (Nicholson's 'ça va' when the President of France calls him up) among the frenetic mugging and world destroying, along with such great laugh lines as 'you can tell the American people we still have two out of three functioning arms of government' after the mass skeletonisation of Congress. It was the first Burton film not to revolve around a central name-in-the-title protagonist, and the diffusion among a large and varied cast certainly means that it seems even more haphazard a bit of story-telling than such straggling items as *Beetle Juice* (1988) and *Batman Returns* (1992). It is clear that Burton invests his own identification in the put-upon Lukas Haas, the lank-haired doughnut counter boy who saves the world with a plot gimmick poached from *Attack of the Killer Tomatoes* (1978), and the film resolves his story through a wonderfully awkward teenage meeting with the sole survivor of the administration, the President's adolescent daughter (Natalie Portman).

However, Burton didn't unleash the skull-headed, big-brained CGI midget monsters to express admiration for much, and the film (following the blithely sadistic 1962 *Mars Attacks!* bubblegum cards) is mainly concerned with blasting a whole parade of detestable images of American 'normality': smug Prezz, fierce First Lady (Glenn Close), slick realtor, militarist goon (Rod Steiger), survivalist trailer trash, lecherous Washington aide (Martin Short), dim bulb scientific expert (Pierce Brosnan), tabloid TV hacks (Sarah Jessica Parker, Michael Fox), lawyers ('you're taking over the Earth, you're gonna need a lawyer,' pleads Danny De Vito), yapping dogs, even a symbolic hippie dove of peace. All are reduced to smoking, coloured skeletons, and one can sense the born anarchist's joy in blasting out of hand an assortment of A-list box office players from mainstream Hollywood, while the survivors are a lovably eccentric parade of exploitation names (Pam Grier, Jim Brown), mixed-up kids, a feisty old-timer (Sylvia Sidney) and Tom Jones.

With Danny Elfman's humming theremin score to accompany the delightfully retro flying saucers, this expertly evokes the 1950s feel of *The Man From Planet X* or the more colourful 1960s look of *First Men in the Moon* (1964). There are a few genuinely surreal images (some from the cards) like a stampede of burning cows, but this is mostly a delight for its pulp SF magazine cover one-offs: the flying saucer ramp unrolling precisely to match the red carpet waiting for it, the giant Martian walking machine, green brain-bursts spattering the inside of the aliens' helmets when Slim Whitman hits high notes. The most sustainedly eerie (and funny) sequence casts Lisa Marie as a voluptuous temptress whose beehive hairdo conceals her Martian brain-pan — chewing gum and wobbling in a tight dress as she invades the White House, the actress achieves the remarkable, disturbing feat of being at once a demonstrably real person

and moving as if she were as computer-generated as the remainder of the alien horde. Less focused than *Dr. Strangelove*, and as interested in childish B picture homages as in lampooning contemporary America, *Mars Attacks!* takes the *1941* influence and runs with it, evoking the Stanley Kramer of *It's a Mad Mad Mad Mad World* (1963) rather than *On the Beach*. It has its moments of quiet humanity (Haas interprets a Martian's circle-in-the-air greeting with 'he's made the universal sign of the doughnut') and flat-out sickness (Martian communication machines barking 'we are your friends' as their owners gleefully raygun fleeing humans), but its main commitment is to chaos. Like *Batman Returns*, it alienates far more people than it converts but has so much sheer verve packed into its admittedly incoherent frame that it's hard not to take something cherishable away from it, whether it be the severed heads of Brosnan and Parker shyly kissing as their flying saucer crashes or the chortling Martians erecting a mammoth and complicated ray-cannon pointed at one little old lady's head.

While these mass invasion movies play on fears of nuclear war, and share clichés with the after-the-bomb films (deserted cities, scavenging survivors, defeated armies), the majority of them serve mainly as retroactive support for the use of the Hiroshima and Nagasaki bombs. Faced with an implacable, hostile, unreasonable, insanely acquisitive enemy prepared indiscriminately to slaughter civilians and flatten cities, we have no choice but to throw whatever ultimate weapon we have at them. The message is that you can't appease a Dalek. It is perhaps to these films' credit that even Cold War era invaders mostly had more in common with the Nazis than the Soviets, though audiences cannot help but read them as arguments for the retention, deployment and (if necessary) use of nuclear weapons.

Disaster!

Visions of mass devastation became common in the big budget films of the fifties. 1956, the height of the Cold War, saw Hollywood's most lavish, apocalyptic versions of *War and Peace* and *The Ten Commandments*. A glance at the cast lists shows how the historical and Biblical epics were given relevance to the years of the Hungarian revolution, the solidification of the Iron Curtain and the erection of the Berlin Wall. In liberal King Vidor's *War and Peace*, American Henry Fonda stands up for a peace-loving democracy

(Czarist Russia!) against an invasion mounted by the totalitarian Napoleon (Czech Herbert Lom). In conservative Cecil B. DeMille's *The Ten Commandments*, American Moses Charlton Heston calls down the righteous wrath of God upon the totalitarian Pharaoh (Russian Yul Brynner). The after-the-battle scenes in *War and Peace* and the smiting of the Egyptians in *The Ten Commandments* have unmistakable overtones of an atomic war, echoed explicitly in John Huston's *The Bible* (1966), where mushroom clouds rise over Sodom and Gomorrah. Vidor contemplates with horror what they could do to us; DeMille contemplates with pride what we could do to them. The remote settings rob the scenes of their specific political references, but do not dilute the power of the anti- and pro-war sentiments.

Even less politicised movies are able to deal more explicitly with atomic disaster. They tended to cost about a twentieth as much as a Biblical epic and were proportionately less spectacular on the screen and at the box office. Curt Siodmak's *The Magnetic Monster* (1953) is a case in point, a cheapie constructed around ten minutes of terrific special effects footage left over from the obscure 1934 German movie, *Gold*. The film is a brisk, pseudo-documentary (with an accent on the pseudo) in the *Dragnet* tradition, celebrating the efforts of the fictional Office of Scientific Investigation (OSI). Richard Carlson and King Donovan note increased radioactivity in the Los Angeles area and trace it to a hardware store where the magnetic field is out of whack. There are also a couple of dead bodies. The culprit turns out to be a newly discovered element, serranium, which is so unstable that it doubles its mass every few hours, converting the energy it sucks from available power sources into physical bulk. Attaching a lump of putty to a spinning top, Carlson demonstrates what the element, if unchecked, could do to the world. However, by bombarding the stuff with more energy than it can assimilate, the OSI neutralises it.

For all its jargon and voice-over explanations, *The Magnetic Monster* is scientifically ridiculous. It is one of a mini-cycle of films about expanding mineral menaces: in John Sherwood's *The Monolith Monsters* (1957), extraterrestrial crystals grow when wet and threaten to crush the world until salt stops them, and in Fred F. Sears's *The Night the World Exploded* (1957), subterranean rocks explode when exposed to the air and threaten to blow up the world until the water stops them. Siodmak's movie, with its banal narration ('The score — four murders in two days. Cause of death

— the element was hungry') and even more banal heroic dialogue ('I like this world. Let's keep it in one piece. At least, let's try') is so stiff and solemn that its implausibilities are all the more laughable. However, the early scenes, in which Homburg-hatted OSI men wander about the crazy hardware store, ignoring the objects stuck to the walls and ceiling, Geiger counters clacking like angry lobsters, are still fairly unnerving. And the Pandora's Box theory of atomic fission gets its motto from Carlson's epitaph for the scientist whose tinkering has unleashed serranium: 'in nuclear research, there is no room for lone wolves.'

Kurt Neumann's *Kronos* (1957) and Lester Berke's *The Lost Missile* (1958) are about troublemaking machines from outer space that head our way. *Kronos* ('Planet Robber Tramples the Earth') is an accumulator in the shape of a giant box robot, sent by a power-starved planet to absorb every unit of energy we've got. Dropping an H-bomb on Kronos doesn't do any good, since it merely absorbs the force of the explosion as the mushroom cloud footage is reversed. *The Lost Missile* ('The Thing That Came From Outer Hell to Burn the World Alive') is an extra-terrestrial nuclear weapon carelessly fired at random into the universe. Whereas Kronos is undisturbed by nuclear attack, the Lost Missile is easily prevented from hitting New York when one of our rockets knocks it off course. However, hero Robert Loggia is fatally irradiated as he gets the warhead in place.

'After Pearl Harbour, it took us months to get ready for war,' announces the narrator of *The Lost Missile*. 'Against attack by missiles, we have only minutes. There may be no tomorrow. There may be no this afternoon.' Loggia is so dedicated to science that he neglects to skip lunch and get married; fiancée/lab assistant Ellen Parker moans, 'and all you can think of is a hydrogen warhead.' Jeff Morrow of *Kronos* is a similarly unromantic soul, putting off a movies-and-necking date with Barbara Lawrence because an unusual asteroid has shown up on his charts. These men save the world but are reminded in the course of their efforts that it is girls like Parker and Lawrence who make the world worth saving. *The Lost Missile* provides an interesting if unlikely sidelight on America's Civil Defence measures in the evacuation scene. Loggia: 'There must be at least ten million children in New York. I wonder how many will get out alive?' Lawrence: 'Under martial law, no car is leaving Manhattan unless it's carrying children. They must have planned it that way.'

In the early sixties, atomic disaster films became more elaborate, with bigger budgets, stronger casts and better special effects. And yet, there is little in Irwin Allen's *Voyage to the Bottom of the Sea* (1961) or Andrew Marton's *Crack in the World* to compare with the grey images of *The Magnetic Monster* or *Kronos*. The bright colours and familiar actors try for excitement but miss out on fear. In *Voyage*, meteors set the Van Allen belt on fire and heat up the world ('no one can doubt that civilisation as we know it will disintegrate if the temperature should rise to 175 degrees'), but Walter Pidgeon launches a thermo-nuclear missile from his submarine and blows the trouble out of the sky. In *Crack*, Dana Andrews sets bombs off underground in the hope of tapping the power of the planet's molten core, but bungles the job and starts a chain reaction which threatens to destroy the world. Kieron Moore is on hand to place a second bomb on the right fault line and save the day. As an interesting side effect, the Earth winds up with an extra moon. Another unwise attempt to drill deep for energy goes awry in 'Inferno' (*Doctor Who*, 1970), where the fiery destruction of a parallel Earth inspires Time Lord Jon Pertwee to intervene and avert disaster in his regular continuum.

Menaces from outer space could sometimes be mineral. As far back as *The Comet* (1910) and *The Comet's Comeback* (1916), which cashed in on Halley's Comet's first twentieth century pass, space rocks were threatening to end the world. Rudolph Maté's *When Worlds Collide* (1951), from the 1933 novel by Philip Wylie and Edwin Balmer, revived the format for the atom age and used the approach of a rogue planet to illustrate not only the devastation of our world as the threat nears but also a Manhattan Project-style race-against-time to create a rocketship which enables a select group of survivors to emigrate to a new planet fortuitously hauled along in the Earth-killer's wake. Privately funded by aged millionaire John Hoyt (who is forced to stay behind — no rich cripples in eugenic Heaven), the rocket is crewed by clean-cut young Americans who have won their places in a lottery (it comes as no surprise that they're all white).

At least *When Worlds Collide* delivers on its title: Bellus, the rogue, hits the Earth, and our home planet is destroyed, as it is in the final shot of the drearily cheap awful warning *End of the World* (1977). Subsequent variations on the theme are resolved with cop-outs: Paolo Huesch's *La morte viene dallo spazio* (1958, *The Day the Sky Exploded*), Ishiro Honda's *Yosei*

Gorasu (1962, *Gorath*), Irwin Allen's *City Beneath the Sea* (1970), 'Allen Smithee's *Solar Crisis* (1990), Bradford May's *Asteroid* (1997), 'Bart's Comet' (*The Simpsons*, 1995). In Steve Sekely's *The Day of the Triffids* (1963) and Thom Eberhardt's *Night of the Comet* (1984), comets don't even hit the Earth, though they do blind or vaporise most of humanity and leave the few survivors at the mercy of killer plants or zombies. 'End of the World' (*The Time Tunnel*, 1966) gets suspense from the fact that the time travelling heroes know Halley's Comet *won't* destroy the world in 1910, and so it *is* worth the effort of rescuing the townsfolk trapped in a mine cave-in.

Ronald Neame's *Meteor* (1979) focuses on the unwillingness of the Russian and American governments to admit that they have put missile launchers into orbit even though the satellites are now needed to save the world from a chunk of rock coincidentally following the lost missile's trajectory. In these films, there is debate about whether the Bomb should be used for therapeutic purposes, but the atom finally turns out to be a good guy. By the time of Mimi Leder's *Deep Impact* (1998), sort of a remake of *When Worlds Collide*, and Michael Bay's *Armageddon* (1998), a jocks-in-space movie, such qualms weren't even worth raising. In both films, space shuttles are despatched to deliver nuclear weapons to meteorites on course to wipe us out and the tension comes from whether or not the bombs can be placed and detonated for maximum effect (ie to save the world, but not before preliminary meteorites have caused enough devastation to make the films worth seeing). Here, as they were as far back as *La morte viene dallo spazio*, nukes are morally neutral tools — no one wonders if a shower of irradiated meteorite fragments would have ill effects on our civilisation.

The same themes are examined, far more ambiguously, in Val Guest's *The Day the Earth Caught Fire*. Atomic tests at the North and South Poles knock the Earth off its axis. At first this just means unusual weather reports, as London swelters in unaccustomed tropical heat. The Thames evaporates, water is rationed, Chelsea beatniks have an orgiastic riot and reporters Edward Judd and Leo McKern fight for the people's right to know exactly what has happened. While most films concentrate on the scientists and military men responsible for handling the crisis (and, if only by association, for causing it), Guest stays with the man in the street and suggests his interests may be last on a list of official priorities. This cynicism is diluted by the naïve treatment of the role of a crusading British press: the film was partially shot in the offices of Lord Beaverbrook's *Daily Express*, and editor Arthur Christiansen appears as himself. By contrast, Téa Leoni in *Deep Impact* initially works hard to break the story but is overwhelmed by the situation and abandons her job to seek a soap-opera reconciliation with her father, hugging him on a beach as a tidal wave looms. *The Day the Earth Caught Fire* may be a variation on endless jokes about the British climate, but it manages to suggest the physical and psychological problems of a disaster-afflicted city. In the end, the world's nuclear powers get together and decide to set off more bombs in the hope of putting Earth back into its proper orbit before it spins into the sun. The film closes with alternative headlines set up for the next day's edition, 'Earth saved!' and 'Earth doomed!' The issue is left undecided, but some prints have a studio-imposed peal of rejoicing bells to suggest salvation. While most atomic disaster movies suggest a rehabilitation of the Bomb by using nuclear weapons to correct global imbalances, *The Day the Earth Caught Fire* simply points out that governments had better be responsible for their actions.

FROM OUT OF SPACE....
A WARNING AND AN ULTIMATUM!
THE
DAY
THE
EARTH
STOOD
STILL
WITH
MICHAEL RENNIE · PATRICIA NEAL · HUGH MARLOWE
SAM JAFFE · BILLY GRAY · FRANCES BAVIER · LOCK MARTIN
JULIAN BLAUSTEIN · ROBERT WISE · EDMUND H. NORTH

Earthlings, Grow Up!

First Angel: Some devilish fellow down on the Earth has actually discovered the secret of the Super H-bomb.

Second Angel: That's impossible! The Super H-bomb is not scheduled for invention by the Devil until the year... let's see... until... here it is... until the year 2016... Why, they're not ready or wise enough to handle it yet! According to our heavenly statistics, if exploded now, the Bomb would blow Man and his Earth sky-high. No one would be left alive. Everyone would be dead.

First Angel: My, my, the housing shortage up here would be terrible... What'll we do?

The Story of Mankind **(1957)**

Science fiction assures us we are not alone in the universe. Intellects vast, cool and unsympathetic regularly cast envious glances at the Earth and lay their plans against the human race. Either they opt unsubtly for mass invasion, as in *War of the Worlds*, arriving amid a super-destructive array of glowing hardware and pummelling terrestrial civilisation into the dirt; or, more sneakily, as in *Invasion of the Body Snatchers*, they shape themselves into emotionless duplicates of our nearest and dearest and subvert human society from within.

During the Cold War, it was easy to identify these invaders with more familiar enemies: the Martians, literally a red army, were Stalinist hordes who had to be stopped in Europe and Asia before they reached Pasadena; the Body Snatchers, outwardly like you and me and Uncle Ira, were a creeping fifth column who had to be exposed and blacklisted before they could undermine the free world. With hindsight, it seems as apt to draw parallels between the monsters and people who were supposed to be on our side: the hawks who would bomb an enemy into the Stone Age or the innocent bystanders who let Senator McCarthy become a national influence. Aliens are rarely simply alien. H.G. Wells, who invented the alien invasion sub-genre, carefully points out that his Martians treat England no worse than European imperialists treated Tasmania. Often, aliens serve as a mirror for the worst of mankind.

There is another breed of alien, however, epitomised by the likes of Doctor Who, Mr Spock, *The Man Who Fell to Earth* (1976), *E.T. The Extra-Terrestrial* (1982) and *Starman* (1984). These visitors are better than the best of us and come to Earth as martyrs or messiahs. Saintly aliens are less common than raygun-brandishing monstrosities, but arrive with some regularity. In the fifties, they were as worried about the Bomb as everyone else and made the hyperspace trip to deliver an Awful Warning. Robert Wise's *The Day the Earth Stood Still*, best and most lavish of the cycle, opens with a slimline saucer settling on the White House lawn ('and none of your nonsense about Tibet or the North Pole,' says Philip Strick). It is immediately surrounded by the US army. 'When a powerful and threatening force lands on our nation's doorstep,' declares a general in *Earth vs the Flying Saucers*, making a policy statement for the genre, 'we don't greet it with milk and cookies.' An aperture appears in the seemingly seamless saucer and a ramp is extruded. Out steps Klaatu (Michael Rennie), an emissary from the interstellar equivalent of the United Nations. He is tall, handsome and speaks impeccable English with a slight British accent (obviously his people have been monitoring the BBC World Service). 'We have come to visit you in peace and with good will,' says Klaatu, reaching into his glittery tunic for the marvellous gift he has to offer President Truman. A fidgety GI, suspecting that the spaceman is going for his blaster, shoots Klaatu down. Welcome to Earth, man of peace and good will.

The Day the Earth Stood Still is informed by nuclear misanthropy. Any species which invents the Bomb is undoubtedly beyond redemption and you wouldn't want them moving into your galactic quadrant. If one of the square-jawed Earthling astronauts of *Destination Moon* had been shot at by the tentacled equivalent of that trigger-happy Private in *The Day the Earth Stood Still*, no one would have complained if his crewmates wiped out its entire planet. Klaatu, however, is inhumanly forgiving. He also has on hand Gort, a twelve-foot robot programmed to restore him to life if

necessary. While his master is lying wounded, Gort shows a bit of muscle by disintegrating a few tanks and mortars. Before the invulnerable robot can wreck the capital, Klaatu calls it off. Though not prepared immediately to terminate the human race, Klaatu is soon pretty fed up with us. He wants to address the Earth's leaders, but the squabbling premiers and presidents can't decide on a neutral venue for the meeting. 'I'm sure you know about the evil forces on our world which have caused trouble,' purrs a White House aide, leaving no doubt as to which large country full of vodka-drinking communists he is referring to. Klaatu coldly states that he isn't interested in such pettiness, and decides that if he is going to get any sense out of the Earth he will have to ignore the great and the good and go among the common people. Escaping from the Pentagon, he takes a room in a typical boarding house. In case anyone has missed the religious subtext, Klaatu assumes the name 'Mr Carpenter'.

The Day the Earth Stood Still, presumably because it was a SF film when nobody took the genre seriously, gets away with markedly un-American attitudes. Klaatu thinks Our Side is no better than Their Side and is understandably cynical about trigger-happy soldiers who represent military preparedness. However, he is soon won over by Mom's apple pie. Klaatu falls in with Helen Benson (Patricia Neal), a commonsensical widow, and her sickeningly cute son Bobby (Billy Gray). Their fundamental decency convinces him that the human race is worth saving. Even if Tom (Hugh Marlowe) rats on Klaatu when he figures the spaceman is waltzing off with his fiancée, it is established that ordinary Americans are basically okay. The hope for the future lies in a combination of mature femininity and childish innocence.

The reason for Klaatu's concern with such an insignificant planet comes out when he gets together with Professor Barnhardt (Sam Jaffe, made up to look like Einstein), a brilliant physicist. 'Soon one of your nations will apply atomic energy to spaceships, and that will threaten the peace and security of other planets.' As a demonstration of his incredible powers, Klaatu shuts off every source of power in the world (except for hospitals, planes in flight and other essential services). Impressed, Barnhardt gathers together the international scientific community to receive Klaatu's lecture. Who better to get the disarmament message than the deep thinkers who split the atom, then turned the Bomb over to the brass hats?

The film's Einstein reference signals just how unorthodox it is. In the fifties, the quintessential scientific genius was hardly a popular figure. His admission that had he foreseen the military applications of his theories he would have been content to live out his life as a simple watchmaker was not calculated to appeal to a Cold War government. Furthermore, the absent-minded professor image of science that Einstein had come to represent was fast being replaced by the patriotic, down-to-earth, crew-cut researcher who would find a faceless archetype in Neil Armstrong. In almost any other film of the fifties, blunt and boring Hugh Marlowe would be the scientist (*Earth vs the Flying Saucers*), while eccentric, interesting Sam Jaffe would be the dangerous lunatic (*The Asphalt Jungle* [1950]). In the finale of *The Day the Earth Stood Still*, Klaatu delivers his awful warning:

> The universe grows smaller every day, and the threat of aggression by any group anywhere can no longer be tolerated. There must be security for all, or no one is secure. This does not mean giving up any freedom except the freedom to act irresponsibly. Your ancestors knew this when they made laws to govern themselves, and hired policemen to enforce them. We of the other planets have long accepted this principle. We have an organisation for the mutual protection of all planets. The test of any such higher authority, of course, is the police force which supports it. For our policemen, we created a race of robots. Their function is to patrol the planets and preserve the peace. At the first sign of violence they act automatically against the aggressor. And the penalty for provoking their action is too terrible to risk. The result is that we live in peace without arms or armies, secure in the knowledge that we are free from aggression and war. We do not pretend to have achieved perfection, but we do have a system, and it works. It is no concern of ours how you run your planet, but if you threaten to extend your violence, this Earth of yours will be reduced to a burned-out cinder. Your choice is simple. Join us and live in peace, or pursue your present course and face obliteration.

Many audiences find Klaatu's rule of robots disturbing. Instead of a divided Earth living in fear of nuclear holocaust, we are offered a united Earth living in fear of Gort. When mankind puts its weapons under the control of dispassionate artificial intelligences in *Dr. Strangelove*, *Colossus: The Forbin Project* (1970) and *The Terminator* (1984), things don't turn out well. The peace of *The Day the Earth Stood Still*, enforced by death rays, is based on a misunderstanding of the relationship between Man and Machine. Klaatu concedes that his civilisation isn't perfect, but doesn't seem prepared to admit the possibility that its technology is similarly flawed. Earlier, he was worried that Gort might spontaneously destroy humanity and gave Helen the famous 'Klaatu barada nikto' code to sway him from the mission, which raises the disturbing question of why an infallible machine would need an emergency override protocol. At the fade-out, the alien flies off in his saucer, leaving no guarantee Gort won't accidentally destroy us like *Strangelove*'s Doomsday Machine, or deliberately destroy us like the CyberDyne Systems computer. Even a 'best case scenario' extrapolation from the end of *The Day the Earth Stood Still* leads to the scary situation of *Colossus*, with the human race as serfs following an omnipotent computer's programme to maximise their efficiency. In *Nuclear Movies*, Mick Broderick offers an unusual but persuasive reading of the Klaatu Ultimatum 'as a then-contemporary metaphoric interpretation of *American foreign policy* — a sort of post-World War II proclamation from the United States to the global community, having monopolised (and demonstrated its willingness to use) nuclear weaponry'.

Considering screenwriter Edmund H. North's insistent Christ references, we can perhaps assume that the Gorts represent an infallible, divine solution to the nuclear stalemate. Irwin Allen's extraordinarily misconceived *The Story of Mankind* is the first Awful Warning film to attempt a genuine heavenly intervention. Following the premature invention of the Super H-bomb, a court is convened in the clouds. The Devil (Vincent Price) and the Spirit of Man (Ronald Colman) argue for and against the extinction of humanity. Like *The Day the Earth Stood Still*, *The Story of Mankind* takes the Bomb as a symptom of mankind's general rottenness and debates the issue by trotting out examples of the good and evil in Man. Interestingly, both films feel nuclear devices *per se* are not necessarily diabolic (after all, Klaatu is allowed an atomic-powered saucer), but that human civilisation is too immature to be allowed to play with them. Allen uses the gimmick mainly as a device to trot out his incredible cast — Harpo Marx as Isaac Newton, Hedy Lamarr as Joan of Arc, Dennis Hopper as Napoleon, etc. Critic Philip K. Scheuer noted, 'In *The Story of Mankind* a High Tribunal is called into session somewhere in Heaven to decide whether or not we folks down here have done anything to make us worth saving. It is my personal observation that if the High Tribunal ever catches this picture, we're goners.'

Reginald LeBorg's *The Flight That Disappeared* (1961) only incidentally puts the entire human race on trial. Here, the accused are represented by three American nuclear scientists, abducted by heavenly powers from a

plane carrying them to a meeting with the President at which they are to present him with the plans for a shiny new Bomb. After much debate, the angels convince them to shred the documents and devote their energies to Peace. Other Awful Warning films generally come out like small-scale re-runs of *The Day the Earth Stood Still* — Burt Balaban's *Stranger From Venus* (1956, *Immediate Disaster*) has alien Helmut Dantine sacrificing himself for Patricia Neal (again cast as the good side of humanity), and Herbert Greene's *The Cosmic Man* (1959) features John Carradine in negative as the peacemaker from outer space.

In Ib Melchior's *The Angry Red Planet* (1960) and David Bradley's *12 to the Moon* (1960), alien civilisations note our irresponsible use of nuclear weapons, give our astronauts a hard time and post 'Earthling, go home' notices on their planets, though Bradley's international crew win cosmic brownie points for self-sacrifice by converting their 'space taxi' into an atom bomb to counteract the aliens' Klaatu-like deep-freezing of North America. Edward D. Wood's *Plan 9 From Outer Space* (1959), often cited as the worst film ever made, also features aliens worried by Earth's atomic policies. Unfortunately, no one is patient enough to endure the head alien's illustrated lecture, in which a tennis ball stands in for the sun, and the hero socks him on the jaw before he can explain precisely what we are doing wrong. Most Awful Warning movies end with question marks, but *Plan 9* uniquely has the human race ignore the aliens and rush headlong towards a presumed destruction.

On the whole, these films are furtively liberal, weakly arguing for nebulous concepts like reason and understanding, but a few Awful Warnings, from the drab but delirious *Red Planet Mars* (1952) on, uneasily reflect Cold War hysteria. In William Asher's *The 27th Day* (1957), from the 1956 novel by John Mantley, a race of Klaatu types, unable because of their 'moral code' to destroy humanity but still intent upon inheriting the Earth, give boxes to five typical earthlings. Only the recipients can open the boxes, which contain capsules capable of disposing of all human life within a radius of three thousand miles of any given spot on the map. The Russian recipient is tortured by the Stalinist premier (Stefan Schnabel), who threatens to use the capsules to snuff out 'all life on the North American continent' unless America withdraws from Europe and Asia, unable to appreciate the well-known fact that Americans aren't as warlike, underhand and cowardly as he is. In the end, the capsules turn out to be part of an alien test to determine the essential worth of humanity. We pass and, as a reward, the capsules make 'every enemy of human freedom' in the world drop dead. *The 27th Day* manages to be wish-fulfilment as well as paranoia, but does suggest progression from the Cold War is possible; it also, perhaps unwittingly, presents Russians and Chinese as good people with bad leaders, and Americans as a panicky mob with good leaders. The unseen Monolith People of Peter Hyams's *2010* (1984), from Arthur C. Clarke's novel *2010: Odyssey Two* (1982), also enforce *détente*, uniting a Soviet-American space crew and solving a Central American crisis which nearly triggers World War Three by turning Jupiter into a new sun. If anything, this instant utopia is even less convincing than the resolution of *The 27th Day*.

Towards the end of the fifties, with the emergence of a respectable anti-nuclear movement and the recession of the McCarthy scare, the nuke angles of Awful Warning films became more prominent. In Robert Gurney Jr's *Terror From the Year 5000* (1958, *Cage of Doom*), a group of scientists invent a time scoop which brings a hideously mutated woman (Salome Jens) from the far future back to our world. The scientific team consists of the regulation elderly professor, a humanist archaeologist and an ordinary joe college boy. The professor's beautiful daughter is on hand to do odd jobs, make cups of tea and remind them to button up their radiation suits. In one now-startling moment, this utterly conventional monster quickie invents the women's peace movement. The mutant, survivor of a disastrous atomic war, corners the bland heroine and tells her where her duty lies: 'Our history clearly records how the women of the twentieth century stood idly by while the atmosphere was contaminated and the children of the future doomed.'

Even more revisionary is Jack Arnold's gloomy *The Space Children* (1958), in which the offspring of a group of nuclear scientists come under the influence of a giant extraterrestrial brain with a vested interest in keeping nuke-happy humanity out of the stars. The parents are the kind of characters SF films had made familiar — ordinary, unimaginative, dedicated, unquestioningly patriotic. But they are also petty, self-absorbed and basically unlikeable. Arnold criticises them for qualities that, a few years earlier, the genre found admirable. At last the warning sinks in and the children persuade their parents to abandon the rocket programme they are working on. *Terror From the Year 5000* and *The Space Children* have the task of dissuading Man from the idiocy of atomic war passing from the hands of messianic aliens and becoming the responsibility of those who would be the innocent victims, the women and children. The rule of Gort might not have appealed to the world's scientists, but the message of Klaatu was not lost on Helen and Bobby Benson.

The World Went... Crazy

The war started when people accepted the idiotic principle that peace can be maintained by arranging to defend themselves with weapons they couldn't possibly use without committing suicide.

Opposite:
Dr. Strangelove,
Peter Bull,
Peter Sellers

Dr Julian Osborn (Fred Astaire), *On the Beach*

The threat of nuclear war is a recurring nightmare in fifties films. Three-eyed mutants, giant ants in the desert, Pandora's boxfuls of fissionable material, billowing mushroom clouds and B-52s scrambling for take-off are common images of the unthinkable. In *Split Second*, clued-up reporter Keith Andes tries to warn hardened criminal Stephen McNally that hiding out in the middle of an A-bomb test site is not a good idea. The villain sneers and suggests the hero swap crazy stories with Dummy, a mentally retarded gangster who does nothing but read comic books and torture people. The film tries to prove McNally wrong, but he represents a grass roots view of the Bomb as something from the pages of *The Magazine of Fantasy and Science Fiction* that remained widespread until the Cuban missile crisis. The effect of this attitude on the SF community is interesting. 'Ever since the day that I first heard that an atomic bomb had been exploded over Japan,' said editor Donald Wollheim, 'I have had the disturbing conviction that we are all living in a science fiction story.'

In the late fifties and early sixties, opinions began to change. Nuclear test footage became a film and television commonplace, the Russians put machines and men into outer space, and in the Caribbean the Cold War was warming up. Amid much bally-hoo, Stanley Kramer made and released *On the Beach*. Adapted from the 1957 novel by Nevil Shute, a writer unconnected with SF, and directed by a man who never made a picture that wasn't Serious, *On the Beach* brought nuclear Armageddon out of the ghetto. Everything about the film shouted its importance to the world. Gregory Peck, Ava Gardner and Fred Astaire wouldn't have appeared in another *Teenage Caveman*. In *Omni's Screen Flights/Screen Fantasies*, Kramer describes how, when *On the Beach* opened simultaneously in fifty cities around the world, he chose to see it in Moscow. 'We know you don't trust us,' a Soviet director told him, 'but, you see, we don't trust you either. Each time we discuss the matter, even ways and means to dissent from the policy of our own government, someone always reminds us, "who are the only people who ever dropped the Bomb?"'*On the Beach* is long and leisurely. In 1964, there has been a brief, incomprehensible war. 'Some poor bloke probably looked at a radar screen and thought he saw something,' says cynical scientist Julian (Astaire). 'He knew that if he hesitated one thousandth of a second his own country would be wiped off the map, and he pushed a button... and the world went... crazy.' (Interestingly, Kramer's least Serious film is *It's a Mad Mad Mad Mad World*). Most of the globe has been depopulated but the people of Australia are, at first, relatively unaffected, though a shortage of petrol fills the streets of Melbourne with bicycles and horses, and club men wonder how they'll ever get through their stock of port before the End comes. Wild winds blow deadly fall-out southwards and the characters have to come to terms with the fact that their survival is only temporary. The Australian government hands out Prescription 24768, cyanide pills to hasten the inevitable. Julian takes part in the last *grand prix*, a daredevil race in which the drivers don't care about fatal crashes; he wins, then revs up his racing car in an airtight garage. At the end, Kramer offers postcard views of empty streets while a mournful version of 'Waltzing Matilda' plays on the soundtrack. The camera notices a bronze statue of 'War, the Destroying Warrior', but closes on a revivalist's abandoned banner which proclaims 'There is Still Time'.

Amid the stiff, forgettable human drama, moments bring home the horror and waste of nuclear conflict without going into the sensationalist/uncompromising business of blasted bodies, summary executions and descent into savagery. The best-remembered sequence is the *Sawfish*'s forlorn voyage to San Diego in order to check out a mysterious, random radio signal. Are there still survivors in the USA? The crewmen explore a completely deserted, completely silent city and find the source of America's last, meaningless, message. A morse code transmitter is accidentally tap-

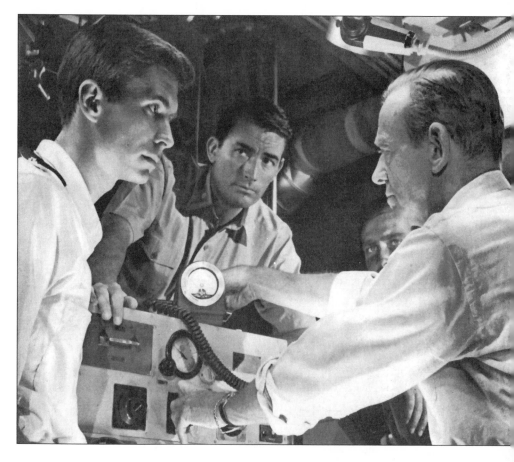

ping gibberish thanks to the breeze, a window sash and a Coke bottle. The continent is dead. Also affecting is a scene when Peck and Gardner retreat to the hills for a last moment of serenity to find everyone else has had the same idea and a party of raucous drunks is belting out 'Waltzing Matilda', an odd comic interlude that chills when Peck finally listens to the last, ghostly verse of the song. Though the lead performances are variable — Astaire, Perkins and Gardner have fragile grasps on their accents, and the Australian actor John Meillon is perversely cast as a phoney-voiced Yank — the film does surprisingly well in its tiny vignettes: the silent barman in the deserted club finally having a drink and taking a shot at snooker just as the lights go out for the last time, the Admiral (John Tate) and his worshipful secretary (Lola Brooks) sharing a poisoned drink.

Above:
On the Beach,
*Anthony
Perkins,
Gregory Peck,
Fred Astaire*

'There are never causes,' said Kramer, 'only feelings, when I select a subject to film.' *On the Beach* is solemn, liberal, sensitive and humane, and achieves an overall effect that alternates between the affecting and the embarrassing. Nevertheless, it is an important and impassioned film. The first voice of dissent came from the US Navy: when Kramer approached the service and asked to borrow a nuclear submarine to stand in for the USS *Sawfish*, which plays an important part in Shute's story, they refused, citing Pentagon estimates that an all-out nuclear war would yield a mere eight or nine million fatalities to prove that the book's end-of-the-world thesis was unnecessarily grim and alarmist. When the film came out, the *New York Daily News* called it a 'would-be shocker which plays right up the alley of a) the Kremlin, and b) the Western defeatists and/or traitors who yelp for the scrapping of the H-bomb... it points the way toward eventual communist enslavement of the entire human race.'

Time was less outraged by the film's politics, but expressed unhappiness with its holocaust, calling *On the Beach* 'a sentimental sort of radical romance in which customers are spared any scenes of realistic horror, and are asked instead to accept the movie notion of what is really horrible about the end of the world: boy (Gregory Peck) does not get girl (Ava Gardner). Aside from its sentimentality, the worst of the film's offences is its reality. Though Kramer and company predict that *On the Beach* will act as a deterrent to further nuclear armaments, the picture actually manages to make the most dangerous conceivable situation in human history seem rather silly and science-fictional. The players look half-dead long before the fall-out gets them. But what could any actor make of a script that imagines the world's end as a scene in which Ava Gardner stands and wistfully waves goodbye as Gregory Peck sails sadly into the contaminated dawn.' Scientist Linus Pauling, however, remarked, 'it may be that some years from now we can look back and say that *On the Beach* is the movie that saved the world.'

On the Beach is not the kind of film that provokes a cycle of imitations, but it did establish World War Three as a subject for important, rather than negligible, films. The Japanese responded to Kramer's holocaust with two of their own: Sigeaki Hidaka's *Dai Sanju Taisen — Yonji-Ichi Jikan no Kyofu* (1960, *World War III Breaks Out*) and Shue Matsubayashi's *Sekai Daisenso* (1962, *The Last War*). Both films concentrate on the Japanese victims of wars the nation was barely involved with and are more interested than *On the Beach* in the causes of the final conflict. Hidaka's film, made in widescreen black and white for the Toei studio, has America accidentally trigger an atomic weapon in flight over Korea. A North/South, East/West confrontation follows and, in the aftermath, Argentina is the world's only surviving country.

Matsubayashi, working in colour for Toei's great rival Toho (which means he has the services of Eiji Tsuburaya, the effects destruction expert of the Godzilla films), also has Korea as the flashpoint, but uses a mid-air collision between Russian and American jets over the South Pole as the immediate cause of the first strike. 'The acting makes the relevant points,' comments the *Aurum Film Encyclopedia: Science Fiction*, 'though it is diffi-cult to assess the performances: what would constitute "appropriate behav-iour" in such circumstances is anybody's guess.'

The first wave of serious nuclear war films are regretful and elegiac, the second are furious and violent: in *On the Beach* and the Japanese movies, irradiated populations wistfully and meekly face doom; in Ray Milland's *Panic in Year Zero!* (1962) and Peter Watkins's *The War Game*, survivors loot, riot and die messily while the authorities brutally attempt to impose martial law. These films have a deeply pessimistic view of human nature (*Panic in Year Zero!*) and the government's ability to handle a crisis (*The War Game*), but still suggest more hope than Kramer's digni-fied, inevitable finality. Once the Bomb is dropped in *On the Beach*, the whole world is finished. There are no survivors. *Panic in Year Zero!* asserts that there will still be plenty of things worth fighting for. Even the despair-ing *The War Game*, because of its speculative, hard-hitting format, is cal-culated to make audiences angry enough to do something about the nuclear situation. Kramer accepts the stalemate, but Milland and Watkins know it has to be broken.

Adapted from 'Lot' (1953) and 'Lot's Daughter' (1954), vicious and ironic stories by the SF writer Ward Moore, *Panic in Year Zero!* is the first of the survivalist movies. Made for American International Pictures, the exploitation outfit who backed many of Roger Corman's films, Milland's movie is a jazzy apocalypse, with finned autos, a loud score, dollops of sadism and Frankie Avalon. Harry Baldwin (Milland), an average joe American, is out in the mountains with his wife (Jean Hagen) and the kids for a weekend of huntin', shootin' and fishin'. A few economical flashes

prove that the cities of America have been destroyed in a sneak attack. Baldwin knows just what to do — rob a convenience store and head for a cave he can turn into a stronghold for his family to hole up in while they wait it out. When irresponsible tearaways ('somebody dropped a bomb, Dad... crazy kick, huh?') rape his daughter, he briskly executes them. Baldwin knows the score and spells it out so even his fuzzy liberal wife can understand.

> **Baldwin:** Every footpath will be crawling with men saying 'no matter what, I'm going to live.' That's what I'm saying too. My family must survive.
> **Mrs Baldwin:** Intelligent people don't just turn their backs on the rest of the world.
> **Baldwin:** Under these conditions, intelligent people will be the first to try.

Though he does his best to act in a spirit of homicidal mania that director John Milius would be proud of, Baldwin is no war lover. When Baldwin Jr (Avalon) gloats over the dead thugs, his Dad upbraids him sharply, refusing to allow him to revel in the brutality of their situation. 'I want you to use that gun if you have to, but I want you to hate it. A big piece of civilisation is gone and your mother wants to save what's left.' Later, after the family have played House in the mountains for long enough ('nothing like eating under an open sky, even if it is radioactive'), they petition for re-entry into decent society. 'You know,' Baldwin tells a country doctor who is doing his best to cope with the situation, 'watching you work is like raising your head out of the mud and slime and seeing civilisation again. I thought we'd lost it for good.'

In the last scene, the family pass a military checkpoint, are proved free of radiation sickness, and join the flow of traffic heading for the tough but hopeful future. 'There Must Be No End', reads the inevitable title screen, 'Only a New Beginning'. In *Future Tense*, John Brosnan sums up the film: 'Milland's message seems to be that if you happen to survive World War Three shoot first and ask questions later, which is exactly the sort of attitude that is likely to cause World War Three.'

Produced, written and directed for BBC TV by Peter Watkins as a follow-up to his successful *Culloden* (1964), 'an account of the most brutal and mishandled battle ever fought in Britain', *The War Game* was famously banned by its sponsors, who rated it 'too horrifying for the medium of broadcasting.' The film became a *cause célèbre*, and won the Academy Award for Best Documentary when released theatrically. Though its initial impact was lessened by the BBC's refusal to air it, the Corporation's decision to turn worldwide distribution rights over to the British Film Institute gave *The War Game* long term availability. The film was frequently screened between its production and a belated telecast in 1985, and was thus more accessible than almost any other British television production of the mid-sixties.

There are more starving citizens, charred corpses, open wounds, summary executions and dying children in *The War Game* than in *Five*, *The World, the Flesh and the Devil*, *On the Beach* and *Panic in Year Zero!* put together, but, for all its explicit horror, it is a television film, designed to have maximum impact on the small screen. The staged documentary imitates and subverts the structure of a traditional current affairs programme. Authoritative newsreaders (Michael Aspel and Dick Graham) provide statistics, comments and analysis, diagrams show there are more nuclear targets per acre in Britain than in any other country, and street interviews with ordinary people reveal public apathy and ignorance ('I would not want us to sit back and do nothing. Yes, I think perhaps I would retaliate'). Meanwhile, we learn of an escalation in international tension through background chatter. The Chinese invade Vietnam, the Russians seal off West Berlin, the communist alliance demands America pulls out of South East Asia, a rioter is shot at Check-point Charlie and soon, sirens are sounding in placid Kent.

The War Game constantly reminds the audience that it is a preconstruction of possible events ('this could be the way the last two minutes of peace in Britain will look', 'this is a possible part of nuclear war'), but it stresses that many of the things it shows have already happened. The firestorms, the widespread civil unrest and the psychological problems of the survivors are all based closely on testimony, not only from Hiroshima and Nagasaki, but also from towns like Dresden and Hamburg that suffered saturation bombing in World War Two. From these sources come the film's most horrifying moments: buckets of wedding rings used to identify the numberless dead, black-faced children who admit that they don't want to grow up.

The imitation of newsreel style is very canny and some of the amateur actors who give interviews (the nurse who claims her patients 'are just falling apart', the bread-hoarding man who resists an offer of money with 'you can't eat a pound note') are uncannily convincing, but Watkins does not just ape the documentary format. In cutting together hand-held 'actuality' footage and staged interviews, he tramples on the BBC's sacred notion of objectivity: a bland parson who claims 'I still believe in the war of the just' is followed immediately by shots of on-the-streets explosions and the announcement that 'within this car, a family is burning alive.'

The most controversial aspect of *The War Game* is its complete mistrust of the authorities. After informing us that 'our side' is likely to push the button first, and giving time to a Strangelove-style strategist ('both sides could stop before the ultimate destruction of cities, so that both sides could retire for a period of ten years or so of post-attack recuperation, in which World Wars Four to Eight could be prepared'), the film shows traditionally unarmed British policemen mercy-killing the hopelessly wounded and executing looters on the spot. Watkins takes pains to point out that the men in

uniform are, after all, men, and shows that they would be even more likely than anyone else to crack under the burden of responsibility. 'If I had made a film about nuclear war,' said Watkins in *Nuclear Films*, 'and people either laughed at it or had I made Britain's recovery from that war quite firm and the Union Jack fluttered on the non-radioactive breeze, I have no doubt the film would have been shown. I must emphasise that it was because there is a feeling of hopelessness at the end that the film was banned.'

Above: The War Game

Watkins has none of the Dunkirk/blitz spirit, and *The War Game* winds down in utter despair. The final reel, though full of memorable images, shows a small screen predilection for words rather than pictures. The narrator calmly provides a summary: 'on almost the entire subject of thermo-nuclear weapons, on the problems of their possession, on the effects of their use, there is now practically a total silence in the press, in official publications and on television. There is hope in any resolved and unpredictable situation, but is there a real hope to be found in this silence?

The world's stockpile of thermo-nuclear weapons has doubled in the last five years and now is the equivalent of almost twenty tons of high explosives to every man, woman and child on the planet. The stockpile is still steadily growing.' Unforgettably, the film closes with a question, paraphrased from a comment by Nikita Khrushchev — 'Would the survivors envy the dead?'

> How are you?... Oh fine. Just fine. Look, Dimitri, you know how we've always talked about the possibility of something going wrong with the Bomb?... The Bomb? The Hydrogen Bomb!... That's right. Well, I'll tell you what happened. One of our base commanders did a silly thing. He, uh, went a little funny in the head. You know, funny. He ordered our planes to attack your country. Let me finish, Dimitri...
>
> **President Merkin Muffley (Peter Sellers), *Dr. Strangelove or: How I Learned to Stop Worrying and Love the Bomb***

General Jack D. Ripper (Sterling Hayden) sits behind a desk in his shadowy office at Burpleson Air Force Base, an obviously phallic cigar clamped between his thin lips. This man has just started World War Three. He explains his reasoning to Group Captain Lionel Mandrake (Peter Sellers), a bewildered RAF officer stranded in an alien land by a NATO exchange scheme. 'I can no longer sit back and allow communist infiltration, communist indoctrination, communist subversion, and the international communist conspiracy to sap and impurify all of our precious bodily fluids.' Stanley Kubrick bought the rights to Peter George's novel *Two Hours to Doom* with the intention of making a serious film about the possibility of an accidental nuclear exchange. He had already made *Paths of Glory* (1957), a film about military ineptitude, maliciousness and hypocrisy; *Two Hours to Doom* seemed like an opportunity to reprise the theme in a contemporary setting. As work on the script progressed, Kubrick realised that the grim story was turning into a horror comedy. In depicting nuclear war as absurd, *On the Beach* had been appealing to our common sense. If the concept of Mutually Assured Destruction is as blind stupid as it sounds, then it can surely be averted. *Dr. Strangelove or: How I Learned to Stop Worrying and Love the Bomb* admits that nuclear war is absurd, but feels that its absurdity only makes it a more likely eventuality given the human race's capacity for idiocy. To push the film over the brink of hilarity, Kubrick called in satirist Terry Southern to lace the script with his poisonous wit.

Unhinged by his impotence, which he puts down to a commie plot involving fluoridation, Ripper orders his bomber wing to attack the Soviet Union. Ineffectual President Muffley (Sellers again) tries to help his Russian opposite number disable Ripper's plans before they can activate the Russian Doomsday Machine, an ultimate deterrent device designed to destroy the world if any superpower launches an atomic attack. One lone plane, under the command of Major T.J. 'King' Kong (Slim Pickens) gets through. The film opens with an echo of *Strategic Air Command* as Kong's B-52 is refuelled in mid-air, the blatant sexual symbolism of jet penetration underscored by a romantic melody, 'Try a Little Tenderness'. Kong is the monstrous alter ego of James Stewart in the earlier film; Pickens, with his Western twang and lumpy grin, actually sounds and looks like a caricature of Stewart. He has all the stubborn ingenuity, patriotic doggedness and unquestioning obedience of fifties heroes, but formerly admirable qualities are here the instruments of Armageddon. There is almost a last minute reprieve (in the novel, the world is saved) when the bomb bay doors jam, but Kong fixes it all with chewing gum and a few kicks. The Major is dropped with his bomb, whooping like a rodeo cowboy as they fall.

As mushroom clouds blossom at the end of *Strangelove*, Vera Lynn sings 'We'll Meet Again', the song she made famous during World War Two. Throughout the movie, ironic references to the last war provide a misleading frame of reference for the far more dangerous nuclear game. Mandrake is unable to sort out the difference between the Japanese who tortured him as a PoW and the Japanese who are currently the West's ally ('the thing is, they make such bloody good cameras!'); SAC General Buck Turgidson (George C. Scott) uses the World War Two records of Russia and America to contrast Slavic guts with American initiative; and Dr Strangelove (Sellers yet again), the Pentagon's resident expert, is a crippled ex-Nazi, unable to stop his metal arm from stiffening in a Heil Hitler salute and wont to absent-mindedly address the President as '*mein Führer*'. Because these men refuse to recognise that warfare has changed, indeed become literally impractical since 1946, the world ends.

Much of the success of *Dr. Strangelove* lies in its escalation of minor idiocies into an unpreventable apocalypse: hawkish Major 'Bat' Guano (Keenan Wynn) is unwilling to shoot a Coca Cola machine in order to get loose change for a phone call which could save humanity; Russian Premier Kissoff has delayed telling anyone about his ultimate deterrent because he wanted to save the surprise for an upcoming Party Congress. The final proof that the world is totally crazy comes when the President finds Turgidson and Soviet Ambassador De Sadesky (Peter Bull) scuffling over a spy camera and declares, 'gentlemen, you can't fight in here... this is the War Room!' While these moments, and the much-quoted lines about 'precious bodily fluids' and 'deviated preverts', reveal comic invention, other funny details ring horribly true: a report on a desk labelled 'Target Figures in MegaDeaths' (a rare grammatically correct use of the prefix 'mega'); Strangelove's survival plan, which involves establishing harems for VIPs at the bottom of mineshafts; and an SAC emergency kit which includes a gun, nylons, gold, chewing gum and a 'miniature combination Bible/Rooshian phrase book.'

There is an announcement at the beginning of *Strangelove* to the effect that the events depicted in the film could not happen, but the relentlessly sick logic of the storyline is more persuasive than the Department of Defence disclaimer. Lawrence H. Suid, an expert on the relationship between Hollywood and the military, writes in *American History/American Film*, 'when *Dr. Strangelove* was released, the Cuban missile crisis was still fresh in people's minds. B-52s still constituted the nation's primary strike force. Audiences could thus readily accept Kubrick's vision of the accidental launching of a nuclear attack, even though Kubrick created his dramatic impact with what was, in fact, a story based on inaccurate premises and factual errors. An SAC base commander has no means of ordering a flight of planes to attack Russia, the script's explanation of events notwithstanding. The attack code came down the chain of command from the President through SAC headquarters in Omaha to base commanders to planes on the ground and in the air. Moreover the code was transmitted to air crews orally, not by means of a black box as shown in the movie. And the Air Force's fail safe mechanisms operated on the principle of positive control — the planes on their missions had to receive a direct order to launch its attack. The absence of such a command would automatically abort the

mission. Unfortunately, at least for the air force and its image, few people either knew or had the time and concern to ascertain how SAC procedures worked. Therefore most viewers could readily suspend their disbelief and accept Kubrick's version of the system and its implied weaknesses. They might well emerge from the theatre not only entertained, but also concerned over the future of the world, at least to the extent that any movie audience thinks seriously about such things.'

Above: Dr. Strangelove, Slim Pickens

In *Past Imperfect: History According to the Movies* (1995), Paul Boyer countered, 'Is *Dr. Strangelove* historically accurate? In a larger sense, yes. The information on the US nuclear arsenal and the capability of B-52 bombers is factual. The billboard at Burpleson AFB proclaiming "Peace Is Our Profession" actually adorned some SAC bases. Gen. Buck Turgidson's rantings about "doomsday gaps" and "mine-shaft gaps" directly echo Kennedy's 1960s "missile gap" rhetoric, and Turgidson's description of US casualties in a nuclear war as "get[ting] our hair mussed" caught the lingo of such military men as former SAC commander Gen. Curtis LeMay... even if *Dr. Strangelove* misrepresented nuclear command policy, it accurately captured deepening popular uneasiness about science and technology, as well as growing fears of an arms race escalating out of control. As nuclear stockpiles mounted and ICBMs cut attack time from hours to minutes, the potential for catastrophe soared.'

For all its comical exaggerations, the characters of *Strangelove* seem horribly close to their real-life equivalents, with Turgidson as LeMay, and Ripper as the general's replacement at SAC, General Thomas Power, whose extremism caused even LeMay to 'worry that General Power was not stable'. Though based on a novel published in 1958, the War Room discussions parallel remarkably debates held in secret by President Kennedy's ExComm group during the Cuban missile crisis of October 1962. Naturally, later re-enactments of this real-life brink-of-destruction scenario — Anthony Page's *The Missiles of October* (1974), Jim Goddard's *Kennedy* (1983), Bert Lovitt's *Prince Jack* (1984) — seem like imitations of Kubrick's film. The most unnerving similarity is that Kennedy's military advisers, like Muffley's, urged him to a first strike against Cuba unaware that retaliation-capable nuclear weapons were already installed on the island and that a supposed tactic of swift American victory would have led instead to a world-devastating all-out war.

Strangelove isn't really about the nuclear situation as it actually was in 1964 (hence the invention of the Doomsday Machine, which later turned out to be a device the Soviets had actually considered), but about the inevitable failings of the soldiers, politicians and scientists we put in charge of our survival. Kubrick's thesis is that the Bomb cannot be disinvented, so we should concentrate instead on getting rid of megalomaniacs like Generals Ripper and Turgidson, ineffectual dolts like Muffley and Kissoff, heroes like Majors Kong and Guano and barely human theorists like Strangelove. By contrast, Sidney Lumet's *Fail Safe* (1964), from the 1962 novel by Eugene Burdick and Harvey Wheeler, exonerates the noble man in public office and blames its *Strangelove*-style crisis on simple mechanical malfunctions. A computer in Omaha accidentally sends B-52s to Russia and orders them to drop the Bomb. Liberal President Henry

Fonda gets on the hot line and explains it all to the Soviet leader. 'No human being made any mistake, and there's no point in trying to place the blame on any one. The disappearance of human responsibility is one of the most disturbing aspects of the whole thing. It's as if human beings had evaporated and their places were taken by computers. And all day long you and I have sat here, fighting, not each other, but rather the big rebellious computer system, struggling to keep it from blowing up the world.'

While *Fail Safe* is a tense and convincing fantasy, its stress on the culpability of the machine is a cop-out. Apart from Groeteschele (Walter Matthau), the film's Strangelove figure ('these are not normal people, these are Marxist fanatics'), everyone is impossibly decent and self-sacrificing, from the President who orders the bombing of New York to prove his good faith to the Russians after they've lost Moscow (a similar exchange is proposed in *Two Hours to Doom*), to the General (Dan O'Herlihy) who executes the order personally to spare any of his pilots the unendurable pain of nuking their loved ones. A few scenes carry an undeniable chill: the whine at the end of the line when the American ambassador in Moscow and his telephone are disintegrated; an officer hastily examining the file of his Russian opposite number as they carry out a long-range negotiation; the freeze-frame overexposures that convey the end of New York; the President's last ditch radio message to the unconvinced pilot who insists his doomsday orders cannot be countermanded. Produced by Columbia, *Fail Safe* was not released until after the company had cleaned up with *Strangelove*; the film was lost in Kubrick's slipstream.

James B. Harris, formerly Kubrick's regular producer (*The Killing* [1956]; *Paths of Glory*; *Lolita* [1962]), made his directorial début with another accidental nuclear war movie, *The Bedford Incident* (1965), from the 1963 novel by Mark Rascovich (which has a non-nuclear ending). Again, World War Two thinking is the problem. Captain Finlander (Richard Widmark, borrowing a few mannerisms from Senator Barry Goldwater) commands the *Bedford*, an American destroyer which comes across a Russian nuclear submarine in NATO waters and hunts it down. Finlander, who wearily states, 'sometimes it's a lot of hard work being a mean bastard', is obsessive in his quest, a Cold War-monger at last given a concrete enemy. His advisor in submarine tracking is Eric Portman, formerly a German U-Boat expert. It is established that the *Bedford* and the

Russian sub are equipped with nuclear weapons, but this is forgotten amid the cat-and-mouse tactics familiar from World War Two submarine movies like *Run Silent, Run Deep* (1958). The enemy is cornered and Finlander says, 'the *Bedford* will not fire first, but if he fires one I'll fire one.' The weapons officer hears only the last two words, confirms the order '*fire one*' and launches a missile. The Russians fire back and *Fail Safe* freeze frame burn-outs show the principal characters are instantly annihilated.

After the Cuban missile crisis, the public image of the Bomb changed. The human race had marched to the edge of the precipice and in panic taken a few steps back. Kennedy's America regained the self-confidence lost during the fearful fifties. There were Americans in orbit, and the commies had been stared down in the Caribbean. Fifties films had revered the Bomb as a peacemaker or feared it as a doomsday device, but there had been little debate. In the general sigh of relief after Cuba, people started treating the Bomb as a neurotic symptom to be confronted and exorcised. Fifties movies are dogmatic and committed to one point of view or the other, but sixties movies are open-ended. There is a general belief that nuclear war is most likely to be an accident, thanks to faulty men ('I admit the human element has let us down here,' says Turgidson) or faulty machines. But even this is played down in early sixties films, which concentrate on showing us just how likely an atomic apocalypse is, but try not to tell the audience what to think. *The War Game* actually ends with a question, but *Strangelove, Fail Safe* and *The Bedford Incident* also finish on notes of uncertainty. Open-minded audiences had been given enough information to form their own opinions.

Learning to Love the Bomb

He frowned. 'Barbara, I'm not as sad over what has happened as you are. It might be good for us. I don't mean us six; I mean our country.'

She looked startled. 'How?'

'Well — it's hard to take the long view when you are crouching in a shelter and wondering how long you can hold out. But — Barbara, I've worried for years about our country. It seems to me that we have been breeding slaves — and I believe in freedom. This war may have turned the tide. This may be the first war in history which kills the stupid rather than the bright and able — where it makes any distinction.'

'How do you figure that, Hugh?'

'Well, wars have always been hardest on the best young men. This time the boys in the service are as safe or safer than civilians. And of civilians those who used their heads and made preparations stand a better chance. Not every case, but on the average, and that will improve the breed. When it's over, things will be tough, and that will improve the breed still more. For years, the surest way of surviving has been to be utterly worthless and breed a lot of worthless kids. All that will change.'

She nodded thoughtfully. 'That's standard genetics. But it seems cruel.'

'It *is* cruel. But no government has yet been able to repeal natural laws, though they keep trying.'

She shivered in spite of the heat. 'I suppose you're right. No, I *know* you're right.'

Robert A. Heinlein, *Farnham's Freehold*

In the early sixties, nuclear war films became a category, like Westerns or musicals. After *On the Beach* and *Dr. Strangelove*, it was no longer possible to see the subject as exclusively the province of low budget SF or militarist propaganda. *Fail Safe* and *The Bedford Incident*, through imitation, confirmed the conventions used in the earlier films as the parameters of a recognisable genre. Ironically, the films are stylistic throwbacks to the fifties: trademarks include high contrast black-and-white photography, newsreel (or staged newsreel) footage to add an air of documentary realism, headline-grabbing based-on-facts subtexts and Big Name Stars emoting intensely in a struggle with a Serious Subject. Joseph Losey's *The Damned*, Frank Perry's *Ladybug, Ladybug* (1963) and John Frankenheimer's *Seven Days in May* (1964) are the same kind of film, concerning themselves not with the World War Two itself but nuclear-induced Cold War anxieties.

The Damned, from H.L. Lawrence's 1960 novel *The Children of Light*, produced by Britain's Hammer Films, is a remarkable, controversial and much tinkered-with movie. 'Columbia refused to release the film for at least two years because of Losey's name on the credits,' said studio head Michael Carreras. 'It could have been a better film; the original script was far better than the released movie. Then Losey came in with Evan Jones and he did something very naughty. It was something like twenty four hours before we were going to shoot the film and he told me he would not shoot the film unless he could shoot his own version of the script. For some reason or another, we just went ahead and shot their script. Disaster.' Columbia sat on the film until memories of the blacklist faded, then let it creep out as a B picture in Britain in 1963, and, trimmed by ten minutes, in America (as *These Are the Damned*) in 1965. Losey's subsequent reputation made some seek it out, but the stigma of cheap SF, Hammer horror and teddy boy bikers still prevents it from being recognised as the flawed classic it is.

In an extraordinary opening sequence, drop-out businessman Simon Wells (MacDonald Carey) tails a pair of tight toreador pants around Weymouth, an English seaside town. He accosts the girl, Joan (Shirley Ann Field), and gets beaten up by a sadistic bike gang led by her brother, King (Oliver Reed). King's well-spoken, umbrella-wielding thug is a precursor of the droogs of *A Clockwork Orange* (1971), and the lyrics of the trashily nihilist theme song that plays over the scene ('Black leather, black leather, smash smash smash! Black leather, black leather, kill kill kill! Got that feeling, black leather rock!') pre-date punk by fifteen years. In a nearby Victorian hotel, Simon is looked after by tweedy civil servant Bernard (Alexander Knox) and committed sculptress Freya (Viveca Lindfors), who bandage his bruises and ply him with a medicinal drink. 'I never expected this to happen to me in England,' moans the American. 'The age of senseless violence has caught up with us too,' replies Bernard.

Above:
The Damned,
*Shirley Ann
Field*

It soon develops that Bernard is involved in a heartless alternative to the age of senseless violence. 'I'm a public servant,' he tells Freya, amid the blasted human figures (actually sculpted by Elisabeth Frink) in her clifftop garden. 'It's too late to do anything in private life. I live with one fact; the power has been released that will melt these stones.' Beneath the tranquil cliffs is a spotless, self-contained complex in which Bernard keeps nine radioactive, cold-blooded children. Contaminated from birth, they are doomed to be the inheritors of a poisonous post-war world. They are victims of purposeful, calculated, supposedly therapeutic violence. The sequences in the children's installation are among the most poignant and chilling in the cinema of the apocalypse. The children construct fantasies of a family life to distract them from regimented education, omnipresent television monitors and the occasional presence of a decontamination-suited adult. Their well-spoken meekness and completely ordered lives provide a pointed contrast to the anarchic, destructive and neurotic sprees of King's leather boys.

The Damned is full of fractured serenity: bikers roaring around a quiet harbour, Frink's anguished sculptures against beautiful seascapes, the children vandalising their controlled environment, ruthlessly efficient government men clearing up after a disruption in their routine. The children are herded back into their shelter, Freya is executed for knowing too much and King's car is forced off a bridge. Simon and Joan are abandoned in a yacht, dying of radiation poisoning as an ominous helicopter circles overhead. All the sympathetic, or even impassioned, characters are casually exterminated, and Bernard's merciless, pessimist plan is back on schedule. In *Science Fiction Movies*, Philip Strick writes of the children, 'their plight is horrifying not only because it is so cold-bloodedly conceived and administered but because they have no future *unless* war breaks out. Thus, paradoxically, they exist as a justification for it instead of as a deterrent.' Perhaps because Losey had more reason to see himself as a victim of the Western world than Kramer or Kubrick, *The Damned* is the angriest, most despairing of the nuclear films.

While *The Damned* conjures up an age of senseless violence of which the Bomb is merely the most fearsome part, *Ladybug, Ladybug*, based on an actual incident that took place during the Cuban missile crisis, is a more concentrated, not to say laboured and heavily symbolic, examination of children and the Bomb. An air raid alert sounds in a rural grade school; the pupils are sent home to find whatever shelter they can. Contrivances keep adults out of the picture, so the kids have to sort out the business of survival among themselves. A bratty rich girl whose parents have invested in a de luxe fall-out shelter invites selected friends to stay alive with her, but she turns away a nice girl she is jealous of. The nice girl, terrified, runs into a dump yard and, ignoring all those safety films, hides in an abandoned fridge. Her young boyfriend rejects the rich kid and searches for her, but is petrified by a USAF jet passing overhead and she suffocates. It turns out to have been a false alarm. *Ladybug, Ladybug* is intermittently haunting and depressing, but its obvious thesis that crises bring out the worst in people works rather better in a half-hour *Twilight Zone* episode, 'The Shelter' (1961), which plays out the same plot with adults.

Seven Days in May is actually about General Burt Lancaster's attempt to effect a military coup in America before President Fredric March can ratify an appeasement treaty with the Soviets. Like *Strangelove* and *Fail Safe*, it spotlights the nuclear pressures on the American President. March is eternally followed by faceless suitcase warriors who are there to give him the attack codes in the event of an emergency. In *The Best Man* (1964), prospective presidential candidate Henry Fonda expresses doubts about rival Cliff Robertson's gutsiness in a possible nuclear confrontation, fearing that he might back down too soon rather than risk getting nuked to help out a bunch of foreigners. Burt Lancaster is back in uniform in *Twilight's Last Gleaming* (1977) as a renegade air force officer who takes over a silo and threatens to start World War Three unless President Charles Durning tells the American people the truth about Vietnam. Our dormant fears that the man with his finger on the button might be too shaky for the job resurfaced in the eighties and the troubled presidencies of Eddie Albert in Joseph Ruben's *Dreamscape* (1984) and Martin Sheen in David Cronenberg's *The Dead Zone* (1983). Albert dreams of a mutated, post-holocaust wasteland, edging near to a nervous breakdown and another appeasement treaty, and Christopher Walken has a psychic vision of Sheen starting a pointless war in the future, which he does his best to forestall.

Sam Fuller's *Shock Corridor* (1963) is a topical anxiety epic in the tradition of *Kiss Me Deadly* and *The Damned*, stirring nuclear neuroses into a whole spectrum of specifically American madnesses. Journalist Johnny Barratt (Peter Breck), another hard-headed but short-sighted Yank, simulates an incestuous desire for his sister — actually his stripper girlfriend (Constance Towers) — in order to get committed to an asylum where he intends to solve a murder mystery and thus win the Pulitzer Prize. To break the case, Johnny needs to get close to three witnesses, madmen who have fleeting moments of lucidity. All three witnesses have been driven mad by America: Stuart (James Best), an abused hillbilly brainwashed in Korea and branded a traitor, takes on the personality of a Confederate general; Trent (Hari Rhodes), tormented as the only black man on an all-white Southern campus, spouts racist Ku Klux Klan rhetoric and leads a race riot in the hallways; and Boden (Gene Evans), 'the most brilliant scientist alive today, went insane working on nuclear fission and rocketry to the moon... now has the mentality of a child of six.'

Fuller's script has the forceful irony of an EC horror comic, as Barratt solves the case and wins the prize but is himself reduced to 'an insane mute'. In his moment of sanity, Boden delivers a startling speech: 'We should take advantage of our ignorance and quit living like tigers in bomb shelters. Today everybody's giving the human race two weeks to get out, and I can't live on two weeks' notice.' *Shock Corridor* is about the dangers of living in constant fear; ultimately, it reduces America to an asylum where only a foolhardy man ventures into 'the Nympho Ward' for fear of succumbing to frightening maenads, the attendants are sadistic scoundrels and every aspect of human behaviour has been meddled with and malformed by shapeless, purposeless terrors and hatreds. Yet, Fuller is torn apart by belief in his country: Stuart laments, 'my folks fed me bigotry for breakfast and ignorance for supper — never, not once, did they ever make me feel proud of where I was born' but learns to revere America (from a very Fullerian tough sergeant) after his brainwashing, while Trent admits, 'it's a blessing to love my country, even when it gives me ulcers'.

Alongside the nuclear *films gris* of the early sixties, there sprang up a livelier, more colourful, insidiously trivial strain of atomic movie. After illustrating the nuke mentality in *The Space Children*, Jack Arnold turned to the whimsical comedy of *The Mouse That Roared* (1959). The Duchy of Grand Fenwick, a pocket-sized Middle European state, declares war on the United States, hoping to lose and qualify for the Marshall Plan. However, General Peter Sellers arrives in an apparently deserted New York during a test alert. While everyone is in the shelters, Sellers wanders into a top secret defence establishment where he is able to gain control of the fearsome Quark Bomb. Grand Fenwick defeats America and comic complications ensue. The nuclear blackmail premise of *The Mouse That Roared* is an update of that of *Seven Days to Noon* (1950), but its light-hearted approach signals the manner in which one of the most potentially horrifying aspects of the atomic age would be treated in later movies.

The villain of Terence Young's *Dr. No* (1962), from the 1958 novel by Ian Fleming, is a megalomaniac descendant of Fu Manchu (Joseph Wiseman) who maintains a private nuclear reactor in his Caribbean stronghold and amuses himself by potting Cape Canaveral space probes as if they were clay pigeons. *Dr. No*, first of the James Bond films, started the popular, escapist and firmly unimportant superspy cycle of the sixties. These films were the big budget equivalents of the Saturday matinée serials of the thirties and forties, but atomic weapons replaced death rays and poison gases as the main attraction of any mad scientist's arsenal. Actually, one serial, Ray Taylor and Lewis D. Collins's *Lost City of the Jungle* (1946), was up-to-the-minute enough to have Lionel Atwill's plan for world conquest hinge on his scheme to harness the power of a newly discovered element, and Walt Disney's Captain Nemo (James Mason) in Richard Fleischer's *20,000 Leagues Under the Sea*, another of Dr No's ancestors, is revealed as a pio-

neer of atomic energy when his island fortress explodes with a mushroom cloud.

Above:
Dr. No,
Ursula
Andress

In the Bond movies, the Bomb co-exists with the fanciful apparatus of the serials — impossible stunts, exotic locations, dastardly villains, plucky heroines, scheming dames, wildly improbable plots and super-scientific devices. Censorship had relaxed enough to allow for the kids' stuff to be spiced up with plentiful sex and violence, but the thrills were much the same. In *Future Tense*, John Brosnan writes of Terence Young's *Thunderball* (1965), but with relevance to the whole genre, 'as the bombs in the film are merely part of the wide range of gadgetry that James Bond has to cope with in the course of the story, the atom bomb itself is thus defused and made safe in the minds of the audience... the Bomb, the Damoclean sword of the 1950s, was being transformed in the 1960s into just another technological toy.'

The domestication of the atom is also evident in a trickle of films (Spencer Bennett's *The Atomic Submarine*; Irwin Allen's *Voyage to the Bottom of the Sea*; Leslie H. Martinson's *Batman* [1966]; James Frawley's *The Big Bus* [1976]; Dan Curtis's *Supertrain* [1979]), which feature nuclear-powered vehicles whose reactors are only there to make them seem more contemporary and impressive. As the Cold War was eclipsed by the hot one in Vietnam, the Bomb became less important. Even those anti-establishment comedies that felt the need to include nukes among the evils of the older generation (William Klein's *Mr. Freedom* [1968]; William T. Naud's *Wild in the Sky* [1972]) treat the Bomb as a comic rather than fearsome symbol of right-wing wrong-headedness. In 1966, a B-52 crash leading to the loss of four H-bombs around the Spanish Mediterranean coast village of Palomares inspired a run of odd dramas: Michael Cacoyannis's symptomatic *The Day the Fish Came Out* (1967); Leslie H. Martinson's Raquel Welch superspy movie *Fathom* (1967); Sidney Hayers's Cliff Richard musical (!) *Finders Keepers* (1966); the 'Survival Code' (1970) and 'You Killed Toby Wren' (1970) episodes of *Doomwatch;* and, much later, David Drury's sober conspiracy movie *Defence of the Realm* (1984). *The Day the Fish Came Out* switches the Spanish locale to Greece, and concentrates on Candice Bergen's trendy jet-setters and their use of the incident as the inspiration for a new dance. The film needs something horrible for its finish, so it adds a biological weapon to the scenario, and closes with a shot of a sea full of belly-up fish. Why not love the Bomb, these post-*Strangelove* films say, when there are more serious things to worry about?

Warriors of the Wasteland

The post-holocaust action movie, dormant since Stanley Kramer took over from Roger Corman as the cinema's prophet of nuclear Armageddon, made an unexpected comeback in *Planet of the Apes*. Astronaut Taylor (Charlton Heston) and his disposable colleagues sleep through centuries of space flight and crash-land on a verdant planet where humans are dumb animals and *simius sapiens* is the dominant species. Franklin J. Schaffner's film of Pierre Boulle's *La Planète des singes* (1964) is a misanthropic *Flash Gordon*, mixing sub-Swiftian satire and serial thrills. It is partially scripted by Rod Serling, who invested the screenplay with his usual gutsy rhetoric and invented an ending not in the novel but familiar from the anecdotes he had presented on *The Twilight Zone* (indeed, the episode 'I Shot an Arrow in the Air' [1960] has a not dissimilar twist). After forcing hidebound orang-utan scientist Dr Zaius (Maurice Evans) to accept the possibility that man could be an intelligent creature, Heston sets out on horseback into the Forbidden Zone. As he trots along the beach, strange, yet familiar, spikes intrude into the frame. Heston howls in anguish, 'the bloody fools finally went and did it!' A reverse angle reveals the astronaut dwarfed by the shattered remains of the Statue of Liberty. The final revelation that the Planet of the Apes is actually the Earth, and that through atomic war man has abdicated his throne as king of the beasts, makes sense of dark hints dropped earlier about the bestiality of humankind ('Beware the beast Man,' reads the sacred scroll, 'for he is the Devil's tool') and adds an anti-nuke subtext that must have caused the staunchly Reaganite Heston some embarrassment during the eighties. The bludgeoning overstatement of *Planet of the Apes* is at least a nod towards seriousness in a SF framework, but the film is really a well-directed, healthily budgeted reworking of the Norms vs Mutates quickies. The punchline isn't all that different from the shock finish of *Teenage Caveman*.

Opposite:
Planet of the Apes, *Charlton Heston*

By 1968, Vietnam had displaced the arms race as a burning issue, and the counterculture was neglecting Ban the Bomb in favour of Hell No, We Won't Go. General anti-war feeling was concentrated on a specific, avoidable, misconceived conflict. These were also the years of radical chic and zero degree cool, of acid rock and Woodstock, and of absurdist literary apocalypses (Kurt Vonnegut's *Cat's Cradle*; J.G. Ballard's *The Crystal World* [1966]; Michael Moorcock's *The Final Programme* [1968]). Apocalyptic movies were common, but the nuclear angle became less important. George A. Romero's *Night of the Living Dead* is a Vietnam apocalypse, with documentary-style sequences of flesh-eating ghouls being snuffed by cheerfully professional National Guardsmen. Roger Corman's *Gas-s-s-s, or Is it Really Necessary to Destroy the World in Order to Save It?* (1970) is a Woodstock Apocalypse, with a spilled bio-weapon wiping out everyone over twenty-five and leaving the world to the Love Generation.

The French, of course, had been exploring the absurdist apocalypse for years. Charles Bitsch's *Le Dernier homme* (1968, *The Last Man*), a post-holocaust eternal triangle, is merely the most mainstream of the Gallic end-of-the-world movies. Jean-Luc Godard's 'Le Nouveau Monde', an episode of the Italian omnibus film *RoGoPaG* (1962), chronicles day-to-day life in Paris after a disorientating war has smashed the Eiffel Tower and the Arc de Triomphe and otherwise distorted the pattern of reality. Godard perfected his technique of misrepresenting contemporary France as an alien future by changing a few vital details in *Alphaville* (1965), before launching into the full-scale apocalypse of *Weekend* (1967), in which automotive carnage becomes (as in Ballard) a central metaphor for the obsolescence of society. Chris Marker's *La Jetée* (1963), a short composed almost but not quite entirely of still photographs, also takes Paris as the epicentre of destruction for its story of survivors in the ruins reaching into a pre-war past at Orly airport in order to propel the race into a safe far future.

While the Americans were putting up with the likes of *Panic in Year Zero!*, the rest of Europe was following the French line and turning out savage, wistful allegories. Peter Brook's *Lord of the Flies* (1963), from William Golding's 1954 novel, shows a group of castaway schoolboys creating a barbaric society when their plane is forced down on a desert island by the outbreak of World War Three. Czech Jan Schmidt's *Konec Sprna v Hotelu Ozon* (1966, *The End of August at the Hotel Ozone*) has a band of women marauding around the ravaged countryside in search of food, nostalgia and a man. The neurotic sexual concerns of Schmidt's gloomy film recur in Marco Ferreri's vicious, hysterical *Il seme dell'uomo* (1969, *The Seed of Men*), in which the traditional post-holocaust ending is ruined when the New Eve (Anne Wiazemsky) refuses to have a baby by the New Adam (Marco Margine) because it would be criminal to inflict more human beings on the planet they've done their best to destroy.

From Spain (though set in America), José Manuel Ulloa's laughable *El refugio del miedo* (1973, *Refuge of Fear*) is a domestic drama of nymphomania and homicide set in a tackily-furnished shelter, with a trip topside to visit a skeleton-filled supermarket; in one amusing moment, Patty Shepard, criticised by her husband for walking around in her skimpy underwear, shows up for dinner in a decontamination suit. Amando de Ossorio's *Planeta ciego* (1975, *The People Who Own the Dark*) is an even more shrieking melodrama as Spanish survivors emerge from their shelter to find the world overrun with mutants blinded by the blast. Both these efforts are essentially lurid trash, but they feel the need to drop in dollops of 'social consciousness' sermonising as if the enormity of the subject matter had got through even the thick skulls of exploitation film-makers. By comparison, Igaal Niddam's Swiss *Le troisième cri* (1974), another drama of shelter-skulking, is restrained, though Carlo Ausino's Italian *La città dell'ultima paura* (1975), a last-man-on-Earth story, is more of the same.

The American art cinema didn't catch up with Armageddon until Jim McBride's extremely boring *Glen and Randa* (1971), a post-holocaust trek in which the hippie hero and heroine wander aimlessly through ravaged rural America in search of Metropolis, the fabled city they have read about in comic books. Meanwhile, the comic apocalypse had found its apotheosis in American Richard Lester's film of Spike Milligan and John Antrobus's 1963 play, *The Bed Sitting Room* (1969). A group of well-known British comedians and character actors gather in the rubbish-strewn remnants of London and try to retain their tattered dignity after a three-minute war, while policemen Peter Cook and Dudley Moore continually exhort them to 'keep moving'. The BBC is reduced to an announcer (Frank Thornton) with the shoulders of an immaculate dinner jacket who can fit into the shell of a television set and recite the news that the new Queen of England is Mrs Ethel Shroake (Dandy Nichols). As in any self-respecting post-nuke movie, there are hideous muta-

tions — Arthur Lowe turns into a parrot, and Ralph Richardson becomes the eponymous bed sitting room. Lester's vision of a raped landscape is so harrowing that the film's non-stop jokes barely raise a laugh, and the punchline — 'Great Britain is a first-class nuclear power again' — is bone-chilling. 'The real awful thing,' said Lester, 'is that we were able to film most of these things in England without faking it. All that garbage is real.'

Opposite:
The Bed
Sitting Room,
Dandy Nichols

The threat of nuclear war seemed remote during the years of *détente*, but film apocalypses were common. Major studios bought up SF disaster novels like Richard Matheson's *I Am Legend* (1954, filmed by Sidney Salkow as *The Last Man on Earth* [1964], and again by Boris Sagal as *The Ωmega Man*, not to mention 'Treehouse of Horror VIII: The HΩmega Man', *The Simpsons* [1997]), John Christopher's *The Death of Grass* (1956, filmed by Cornel Wilde as *No Blade of Grass* in 1971), John Wyndham's *The Day of the Triffids* (1951, filmed by Steve Sekely in 1963, remade for television 1981), Harry Harrison's *Make Room! Make Room!* (1966, filmed by Richard Fleischer as *Soylent Green* in 1973), William F. Nolan and George Clayton Johnson's *Logan's Run* (1967, filmed by Michael Anderson in 1975), Michael Moorcock's *The Final Programme* (1968, filmed by Robert Fuest in 1973) and Roger Zelazny's *Damnation Alley* (1969, filmed by Jack Smight in 1977). In a minor way, this trend has continued with Ursula K. Le Guin's *The Lathe of Heaven* (1971, televised by Fred Barzyk in 1980), John Varley's *Millennium* (1977, filmed by Michael Anderson in 1989), Margaret Atwood's *The Handmaid's Tale* (1985, filmed by Volker Schlöndorff in 1990) and David Brin's *The Postman* (1985, filmed by Kevin Costner in 1997). All these writers have produced a great deal of 'serious' science fiction on various themes, but only their apocalypse novels have been filmed, with few exceptions — which suggests that this particular theme has an accessibility that general audiences do not find in, say, Greg Bear or Paul J. McAuley.

Contributing to this mini-trend of after-the-end movies were a batch of *Planet of the Apes* sequels and a few screen originals like David Cronenberg's glacial *Crimes of the Future* (1970), John Boorman's funkily mythmaking *Zardoz* (1974), Robert Clouse's trashy *The Ultimate Warrior*, Timothy Bond's cheap *Deadly Harvest* (1976) and Richard Compton's dull *Ravagers* (1979). The holocaust became palatable enough for television, as witnessed by Gene Roddenberry's pitiful attempts to get a post-*Trek* series on

the air (*Genesis II* [1973]; *Planet Earth* [1974]; *Strange New World* [1975]), shows like the *Logan's Run* (1977-78) and *Planet of the Apes* (1974) spin-offs, and Terry Nation's *Survivors* (1975-77). A rare apocalypse TV movie is John Llewellyn Moxey's *Where Have All the People Gone?* (1974), with Peter Graves and family returning from a back-packing trip to the mountains to find that everyone else has been powderised by what seems like a neutron bomb attack but actually turns out to be a natural phenomenon (a solar flare).

In *The Ωmega Man*, Charlton Heston, instant icon of the survivor type, spends his days hunting down the cowled albinos who replace the vampire villains of Matheson's novel, trying to cement an alliance with a group of multi-racial hippies, and watching his favourite film, *Woodstock* (1970). Reflecting a post-Manson schism within the counterculture, the survivors are divided into the flower children Heston has to save at the cost of his own life and the hooded cultists who call themselves The Family and follow a Luddite guru (Anthony Zerbe). In the early seventies, we were all into ecology. After the oil crisis, big studio holocausts concentrated on dwindling resources and biological imbalance. *No Blade of Grass*, *The Ultimate Warrior* and *Deadly Harvest* feature ecological breakdowns and worlds in which food is currency; *The Ωmega Man*, *The Crazies*, *Plague* and *Fukkatsu No Hi* feature bio-weapons-related ends of the world; *Soylent Green* has Charlton Heston turning his attention to the problem of over-population; and Robert Altman's *Quintet* (1979) finds Paul Newman playing a murderous form of ludo in a frozen city during a future ice age.

However, the Bomb was not completely neglected. Ted Post's *Beneath the Planet of the Apes* (1970) takes the future world of the first film and elaborates on its post-atomic mutants. In a few impressive scenes, we are given a tour of a subterranean New York, dominated by a fractured stock exchange, and are introduced to Victor Buono's gang of telepathic mutants. Having come into being during World War Three, the mutants worship the Bomb as their maker. 'Glory be to the Bomb, and the Holy Fallout,' they sing, gathered around their idol, a gleaming missile. In the finale, Heston gets to make movie history again by being the first actor personally to destroy the world. As the grouchy gorillas and the mad mutants shoot it out in the cathedral of the Bomb, Chuck decides planet Earth just isn't worth it any more, and pulls the fatal lever. A disembodied narrator (genre stalwart Paul Frees) informs a shocked audience that 'a green and insignificant planet is now dead', which put screenwriter Paul Dehn on the spot when further sequels were required, though a timewarp enabled the saga to achieve circularity with Don Taylor's *Escape From the Planet of the Apes* (1971), and J. Lee Thompson's *Conquest of the Planet of the Apes* (1972) and *Battle for the Planet of the Apes* (1973).

The atomic wars of these movies have usually taken place in the distant past. In *Planet of the Apes*, *Logan's Run*, *Genesis II* and *Deathsport* (1976), the devastation is hundreds of years old by the time the stories start and we are shown alien societies that have sprung up in the ruins of our world. Even L.Q. Jones's grim *A Boy and His Dog* (1975), from Harlan Ellison's 1969 novella, doesn't go into the business of 'World War Four', choosing instead to cover the Earth in mud and invent a 2024 society stratified between surface scavengers and subterranean sybarites. Like *Beneath the Planet of the Apes*, *A Boy and His Dog* scrambles the roles of the Norms and the Mutates, presenting two differing but ghastly post-holocaust societies — a topside of wandering outlaw rapists who barter canned goods and a downunder of Nixon-era folksy fascists who decree that troublemakers be executed in 'farm accidents'. The only hope is in the central relationship, between Vic (Don Johnson), a solo rover who is humane enough to lament the murder of a rape victim ('she could've been used two or three more times'), and Blood (voiced by Tim McIntire), an erudite telepathic dog who guides and educates his master. In the end, given the choice between his manipulative downunder sweetheart (Susanne Benton) and a wounded Blood, Vic kills and cooks the girl (off-screen, in a rare moment of tact), then feeds her to the dog.

Sutton Roley's *Chosen Survivors* (1974) is set in a deep-level fall-out shelter where an ill-assorted bunch of selected citizens find their survival of a thermo-nuclear war raging above the ground imperilled by an infestation of vampire bats. In the end, Bradford Dillman admits it has all been an experiment to see how people would react, an ill-advised test also carried out in *Operation Dead End* (1985) and *Control* (1987). A rare film to give a before-and-after view of World War Three is Jack Smight's anodyne *Damnation Alley*, a disappointing version of Zelazny's gritty novel, in which Jan-Michael Vincent and George Peppard, a pair of air force officers who replace Zelazny's biker hero, emerge from their bunker in a tank-like RV and search amid the giant scorpions and killer cockroaches for other survivors. Early in the film, an embittered inhabitant of the radioactive desert comments, 'nothing good ever happens by itself', but the cop-out finale has a sudden climatic shift returning the world to idyllic normality.

The common denominator, even in *Damnation Alley* and the TV movies, is savagery. Our world may be unfair and self-destructive, but when it goes up in smoke things get a lot worse. Going one better than *A Boy and His Dog*, *The Ultimate Warrior* sees survivalist guru Max Von Sydow order hero-for-hire Yul Brynner to save a packet of seeds rather than the heroine. By the end of the film, Von Sydow has had his head bashed in with a typewriter and Brynner has had to cut off his own hand to win a fight. These downbeat films complement the cynical, post-*Night of the Living Dead* horror films in which unhappy endings are the convention. The genres come together in Wes Craven's *The Hills Have Eyes* (1977), a Norms vs Mutates story which would have been the first post-holocaust Western if the producers had had the money to depict a large-scale societal breakdown, and George A. Romero's *Dawn of the Dead* and *Day of the*

Dead, which take the undead apocalypse of *Night of the Living Dead* as far as it can go and hint that a tougher, but kinder, world could arise from the flesh-eating remnants of the sick society.

Roger Corman's hippie-influenced *Gas-s-s-s*, scripted by George Armitage, parodies all this savagery with a post-collapse world in which all-American football teams, complete with cheerleaders ('Two-four-six-eight, who do we annihilate? Everybody!), devastate the South-West ('...and now the big one, we're gonna sack El Paso!'), while Hell's Angels take over the golf clubs and become the New Conservatives. In a development perhaps possible only in 1970, though vaguely echoed by *The Postman*, the hero (Robert Corff) rejects the theory that 'the only way we can beat these warriors once and for all is to become better fascists than they are'. Demonstrating that a society founded on dog-eat-dog will inevitably collapse, dragging the predators under with the prey, he proposes that rather than the barbarians overrunning the pacifist pueblo commune and stealing their food, a barter system be set up whereby the thugs raise cattle and the hippies produce fruit and vegetables. With this revelation, the survivors are rewarded by the return to Earth of their heroes: Lincoln, JFK, Martin Luther King, Che Guevara and Alfred E. Neuman. Edgar Allan Poe (Bruce Karcher), passing by on a motorcycle, listens as his Lenore asks, 'aren't they going to rape, cheat, steal, kill, lie any more, Edgar?' only for his raven to provide the punchline 'nevermore!'

> *Mad Max* stands alone, the first and only film of a genre that surely could be explored and exploited, with interesting results, by action-oriented filmmakers. It is extremely probable, I believe, that if Australian filmmakers began churning out similar violent, futuristic car-motorcycle films full of spectacular chases and crashes — films in which the stuntmen are the stars — it could be the start of an international craze equal to that caused by Italian Westerns and Chinese kung fu movies a few years back.
>
> **Danny Peary, *Cult Movies***

'There are no heroes any more,' a post-holocaust police chief tells his Number One man, Max Rockatansky (Mel Gibson), 'well... we're going to give them back their heroes.' The vaguely liberal eco-catastrophe films had emasculated their Chuck Hestons, but apocalypse action films need colourful, larger-than-life Marvel Comics-style characters to strut their stuff in the ruins. Mad Max is the only law in a world gone crazy and the film's poster insists that we 'pray he's out there.' The film opens shortly after most of the world has been devastated in an off-screen war. In a dynamic chase, featuring spectacular stuntwork and razor-sharp editing, the Australian highway cops tackle The Nightrider, an insane killer, as he bombs down the Old Arnachie Road. 'I'm a fuel-injected suicide machine,' screams The Nightrider just before he makes his exit in a massive explosion.

Unfortunately, George Miller's *Mad Max* (1979) makes its strongest impression with its opening — not only does the rest of the film fail to come up with a villain to equal The Nightrider, but none of its action scenes are quite as exciting as its first. Indeed, there is a particularly soggy stretch in the middle when Max quits the force and settles down in soft focus with his wife and child. The remains of The Nightrider's vicious bike gang kill the woman and baby, and the maddened Max is back on the road

Below:
Mad Max,
Mel Gibson,
Tim Burns

in his Interceptor Vehicle. Though Max on the vengeance trail provides plenty of rip-roaring action, and a sadistic punchline (Max cuffs a minor thug to a wrecked car and tells him to saw his foot off or die when the spilled petrol ignites), the film still fails to live up to its original verve. Because *Mad Max* was made cheaply in horrendous conditions, Miller had to redub the Australian cast with bland, mid-Atlantic voices, and was never really satisfied with the finished product, which is why he took the opportunity, when the movie became an international success, to make a sequel and do everything right.

By the time of *Mad Max 2*, civilisation has completely decayed. The police force no longer exists and Max roams the deserts in his battered Interceptor, accompanied by a mangy dog and a loopy autogiro captain (Bruce Spence in long johns, Richthofen helmet and sunflower boutonnière). An old-timer narrates the legend of the road warrior who threw in with the hippie good guys against the punk/monster villains in order to clear the way for the re-establishment of decent society. While the first film presents Max as a Clint Eastwood-style rogue cop, *Mad Max 2* has him as the kind of doomed Western hero played by John Wayne in *The Searchers* (1956) and *The Man Who Shot Liberty Valance* (1962), a man of action who is prevailed upon to help lesser mortals destroy the only world he is capable of living in. Like Wayne, Mad Max finally disappears into desert obscurity. The sequel is actually a ninety-minute action sequence, which rather cramps the style of several intriguing supporting characters who are introduced and then brushed off, but Miller handles the whole thing with the verve of the opening twenty minutes of the first film. *Mad Max 2* was retitled *The Road Warrior* in the United States (the one territory where *Mad Max* flopped), and served to establish Miller as a director of note (his segment of *Twilight Zone: The Movie* [1983], is worth the rest of the film put together), Gibson as an international star and the futuristic action/adventure as genre flavour-of-the-month.

Miller brought in George Ogilvie to co-direct the third, and so far final, film in the series, *Mad Max Beyond Thunderdome* (1985), which mellows out after *Mad Max 2* and tries to get Max to show a little sensitivity as he does his best to help out a community of marooned children. Sadly, this positive stuff is less engrossing than the more traditional scenes as an embittered Max, robbed of his camel cart in the desert wastelands, stumbles into Bartertown, a hellhole run by the tyrannical Auntie Entity (Tina Turner) and kept going by methane gas derived from pigshit by tiny genius Angelo Rossitto. Auntie puts Max into the Thunderdome, a combat arena where gladiators on bungee-cords duel with sputtering chainsaws. After the energy and cynicism of the Bartertown sequence, which is bristling with bizarre characters, the film struggles when it gets down to helping the kids, who have a convincing argot and have been mythologising their situation with cave paintings and an idol dressed as a pilot. For a finale, it trots out yet another chase, with more machines and less violence. Though it ambitiously ventures into the linguistic territory charted by Russell Hoban's novel *Riddley Walker*, *Mad Max Beyond Thunderdome* is hampered by its need to develop the lead character to the point where he isn't mad any more and therefore unpicks the premise of the whole show.

The key ingredients of the post-holocaust action movie are weird costumes and ultra-violence. Stanley Kubrick proved in *A Clockwork Orange* that the cinema could have these without an expensive-to-simulate nuclear war. In Kubrick's version of Anthony Burgess's 1962 novel, the future has become hell through simple deterioration. With inner city decay and a rising crime rate, it is not hard to envision the kind of near future in which Alex (Malcolm McDowell), a droog in white boiler suit, bowler hat and eye make-up, can lead his gang of thugs through a vicious, decadent London. In America, the urban decay horror movie grew out of the Charles Bronson/Clint Eastwood action film; both actors were considered by John Carpenter for the role of Snake Plissken in *Escape From New York* (1981) before he settled on his (then) cheaper friend Kurt Russell. In 1997, Manhattan is walled off as a maximum security prison and Plissken, a bank-robbing World War Three veteran, is sent into the city to rescue creepy President Donald Pleasence. Elaborate depictions of near future American cities on the skids are featured in John Frankenheimer's *99 and 44/100% Dead* (1974, *Call Harry Crown*), Walter Hill's *The Warriors* (1979), the 'Harry Canyon' segment of Gerald Potterton's *Heavy Metal* (1981), Ridley Scott's *Blade Runner* (1982), Francis Ford Coppola's *Rumble Fish* (1983), Hill's *Streets of Fire* (1984) and Carpenter's tardy *Escape From L.A.* (1996). Italy's Enzo G. Castellari contributed a cheap, lively rip-off in *1990: I guerrieri del Bronx* (1982, *Bronx Warriors*), which spawned an even more blatant rip-off of a sequel, *Fuga dal Bronx* (1983, *Bronx Warriors 2*).

Castellari struck back with *I nuovi barbari* (1982, *The New Barbarians/Warriors of the Wasteland*), an imitation of *Mad Max 2* in which the Cinecittà rubbish dump stands in for the ravaged post-holocaust landscape, and the fate of the Earth is fought over by a handful of ragged dune buggy drivers in leather codpieces. Luigi Montefiore/George Eastman began a mini-career in the genre as One, leader of the Templars, a band of fanatical gay libbers who believe in finishing off what World War Three started by killing everyone left over in the aftermath. Just about the only remarkable thing about the film is that the heroine doesn't get raped but the hero does. 'Once you've survived the holocaust,' read the ad lines, 'you've got to be tough!' Montefiore was back as Big Ape in Sergio Martino/Martin Dolman's *2019: dopo la caduta di New York* (1982, *2019: After the Fall of New York*), helping hero Parsifal (Michael Spokiw) rescue the last fertile woman in the world from the fascist Europeans who have invaded what is left of New York. In the end, the Pan-American Confederacy pack Parsifal and his deep frozen bride into a spaceship and give them a shot at a less nuked planet in a distant galaxy.

Above: I guerrieri del Bronx

Most of the Italian apocalypse movies are more earthbound, concentrating on a leather-clad lone wolf warrior hero who falls in with and protects a small group of roving scuzzbag troublemakers and Nazi-style armies, often encountering Fred Williamson, Sabrina Siani, Pier Luigi Conti/Al Cliver or the ubiquitous Montefiore/Eastman and carrying over a great many costumes, props and vehicles between films. Among the guilty are Giuliano Carnimeo/Jules Harrison's adequate *Giustiziere della strada* (1983, *The Exterminators of the Year 3000*), Antonio Margheriti/Anthony M. Dawson's lightweight *Il mondo di Yor*, Tonino Ricci/Anthony Richmond's mind-numbing *Rush* (1983) and its even worse sequel *Fuoco incrociato — Rage* (1983, *Rage*), Aristide Massaccesi/Steven Benson's initially promising *Endgame: Bronx lotta finale* (1983, *Endgame*), Aristide Massaccesi/Kevin Mancuso's dreary *Anno 2020: Il gladiatori del futuro* (1983, *2020: Texas Gladiators*), Ruggero Deodato/Roger Franklin's silly *I predatori di Atlantide* (1983, *The Atlantis Interceptors*), David Worth's boring *I predatori dell'anno omega* (1984, *Warrior of the Lost World*), Romolo Guerrieri's best-of-a-bad-lot *L'ultimo guerriero* (1984, *The Final Executioner*) and its ghastly semi-reprise Vanio Amici/Bob Collins's *Il giustiziere del Bronx* (1989, *The Bronx Executioners*), Bruno Mattei's endearingly ropy *Rats, notte di terrore* (1985, *Rats: Night of Terror*), Deran Sarafian's dull *Interzone* (1989), Giuseppe Vari/Joseph Warren's negligible *Urban Warriors* (1989), Ettore Pasculli's obscure *Fuga dal paradiso* (1990) and Enrico Caria's unusual tale of futuristic Naples *L'incredible e triste storia del cinico Rudy, ovvero: diciassette* (1991).

It had all been done before in Henry Suso and Allan Arkush's *Deathsport*, with David Carradine and Claudia Jennings as warriors on the run and Richard Lynch as the traitor who has sworn to kill them, and the Italian explosion was accompanied by bursts of extremely similar films from unexpected corners of the globe. Films in the *barbari del futuro* tradition emerged from many countries, including Australia (Gary Keady's *Sons of Steel* [1988]; Alex Proyas's *Spirits of the Air, Gremlins of the Clouds* [1988]), France (Pierre William's *Terminus* [1986]), Hong Kong (Johnny To's *Xiandai Haoxia Zhuan* [1996, *The Heroic Trio II: Executioners*]), Israel (Avi Nesher's *She* [1983]; David Engelbach's *America 3000* [1985]), Japan (particularly animated films — Hayao Miyazaki's affecting *Kaze no Tani no Nausicaa* [1984, *Warriors of the Wind*]; Toyo'o Ashida's thuggish *Hokuto* no Ken [1986, *Fist of the North Star*]; Ichiro Itano's appalling *Violence Jack* series), New Zealand (Harley Cokliss's *Battletruck* [1981, *Warlords of the 21st Century*]), the Philippines (never-let-go-of-a-good-thing Ciro H. Santiago's *Stryker* [1983], *Wheels of Fire* [1985], *Equalizer 2000* [1986], and *Sisterhood* [1988]), Russia (Rasdhid Nugmanov's *Diki Vostok* [1993, *The Wild East*]), South Africa (Percival Rubens's *Survival Zone* [1983]; Lance Hool's *Steel Dawn* [1988]) and Britain (Richard Stanley's robo-carnage quickie *Hardware* [1990]; Ngozi Onwurah's agonising *Welcome II the Terrordome* [1994]). Any territory that could boast a rubbish-strewn desert or a couple of rustily abandoned factories was also likely to find a band of leather-clad extras to run around popping off pretend guns at each other while sneering grimly. Rainer Erler's German *Operation Ganymed* (1977) is a depressing but ingenious reversal of the astronauts-return-to-a-blasted-Earth cliché originated in *World Without End* and *Planet of the Apes* and reused by Steve Barkett's *The Aftermath* (1980), Paul Donovan's *DefCon 4* and Michael Shackleton's *The Survivor* (1988). Here, the astronauts crash-land in a desert wilderness they come to believe is a post-holocaust Earth only to find they have been stranded in an ordinarily inhospitable part of Mexico.

The most interesting of the eighties post-apocalypse films is Luc Besson's *Le Dernier combat* (1984, *The Last Battle*), a black and white widescreen exploration of a Parisian desert where the speechless survivors of an unspecified catastrophe kit themselves up in leg-warmers and improvised armour and play power games with a patience and concern for symbolism that recalls mid-sixties art cinema. Whereas the struggles in Italian future schlockers are supposed to be epic battles for the fate of humanity but come over as petty squabbles thanks to the measly budget, Besson deliberately plays up the forlorn way his characters go through the motions of trying to find water, wishing there were women around and living on because there is nothing better to do. Heroes and villains alike are half-hearted about the roles they are called on to play, and the tone, while playful, is deeply pessimistic. The hero (Pierre Jolivet) finds the last woman on earth but the villain (Jean Reno) kills her and the human race is left to die out quietly. Many apocalypse movies use the words 'last', 'ultimate' or 'final' in their title; *Le Dernier Combat* actually means it.

In the meantime, post-nuclear America made a comeback as the setting for a few lively cheapies. *The Lathe of Heaven* opens with George Orr (Bruce Davison) stumbling about the usual radioactive ruins, but he is a psychic prodigy with the ability to reshape reality through his dreams and proceeds to alter 'the world after April', under the guidance of an incipiently megalomaniac therapist (Kevin Conway), towards a utopia that eventually threatens to be worse than the standard-issue holocaust that precipitated the plot. Rinse Dream's *Cafe Flesh* (1981), a well-reviewed hard-core porno movie, is set in a post-war world where ninety-nine per cent of the population are unable to have sex, and the remaining one per cent are forced to perform in the floor show at the titular dive in order to titillate an audience of impotent voyeurs. 'If the future portrayed in *Cafe Flesh* is an obscene one,' writes co-scenarist Jerry Stahl, 'it may be because the present long ago became unspeakable.' The film's inevitable self-hatred limited its appeal and its influence, but Frederic Lansac's French *Shocking* (1983) features an edge-of-doom orgy as the final war starts, C.C. Williams's *The Load Warrior* (1987) and Bruce Seven's *Mad Jack Beyond Thunderbone* (1986) are typically parodic pornos, and Antonio Passolini eventually made *Cafe Flesh 2* (1997).

There were a great many other American post-nuke warrior efforts, including: Charles Band's 3-D duo *Parasite* (1982) and *Metalstorm: The Destruction of Jared-Syn* (1982), Aaron Lipstadt's youth-themed *City Limits* (1984), Peter Maris's *Land of Doom* (1985), genre specialist Albert Pyun's eccentric *Radioactive Dreams*, inconclusive *Knights* (1993) and post-plague *Adrenalin: Fear the Rush* (1995), Bobby A. Suarez's *Warriors of the Apocalypse* (1985, *Searchers of the Voodoo Mountain*), Carl Colpaert's *In the Aftermath* (1986), Lindsay Shontoff's *The Killing Edge* (1986), Fred Olen Ray's *Warlords* (1986), Franky Schaeffer's post-plague *Wired to Kill* (1986), Tim Kincaid's *Mutant Hunt* (1987), 'the other' George Miller's TV pilot *Badlands 2005* (1988), Luis Llosa's *Crime Zone* (1988), Jon Hess's *Lawless Land* (1988), David Heavener's *Deadly Reactor* (1989), Brian Thomas Jones and James McCalmont's *Escape From Safehaven* (1989), Tom Gniazdowski's *Tin Star Void* (1989), Augusto Tamayo's *Welcome to Oblivion* (1990), Frank Harris's *Aftershock* (1990), Rick King's silly *Prayer of the Rollerboys* (1991), Philip Roth's *Prototype X29A* (1992) and *A.P.E.X.* (1993), Steve Barnett's *MindWarp* (1992), Augustin Tamayo and Kevin Tent's patchwork *Ultra Warrior* (1993).

Amid all these busily repetitive or penny-pinching pictures, the few that stand out tend to get by on oddball wasteland humour, like Steve DeJarnatt's lively and satirical *Cherry 2000* (1987), which has bounty tracker Melanie Griffith helping hapless hero David Andrews (from an enclosed city where casual singles bar pick-ups have to exchange fat contracts before anonymous sex) search the wilderness for his lost loved one, a robot sex-doll (Pamela Gidley), and coming up against a rubbish tip tyrant played in a Hawaiian shirt by sub-genre stalwart Tim Thomerson (along with Brion James, the most common performer in wasteland SF). One of the charms of *Cherry 2000* is that it features substantial performances from John Ford rep company members Ben Johnson and Harry Carey Jr as desert rats, and the Western motif recurs throughout the cycle, with a surprising number of films lifting their plots whole from classic oat operas: Gregory Brown's *Dead Man Walking* (1987) is Ford's *The Searchers* with Wings Hauser as John Wayne and Brion James as Henry Brandon; Lee H. Katzin's *World Gone Wild* (1988) is John Sturges's *The Magnificent Seven* (1960) with Michael Paré as James Coburn and Adam Ant as Eli Wallach; Monte Markham's *Neon City* (1991) is Ford's *Stagecoach* (1939) with Vanity as John Wayne and Michael Ironside as George Bancroft.

If no Western inspiration was available, filmmakers could rip off or remake foreign-originated properties — David DeCoteau's *Creepozoids* (1987), with post-holocaust soldier girl Linnea Quigley and company chased around a military-bunker by a genetic experiment mutated into a giant rat, is an unashamed imitation of *Rats, notte di terrore*, while Tony Randel's *Fist of the North Star* (1995), with guru Malcolm McDowell tutoring wanderer Gary Daniels in the skills he needs to best a wilderness tyrant, is a remake of the anime original, complete with Chris Penn as the thug who has received a fatal martial arts blow which will explode his head if he ever lets the bandages loosen.

The cycle lasted long enough to throw out a few series of films — Donald Jackson's *Roller Blade* (1986), R.J. Kizer and Jackson's *Hell Comes to Frogtown* (1987) and Pyun's *Cyborg* (1989) all led to minor franchises: Jackson's *Rollerblade Warriors: Taken By Force* (1988), *The Rollerblade Seven* (1992), *Legend of the Rollerblade 7* (1992) and *Frogtown II* (1992), Michael Schroeder's *Cyborg 2: Glass Shadow* (1993) and *Cyborg 3: The Recycler* (1994). Stuart Gordon's childish but fun *RobotJox* (1989), with the Superpowers conducting their wars through gladiatorial conflicts between piloted giant robot warriors, had a spin-off (Charles Band's *Crash and Burn* [1990]) *and* sequels (Albert Band's *Robot Wars* [1993]; Ian Barry's *Robo Warriors* [1997]). The burst of activity in the mid-to-late eighties more or less petered out around 1992, as Pyun and pals forgot *Mad Max* and started imitating *The Terminator* or *Die Hard* (1988).

The few healthily-budgeted, studio-financed efforts were little different: Alan Johnson's more than ordinarily bad *Solarbabies* (1986) is about post-holocaust teens on skates (cf *Roller Blade, Prayer of the Rollerboys*), with the likes of Jason Patric and Jami Gertz tutored by a glowing alien presence to set aside their roller derby antics and concentrate on overthrowing militarist dictator Richard Jordan; David Webb Peoples's grim *Salute of the Jugger* (1990, *Blood of Heroes*) has Rutger Hauer and Joan Chen taking part in another of those gladiatorial sports the movies imagine will take the place of entertainment after a collapse of civilisation (cf Norman Jewison's *Rollerball* [1975]; Paul Bartel's *Death Race 2000* [1975]) and which allow the filmmakers to condemn the public's taste for ultraviolence while simultaneously pandering to it. Simon Wincer's *Harley Davidson & the Marlboro Man* (1991) has Mickey Rourke and Don Johnson as the eponymous pals tangling with a crooked corporation and a new drug in run-down 1996 (just like Corey Haim and Patricia Arquette in *Prayer of the Rollerboys*), taking care to include in its credits a disclaimer that no real-life corporation has endorsed the use of their names.

Rachel Talalay's *Tank Girl* (1995), the flop Lori Petty vehicle derived from Alan Martin and Jamie Hewlett's comic series, is a medium-budget revival of the genre, with *Mad Max 2*-style car chases in the desert and a streak of nastily absurdist humour not quite incarnated by Petty's supposedly spiky punk survivalist heroine. Along with Kevin Reynolds's troubled *Waterworld* (1995) and *Waterworld* star Kevin Costner's commercially disastrous *The Postman*, which aren't quite the artistic write-offs their out-of-control budgets and inflated star ego indicate they ought to be, *Tank Girl* suggested the genre was exhausted by the mid-to-late nineties.

Waterworld, which did finally make back its huge budget, is symptomatic of the bloat of the genre. Scripted initially by David Twohy as a Roger Corman-scale quickie, it became an epic almost against its will. The film opens with one of the neatest of all movie set-ups as the ice caps melt on the Universal globe logo, drowning the world and establishing its water-logged future. Then, at a price tag of an alleged $200,000,000, Costner delivers a big summer action movie with a derivative high concept — it's *Mad Max 2* with waterwings.

The Mariner (Costner), a glum mutant drifter with gills behind his ears, wanders endless seas in his cool trimaran, showing off its gimmicked-up sail-raising devices and drinking his own urine. The hero drops by a floating settlement of beleaguered hippies and is sentenced to be recycled in yellow sludge but saved from death when the settlement is overrun by 'Smokers' (power-boat baddies under the direction of Dennis Hopper's Deacon, who lives in the *Exxon Valdez*), and a woman (Jeanne Tripplehorn) rescues him on the condition he look after her and a tag-along little girl (Tina Majorino) who has an arcane symbol tattooed on her back which might be the key to finding the last bit of dry land in the world. The Mariner is so unpleasant a hero that he tosses the non-swimming moppet overboard at one point, but slowly cosies up to his ersatz family while Hopper's ranting madman and his oar-driven oil tanker follow in their wake. Packed full of silly business and cliché plot points, it at least offers an unfamiliar post-holocaust world, a gritty hero who doesn't make cheap jokes or need a comedy sidekick, and more thrilling stunts and action scenes than dodgy CGI effects. Hopper's entertainingly over-the-top turn is pure comic book, reducing the menace of the villains, and there's a bathetic landfall at the end — which, logically, should take place at the site of Mount Everest but offers instead a Hawaiian-style paradise island — but *Waterworld* is by no means the disaster its escalating budget and problematic production history suggested it might be.

Given that the end of the Cold War scuppered the premises of most post-nuclear-apocalypse action movies, Lance Mungia's *Six-String Samurai* (1998), a rare film venture into the established literary form of alternative history, may suggest a way forward for the sub-genre. The set-up is that an all-out atomic war took place in 1957 and the Russian army attempted to occupy a fragmented America, and that Elvis Presley was literally crowned King of the free city of Las Vegas. Forty years later, Elvis has just died and wandering rock 'n' roll warriors from the wastelands make a violent pilgrimage towards Vegas in an attempt to become the new King. Betraying the influence of the Japanese 'Baby Cart' series and Robert

Rodriguez's *El Mariachi* (1992), the actual story concerns Buddy (Jeffrey
Falcon), a wandering rocker with a samurai sword taped to the back of his
six-string guitar and a look that combines Buddy Holly with Mad Max,
and his partnership with a mostly silent Kid (Justin McGuire), who sticks
by him as he faces off against a succession of bizarre enemies: a bowling
team, regular desert rat mutants, a cannibal sitcom family, the Red Army,
windmill worshippers and the minions of his deadliest rival, a heavy metal
rocker who calls himself Death (Stephane Gauger).

Made on a limited budget, this has a pleasantly restless energy and manages to cover up its multiply derivative script by striking subtly different poses. By making the villain a metalhead, the film rejects the predominant leather/biker aesthetic of most post-apocalypse movies, and works out a fifties-gone-nuclear style that is especially well conveyed in a music score by Brian Tyler, with on-screen and soundtrack performances by Russian-flavoured rockabillies the Red Elvises. However, the progression of the quest from fight to fight becomes a touch monotonous, with the supposedly weightier final conflicts rather less impressive than the initial action scenes as the film's basic licks are repeated a few too many times. In the finale, Buddy succumbs but the Kid defeats Death, who is as allergic to water as the Witch of *The Wizard of Oz* (1939) was, and adopts the costume of his role model to enter the gleaming free city.

Side Issues

Bombing the Ban?

Basically, it's about a group of fraternity guys on 'hell night'. They send some of their pledges down into the bad side of town to kidnap the leader of an anti-nuke group. Before they can kidnap him, a psychotic, violent, anti-nuke person — myself — enters the scene. Now this man is bad. He's taken up permanent residence in the ozone. He's nick-named 'Splatter'. The leader of the anti-nuke group is violent, so, see, we get both sides in there. We didn't want to slant it one way or the other, we just wanted people to think about it... The killer is not just another demented psycho without the audience ever knowing why he's a psycho. The guy's trip is that he was once a nuclear scientist, terribly pro-nuke. And then he lost his entire right arm in a nuclear accident. Part of his upper body and face area are now covered by a helmet, and his right arm is hydraulic.

Edwin Neal, on acting in *Future Kill* (1984), *Fangoria*

Opposite:
The Manhattan Project, *John Lithgow*

Though protest against nuclear weapons was widespread in the West throughout the Cold War, the cinema took a long time to take notice of the organised peace movement. In the late fifties, the Campaign for Nuclear Disarmament became an organised, if not mass, movement. Almost immediately, CND was saddled with an image of well-intentioned wrong-headedness. In Russia, dissidents ended up in labour camps; in Britain, they looked ridiculous in newspaper cartoons. In John Christopher's novel *The Death of Grass*, a Citizen's Emergency Committee takes over London and announces that a ruthless government has decided to bomb Britain's population centres in order to avert famine. 'At my guess,' asserts a tough but right-minded character, 'the Emergency Committee's a triumvirate composed of a professional anarchist, a parson, and a left-wing female school teacher. It would take that kind of combination to show such an ignorance of elementary human behaviour.' These dismissive stereotypes remained dominant in the media view of the peace movement; in the eighties, Christopher's committee could easily have been read as a demeaning reference to Ken Livingstone, Monsignor Bruce Kent and the Greenham Common women. Rather more to the point are the dying survivors of Peter Van Greenaway's novel *The Crucified City* (1962), a similar if less caricatured cross section of Ban-the-Bomb types, who go on the very last Aldermaston march, after a final war that takes place on Good Friday, 1970.

In the early sixties, the general Establishment attitude to CND was that the movement was fundamentally harmless, a ripple of duffle-coated eccentricity along the lines of wartime conscientious objection. Aldermaston marches were precisely the kind of polite, orderly, non-influential protests that the West liked to point to as examples of the relative freedom of its society. Hardly a debate on the nuclear issue went by without a well-groomed pro-nuke spokesman mentioning that there weren't any Ban-the-Bomb rallies in Russia. Wellington boot radicalism was seen as irrelevant to the great mass of public opinion. If Jimmy Stewart was committed to the Deterrent and Jack Kennedy could face up to Khrushchev over Cuba, their audiences would go along with them and keep the Bomb. The only nuke demonstration in sixties cinema is outside the White House in *Seven Days in May*, and that is a protest *against* President Fredric March's disarmament treaty. In Henry Koster's *Take Her, She's Mine* (1963), we're expected to identify with James Stewart again; he's the baffled father of a daughter who takes up with 'beatniks and Ban-the-Bomb protesters' after going to college, but the film is about sex — no one could take Sandra Dee's political opinions seriously.

Of course, the nuclear war films of the early sixties were taken up and championed by CND. The BBC's refusal to screen Peter Watkins's *The War Game* led to a minor battle with the peace protesters. 'I believe there is a silence on why we possess nuclear weapons,' said Watkins. 'It's not a Ban-the-Bomb film. We don't ask any more, we don't criticise. We accept. I wanted to make the man in the street stop and think about himself and the future.' When *The War Game* was released theatrically, it became a staple of CND meetings. Despite Watkins's supposed objectivity, the film served as a recruitment film for the peace movement. It is an attempt to shock comfortable people into an awareness that they could easily lose their lifestyles at the push of the button. Shown on television, it would certainly have won many subscriptions for CND, and perhaps turned the organisation into the broad-base mass movement it would not become for another fifteen years.

Perhaps the nuclear debate was too big, too important an issue to be made the subject of film drama. Or maybe it was difficult to make an interesting dramatic conflict out of an argument in which both sides had the same ultimate objective. After all, there was no one (except maybe Curtis LeMay) *in favour* of nuclear war. It was not until the fate of the planet became a less hot item than the fate of South East Asia that protest movements had films about them. In the wave of generally embarrassing campus protest movies (*Getting Straight*, *The Strawberry Statement*, *RPM*, all 1970), there is no mention of the Bomb, unless you count the probably symbolic explosions Michelangelo Antonioni uses to finish off *Zabriskie Point* (1970).

After Vietnam, Watergate, the decline of *détente* and the temporary obsolescence of ecology as a hip issue, the Peace Movement made a comeback. Ageing campus crusaders handed back the inverted trident in a circle emblem they had appropriated (the peace sign is semaphore for ND, nuclear disarmament). When President Carter asked daughter Amy what the most important issue in the 1980 election was, she said, 'nuclear weapons, I guess'. But we all know what happened to the Carters. Though CND grew into an across-the-board, genuinely representative organisation in the eighties, Britain and America elected hardline pro-nuke, anti-commie governments. The difference between the nuclear debates of the sixties and the eighties was that there were fewer 'don't knows'. Opinion was polarised. The CND of the eighties was seen as more dangerous — the British Labour Party's passing commitment to disarmament is mentioned in *The Day After* as a possible threat to the NATO alliance, and the Russian press, tired of Western gulag stories, gleefully cited CND as an example of dissidence in the supposedly free world. It now seemed conceivable that the peace movement could influence national politics.

It is probably not coincidental that, when CND was too widespread to be ignored, the movement featured in a handful of films and was grossly maligned in most of them. Ian Sharp's *Who Dares Wins* (1982, *The*

Final Option), a glorification of the SAS, has a highly unbelievable cadre of hard-core terrorists within the peace movement as its villains. They take over the American embassy in London, holding Secretary of State Richard Widmark and Chief of Strategic Air Command Robert Webber hostage, threatening to execute everyone in sight unless a nuclear missile is launched against the Holy Loch submarine base in Scotland 'as a demonstration of the horror of nuclear war.' John Glen's *Octopussy* (1983) has Steven Berkoff as a renegade Soviet general who plans to detonate a nuclear device at an American air force base in West Germany, putting the blame on faulty Yankee safety procedures. James Bond (Roger Moore) gets the point immediately, 'Europe will insist on unilateral disarmament, leaving every border open for you to march through at will!' While Judy Davis in whiteface, chanting 'Two four six eight, we don't want to radiate' in *Who Dares Wins*, and Berkoff gasping 'they would have made me a hero of the Soviet Union' as his scheme is foiled by 007, might seem implausible CND supporters, they are positively reasonable compared with the anti-nuke protesters of Ronald W. Moore's *Future Kill*. Here, CND has become a mutant punk street gang much given to ultra-violence.

There was no attempt to present a fictional but realistic view of the peace movement in mainstream cinema. Richard Eyre's *The Ploughman's Lunch* (1983), scripted by Ian McEwan, supposedly a radical dissection of the malaise of Thatcherite Britain, has its right wing bastard anti-hero (Jonathan Pryce) stumble through the mists into a women's peace camp set up outside an American air base. The women are characterised as naïve angels in anoraks. Though the film is full of hatred for its horrible Tories, it is far more interested in them than in the people it presumably agrees with. A pointed contrast is *Carry Greenham Home* (1983), a documentary by Beeban Kidron and Amanda Richardson which chronicles the lives of the women camping for peace at the USAF base on Greenham Common over a seven-month period from 12 December 1982, the day 30,000 women joined hands and ringed the base. In one of the film's most interesting scenes, the women combat their demeaning media image by reading aloud and communally ridiculing newspaper accounts of their activities.

Edge of Darkness (1985) presents a credible CND meeting in its first scene but edges into strange mysticism signalled by naming its protest movement Gaia. The activist heroine (Joanne Whalley) is swiftly murdered and reduced to the status of saintly ghost, advising her less aware policeman father (Bob Peck) about nuclear threats to an apparently sentient planet. In a spectacular bit of cynicism, the founder of the Gaia movement is revealed to be flamboyant CIA agent Darius Jedbergh (Joe Don Baker), acting on the temporarily anti-nuclear policies of the Carter administration. Martin Campbell's remarkable miniseries, scripted by Troy Kennedy Martin, climaxes with the rogue Jedbergh convinced after one betrayal too many that the Gaians have a point. He exposes a roomful of nuclear industry spokespeople to a small implosion of weapons-grade plutonium with the announcement, 'twenty-four people have died for this, including me'.

The peace movement was involved in many documentary films, mostly on video or 16mm, intended for distribution outside the usual channels, including *Prophecy* (1980), Terri Nash's Oscar-winning *If You Love This Planet* (1983) and *No More Hibakusha* (1983). A rare feature film made with major participation from anti-nuclear protesters themselves, Emile De Antonio's *In the King of Prussia* (1983) is a peculiar cocktail of the real and the recreated, which stages the trial of the Ploughshares Eight, a group of militant Catholics who invaded a GEC factory in Pennsylvania where warheads were stored. The Eight play themselves, but the judge who hands out disproportionately severe sentences is an actor, Martin Sheen. The script is simply an edited version of the court records. Though well-intentioned, *In the King of Prussia* is an oddly beside-the-point film — the trial hinges on a particularly obscure point of law and so much time is spent debating it that the nuclear issues never come into focus. The sincere TV movie *The Rainbow Warrior Conspiracy* (1988) dramatises covert actions taken by the French secret service against a Greenpeace vessel to forestall a protest against a Pacific nuclear test. Again, the focus is on the perfidy of the nuclear powers, which extends to America and Britain, who refuse to help the New Zealand authorities investigate the crime, but not on the issues raised by the protests.

Nuclear Terrorism

'I don't know what's scarier — losing nuclear weapons, or that it happens so often there's actually a term for it.'
Broken Arrow (1996)

The only peace protesters in the cinema taken seriously are those who, like Darius Jedbergh, choose to fight for peace with the threat of violence. The movies first nuclear terrorist is Professor Willingdon (Barry Jones) in *Seven Days to Noon*. Unhinged by guilt and anxiety, Willingdon walks out of his government research laboratory one evening with a small nuclear device in his briefcase. He threatens to detonate it in central London unless Britain ceases the manufacture of atomic weapons. Willingdon is treated sympathetically, but is still a mental case. *Seven Days to Noon* admits the arms race is a dangerous game, but uses this to argue that it should be put in the hands of iron-willed, stiff-upper-lipped, tweedy patriots like the policeman (André Morrell) who coolly deals with the crisis. Nuclear war is too important to be left to the physicists. Produced and directed by Roy and John Boulting (whose films, like *I'm All Right, Jack* [1959], tend to the reactionary), from a story by Paul Dehn (who would write the *Planet of the Apes* sequels) and James Bernard (who would score the major Hammer horrors), *Seven Days to Noon* draws on memories of the blitz for powerful scenes of the evacuated city, but its gloomy, neurotic feel looks forward to the years of Suez and downbeat British SF films to come, like *The Quatermass Xperiment*, *X the Unknown*, *Quatermass 2* and *The Damned*.

Willingdon's tactics were imitated in Jimmy Sangster's TV play *I Can Destroy the Sun* (1958) and 'Say Knife Fat Man' (*Doomwatch*, 1972), and echoed in Edward Zwick's shot-on-video TV movie *Special Bulletin* (1983). Here, concerned scientists Bruce Lyman (David Clennon), 'former strategic weapons planner for the Pentagon', and Dave McKeeson (David Rasche) threaten to detonate a home-made nuclear device in Charleston Harbour unless the government unilaterally disarms the South-Eastern United States. A SWAT raid takes out the terrorists, but the defusing is bungled and the Bomb goes off, obliterating a chunk of picturesque South Carolina. Scripted by Marshall Herskovitz, *Special Bulletin* is told entirely through media coverage of the event; the precedent of the Welles *War of the Worlds* broadcast means the fictional network has to run several announcements that this is just a made-up story to prevent panic. The major contrivance is that the initial Coast Guard skirmish with the terrorists happens to be filmed by a two-man team doing a story on a dock strike. Lyman, whose cell includes a black radical (Rosalind Cash), a jittery ex-con (Ebbe Roe Smith) and a housewife (Roberta Maxwell), demands a network feed so he can address the nation, while anchor-persons John Woodley (Ed Flanders), 'the dean of RBS news', and Susan Myles (Kathryn Walker) provide updates, background material and testy interviews with the hostage-takers and experts.

An unnamed President clearly stands for Ronald Reagan, and the film consistently attacks his administration policy, all but accusing the government of driving the terrorists mad in the first place and then showing how official overconfidence and callousness push the situation over the edge. In the end, however, *Special Bulletin* is less concerned with nukes than the news, indicting a system which handles crises 'as if the coverage of the event were more important than the event itself.' The incorporation of the media into the story is underlined when a Presidential press aide issues a statement that Lyman's demands will be met, but only as a feint to distract the terrorists just before the SWAT assault on their tug-boat, which is cued by the cutting-off of their TV picture. The most chilling aspect of *Special Bulletin* is that, after a few days, the story no longer dominates the bulletins, the memory of Charleston receding as the anchors move on from the catastrophe with 'in other news...'

The character of the militant pacifist is a stubbornly persistent cliché, with a clutch of films and novels (Alan Gardner's *The Escalator* [1963]; Bob Shaw's *Ground Zero Man* [1971]) depicting fumble-fingered protesters interfering with the legitimate deterrent as a likely cause of nuclear disaster. Even more far-fetched are those cabals of scientists and planners who decide that the only way to forestall a world-destroying war is to manufacture a paper dragon threat from alien invaders — a possibility that Ronald Reagan once mused about in public — that frightens the superpowers into pointing all their weapons out into space rather than each other. The concept seems to originate with Theodore Sturgeon's short story 'Unite and Conquer' (1948), but novels on the theme include William C. Anderson's *Pandemonium on the Potomac* (1966) and Martin Caidin's *The Mendelov Conspiracy* (1969). Such a scheme is dramatised quite movingly in 'The Architects of Fear' (*The Outer Limits*, 1963), in which Robert Culp volunteers to be surgically transformed into a hideous alien to shock complacent humanity, and Alan Moore and Dave Gibbons replay the scenario, with an almost subliminal credit to the TV episode, in the Cold War superhero comic book *Watchmen* (1986-7).

Willingdon and Lyman threaten to use nuclear weapons for a very specific end (Lyman wants the '968 detonating modules' of nuclear weapons in the Charleston area delivered to him for disposal), but high school genius Paul Stevens (Christopher Collet) of Marshall Brickman's *The Manhattan Project* (1986, *Deadly Game*) puts together a functioning atom bomb just to ace a science fair and put his single Mom (Jill Eikenberry) in her place for dating a nuclear physicist (John Lithgow). In *Special Bulletin*,

Dave McKeeson, who contracts fatal radiation poisoning in the process, has rigged up his bomb off-screen before the film starts; but Paul Stevens takes us through the construction of his device with *Blue Peter* meticulousness. Brickman comes up with some smart lines ('they could lock you in a room and throw the room away') and Lithgow manages to get a real impact with, 'well, that was interesting' just after the countdown is averted, but *The Manhattan Project* is one of the most ideologically confused films of all time. Here, the maker of an atom bomb is an adolescent whiner out to get his Mom's attention, who (as in *WarGames* [1983]) finally has to wake up to responsibility during a suspense sequence by defusing the device he has created. Crucially, however, we're expected to like Paul and think the adults who give him a hard time are stuffy fools. After all, the film shows how a clever kid with a remote-control gadget can heist a canister of plutonium from a government plant.

Most nuclear terrorists in the movies are more simple-minded baddies, often in the employ of a 'foreign power' or out to extort a fortune. Their archetype may well be the serial villain played by Bela Lugosi in *The Phantom Creeps* (1939), who, as William K. Everson has it, spent the last chapter 'zooming over New York in a tiny plane with a thin vial of his explosive formula', gleefully planning 'to throw it overboard and "blow up the entire world"', happily unmindful that this might affect him too!' Equally as cracked or melodramatic are the schemes exposed in Fred F. Sears's *The 49th Man* (1953), where a spy ring smuggles the individual components of an atom bomb into the America for assembly and eventual detonation; Harold Schuster's *Port of Hell* (1955), where the bomb is in the hold of a ship docked in Los Angeles and set to go off in twelve hours; Jack Arnold's *The Mouse That Roared*, in which bumbling invaders get hold of the 'Q-bomb' and bring the United States to its knees; Franklin Adreon's *Dimension 5* (1966), in which Jeffrey Hunter foils a Chinese plan to sneak a H-bomb into America in a shipment of rice; Montgomery Tully's entertainingly demented *Battle Beneath the Earth* (1967), in which a renegade Chinese warlord tunnels under America and places bombs beneath the major cities, thus saving a fortune on air force appropriations; Eddie Davis's *Panic in the City* (1968), in which Howard Duff saves Los Angeles from another concealed bomb; and Kazuhiko Hasegawa's outright comic *Taiyo o Nusunda Otoko* (1980, *The Man Who Stole the Sun*), in which Kenji

Sawada threatens to set off his home-made atom bomb unless the Japanese government allows the Rolling Stones to give a concert despite their drug convictions and televises overrunning live baseball matches to the end rather than returning to scheduled programming.

These films concentrate on the threat of the Bomb itself, with no suggestion of any motive beyond sheer rottenness for scheming to use it. Nigel Kneale's TV play *The Crunch* (1964) is more sophisticated, with a Middle Eastern state threatening London with a bomb that has been assembled in the basement of their embassy from parts smuggled into Britain in diplomatic pouches, demanding one billion pounds as reparation for the period the country spent as a colony. James Glickenhaus's *The Soldier* (1982, *Code Name: The Soldier*) sees the Russians conceal an atomic weapon in the Saudi oil fields and try to pick on Israel, with a covert CIA/Zionist gang pointing a borrowed missile at Moscow to face the commies down. The most elaborate of the bomb-in-the-basement movies is John Mackenzie's *The Fourth Protocol* (1987), from the 1984 novel by Frederick Forsyth, in which glum Soviet agent Pierce Brosnan, another avatar of Forsyth's Jackal character, puts a bomb together in a semi in Milton Keynes. His scheme is much the same as that of Steven Berkoff in *Octopussy*, to make a big bang during a peace rally and blame it on the Americans, prompting Western Europe to disarm and pull out of NATO. The title refers to a secret gentleman's agreement between the superpowers not to do things like this, and, as often in the eighties, the villains are rogue KGB hard-liners disturbed by *détente*.

Of course, variations on the hijack-and-threat nuke routine have been common in James Bond adventures, to the extent that Dr Evil (Mike Myers) in Jay Roach's spoof *Austin Powers: International Man of Mystery* (1997), after all his other outdated schemes have been shot down by his board of directors, decides that 'we'll just do what we usually do', get hold of a nuclear weapon and threaten the world. In Terence Young's *Thunderball*, Adolfo Celi steals a pair of bombs and threatens to blast selected cities off the map unless the United Nations fork over heavy payola; in Lewis Gilbert's *You Only Live Twice* (1967), Donald Pleasence kidnaps spacecraft from both sides of the Iron Curtain in the hope of triggering World War Three; in Gilbert's *The Spy Who Loved Me* (1977), the imitative Curt Jurgens kidnaps nuclear submarines, again in the hope of triggering World War Three; in Irvin Kershner's *Never Say Never Again* (1983), a remake of

Thunderball, the stolen bombs are updated into cruise missiles; and in Martin Campbell's *GoldenEye* (1995), Sean Bean plans to use the electro-magnetic pulse effect of nuclear explosions to crash the world's financial computer system. The difference in style between Connery and Moore is illustrated by their reactions to identical situations: in Guy Hamilton's *Goldfinger* (1964), Connery's Bond, handcuffed to a nuclear device in the vaults of Fort Knox as part of Gert Frobe's scheme to up the value of his gold stocks by making everyone else's reserves unapproachable for a few thousand years, is on the point of yanking out all the wires of a nuclear device when an anonymous expert walks up and calmly flicks a disarming switch; but in *Octopussy*, Moore's Bond, discovering Berkoff's bomb in a carnival, goes through the tricky business of defusing the device himself with many an elegantly perspiring close-up and the red-wire-no-the-blue-wire snip gambit.

Related superspy-vs-the-Bomb efforts include Mario Bava's *Dr. Goldfoot and the Girl Bombs* (1966), in which Vincent Price unleashes sexy robots with thermo-nuclear navels on unwary heads of state; Phil Karlson's *The Silencers* (1966), in which Dean Martin's Matt Helm prevents Victor Buono from sabotaging American atomic missiles and the villain's HQ ends up as ground zero; Michel Boisrond's *A Tout coeur à Tokyo pour O.S.S. 117* (1966, *Terror in the Sky*), with Frédéric Stafford as 'le Bond Français' thwarting a *Thunderball* rip-off plot; John Gilling's *Where the Bullets Fly* (1966), in which the second best secret agent in the world tracks down an atom-powered plane; Ferdinando Baldi's *Goldsnake 'Anonima Killers'* (1966), whose MacGuffin is 'a formula for pocket-sized A-bombs'; Lucio Fulci's *Come rubammo la bomba atomica* (1966), in which low comedians Franco and Ciccio steal an atom bomb; and Nick Nostro's *Superargo versus Diabolicus* (1966), with a wrestler taking on a mad scientist who wants to use his 'radioactive gold isotope' to rule the world. Antonio Isasi's slightly more credible *That Man in Istanbul* (1966) sees terrorists force an American physicist to build a bomb; Gordon Douglas's *In Like Flint* (1967), has feminists who threaten the world with orbiting nukes; and in Ray Austin's *The Return of the Man From UNCLE* (1983), THRUSH becomes a nuclear power. Sometimes, superhuman effort is required to see off the threat — in Richard Donner's *Superman* (1978), Superman (Christopher Reeve) foils Lex Luthor (Gene Hackman) and his plot to destroy California with cruise missiles, thus making his desert holdings valuable beach front property; more briskly, in Richard Lester's *Superman II* (1980), he defeats terrorists who have planted a bomb in the Eiffel Tower.

With the thawing of the Cold War and the limited success of disarmament programmes, the nuclear terrorist film revived somewhat, entering into a perhaps more believable, more frightening phase. In Richard Brooks's *Wrong is Right* (1982, *The Man With the Deadly Lens*), our old friend Sean Connery finds out that an international troublemaker is offering a pair of black market atom bombs to the highest bidder, suggest-

Above:
Wrong is
Right, *Leslie
Nielsen*

ing that there will be problems to come when surplus nuclear devices somehow pass from the control of superpower governments with a vested interest in maintaining an undevastated world into the hands of various grudge-holding terrorist groups or dictatorships. The cold war surplus warhead has become an essential in the armoury of many large-scale movie villains, as demonstrated by the resale of former Soviet weapons to Saddam Hussein, all-purpose Islamic Jihads, or a despairing Bosnian in David S. Jackson's *Death Train* (1993, *Detonator*), James Cameron's *True Lies* (1994), Rod Holcomb's *Royce* (1993), Stanley Tong's *Jingcha Gushi 4 Zhi Jiandan Renwu* (1996, *First Strike*) and Mimi Leder's *The Peacemaker* (1997). In Andrew Davis's *Under Siege* (1992) and John Woo's *Broken Arrow*, renegade American Cold Warriors (Tommy Lee Jones and John Travolta, respectively) steal American warheads as part of pleasingly old-fashioned extortion schemes, out for money rather than political gain. Frederic Forestier's *The Peacekeeper* (1997) has some novelty value, with villains who steal the 'football' (a case containing launch codes for the American nuclear missile fleet) and threaten to take out major cities unless President Roy Scheider commits suicide on television. Jim Wynorski and John Terlesky's *The Pandora Project* (1998) has a renegade American agent (Richard Tyson) stealing and deploying an absurd portable neutron bomb that is reusable and has an adjustable kill zone.

The overwhelming majority of nuclear terrorism movies wind up with a happy disarming of the device, in flagrant violation of the Chekhov dictum that a pistol shown to the audience in Act One must be fired by Act Three. The Bomb was once thought to be such a fearsome MacGuffin that the inevitable climax would come with our hero thwarting the villains, often by going through the tortuous process of defusing the device himself. A nineties frill, concomitant to an escalation of expectation in the audience, is that thrillers on this pattern often include actual detonations. *True Lies*, *The Peacekeeper*, *The Peacemaker*, *Broken Arrow* and *The Pandora Project* all have preliminary explosions that blow up underpopulated or non-American sites to illustrate an ultimate threat to somewhere the audience is expected to care about. *The Peacekeeper* vaporises Mount Rushmore to make a symbolic point before disgraced secret serviceman Dolph Lundgren saves the day, while *The Peacemaker* opens with a spectacular explosion in the Urals, that reminds us of Chernobyl and the traditional Russian clumsiness in handling nuclear devices, but saves all its suspense for a finale in which a bomb counts down in New York, and only macho military man George Clooney and unlikely physicist Nicole Kidman can save the city.

The Power

> Johnny had three truckloads of plutonium. He used three of them to light New York for one year. How much plutonium did Johnny have left? Answer: Four truckloads.
>
> **AEC poster promoting breeder reactors, quoted in *The Little Black Book of Atomic War***

Nuclear power is the acceptable face of atomic fission. In the fifties, many guilt-ridden scientists assuaged their consciences by getting out of the weapons business and dedicating themselves to the peaceful use of the atom. In this they were deluding themselves, for military and civilian applications of nuclear reactors are almost completely interdependent. *Edge of Darkness* is again the major text on this argument, with a secret underground plant reprocessing waste from power plants into weapons-grade material, and Jedbergh declaiming 'that's the trouble with plutonium... it's limited in its application'. Once seen as symbols of technological might, a monstrous force tamed for the benefit of humanity, nuclear power stations earned a very poor public image. There has never been a film about a smoothly run, safely operational nuclear power plant, just as there has never been a film about a smoothly run, safely operational commercial air flight. Disaster is always more cinematic.

Not inappropriately, the first major nuclear power anxiety film is Russian, Mikhail Romm's *Dveyat'dney Odnogo Goda* (1961, *Nine Days in One Year*). It deals with the plight of a physicist (Alexei Batalov) who is exposed to a dangerous level of radiation during an experiment. An American film, like *Silkwood* (1983), would have its hero turn against the institution which has poisoned him, and become an anti-nuke champion. Batalov accepts his fate as one of the risks of the job, and the central crisis of the movie has him torn between a safe, cosy, unproductive retirement or a dangerous, challenging, useful return to work. He chooses to go back to the cyclotron-lined bunkers of his research establishment, and suffers the inevitable second, probably fatal, dose of radiation. The ending leaves a glimmer of hope — an operation that has only been successful on dogs — but Romm refuses to condemn or condone Batalov's dedication to nuclear experimentation.

Devyat'dney Odnogo Goda is melancholy where later films are angry, but it was made before public concern over nuclear power plants that, in Stephen King's words, 'have apparently been put together from Aurora model kits by ten-year-olds with poor hand-eye co-ordination' eclipsed the bland reassurances of white-coated spokesmen who hawk atomic energy in much the same way that other white-coated spokesmen hawk headache pills. The movies have given us power plants employed by the Antichrist as an instrument of Armageddon (Alberto de Martino's *Holocaust 2000* [1977, *The Chosen*]), power plants that melt down because José Ferrer has carelessly forgotten to take precautions against an attack by killer bees (Irwin Allen's *The Swarm* [1978]), power plants that turn everyone in seeping distance into flesh-eating zombies (Umberto Lenzi's *Incubo sulla citta*

[1980, *Nightmare City/City of the Walking Dead*]) and power plants proposed to be developed on the Chatterley Estate but protested against by the sex-happy inhabitants (Alan Roberts's *Young Lady Chatterley II* [1984]). Television offers an atomic pile in the Batcave on *Batman* (1966-68) — mostly just another gadget, though Jill St John falls into the thing and is vaporised in the pilot; *The Outer Limits* has nuclear energy research facilities create dangerous beings of living radiation twice ('It Crawled Out of the Woodwork' [1963]; 'The Production and Decay of Strange Particles' [1964]); and the *Doom Watch* (1999) revival investigates a power plant with a miniature black hole at its heart.

The major power paranoia movie is James Bridges's *The China Syndrome*, which takes its title from the facetious term for what would theoretically happen if a nuclear reactor went into meltdown — the plutonium would eat through the world and turn up in China. The film is a tribute to Jane Fonda's aerobic radicalism, casting her as a decorative television commentator who, while shooting a filler on atomic energy, witnesses a minor mishap in the local power station. Digging deeper, she finds out that the glitch could easily have turned into a major mishap and wiped out most of the state. AEC genius Jack Lemmon is racked with doubts about the faceless zombies he is working for, and his own investigation into the workings of the plant reveals an officially tolerated relaxation of the safety procedures. Once the message that nuclear power stations are potentially more dangerous than nuclear weapons has been delivered, the film turns into a typical thriller in which the heroic newspersons try to bust the big story while the government's squad of anonymous hit men try to stop them. *The China Syndrome* is a hard-edged, liberal movie, but its commercial success doubtless had something to do with the fact that it happened to get released shortly after the Three Mile Island incident. Sooner or later, the film says, it will happen...

The concerns of *The China Syndrome* are reflected in William Hale's TV movie *Red Alert* (1977) and Ian Barry's *The Chain Reaction* (1979). In *Red Alert*, a disgruntled power plant employee (Jim Siedow, one of the maniacs from *The Texas Chain Saw Massacre* [1974]) sets a series of small bombs in the installation, and tinkers with the master computer so that safety precautions will ensure rather than prevent the disaster. In *The Chain Reaction*, another disgruntled scientist discovers that nuclear waste has per-

meated the water table and could blow up a large section of the Australian outback. Both films align themselves with *The China Syndrome* by stressing the government cover-up. There is a strong scene in *Red Alert* of an airport thronging with people who have heard rumours of an impending atomic catastrophe, and *The Chain Reaction* is primarily a chase thriller with the irradiated scientist taken in by a young couple who then have to evade the Establishment's decontamination-suited wipe-out squads.

In these films, word gets out and the disaster is averted, but only just. *Red Alert* has the best man vs machine sequence, as William Devane has to become a human spanner in the works, shutting off the auto-destruct mechanism by shoving his body between the contacts. Rainer Boldt's West German *Im Zeichen des Kreuzes* (1983, *Due to an Act of God*) is about a spill of nuclear waste being transported through the countryside, and follows a great many American paranoia movies by depicting the irradiated population herded behind barriers and left to die on their own. Mike Nichols's *Silkwood*, based on an actual case (inspiration also for Richard Michaels's TV movie *The Plutonium Incident* [1980]) while the other films are speculative, personalises the issue to zoom in on a single, individual victim. Karen Silkwood (Meryl Streep) discovers that the factory where she works, making plutonium rods for reactors, is as cavalier about elementary safety systems as the power stations in *The China Syndrome* and *The Chain Reaction* (all the films feature doctored safety record photographs). The happy-go-lucky blue collar girl becomes politicised, and dies in a mysterious 'one-car accident' before she can dish the dirt to the *New York Times*. 'We know how much plutonium can kill you,' announces a union official, 'but we don't know how little.'

Unstable Elements (1985), directed by Andy Metcalf and Paul Morrison, is half-documentary, featuring oral history interviews with mainly dissatisfied and disillusioned nuclear scientists and the affected people of Sellafield, where the Windscale reactor has been leaking deadly goo for years. It is also half-fiction, the story of a scientist (Donald Sumter) due to testify before the Sizewell B inquiry. His troubled relationship with his young daughter prefigures his eventual turn against the system which sponsors him. Establishing at the outset that 'nearly half of Britain's scientists work for the military', *Unstable Elements* contrasts the optimistic jingoism of fifties newsreels ('America has practical experience of operating the Bomb,' boasts a commentator, 'a fact which the men behind the Iron Curtain would do well to remember') with the questioning and self-doubt, not only of the innocent bystanders exposed to nuclear waste, but of the men inside the atomic energy industry.

The 1986 disaster at Chernobyl in what was then the Soviet Union, which spread radioactive material across a great swathe of Europe, one-upped Three-Mile Island, and triggered a wave of angrier, more extremist movies. Chernobyl itself has been under-represented in the movies, featuring obliquely in the Egyptian *Anbar el Mawi* (1988, *Death Ward*), in which a child is poisoned by irradiated, exported milk from the region, and the 1998 *Godzilla*, where Matthew Broderick is found poking around in the ruins looking for mutant insects. Another *Chain Reaction* (1996), directed by Andrew Davis, depicts the devastating explosion of an American research centre, which was supposed to be working on safe alternatives to nuclear power, but then concentrates on the familiar conspiracy business of Keanu Reeves running from pillar to post. It may be that the ultimate cultural legacy of Chernobyl is the Springfield nuclear power plant of *The Simpsons*. Owned by senile monster C. Montgomery Burns, this establishment employs the utterly incompetent Homer Simpson as safety officer, and specialises in unethical procedures that range from dumping radioactive waste in a local playground to suggesting a three-eyed mutant fish ('Blinky') be adopted as state animal.

The Atom
Strikes Back

There is a strain of cinema caught between the post-holocaust action movie and the serious, television-generated nuclear drama. In the eighties, David Cronenberg's *The Dead Zone*, Joseph Ruben's *Dreamscape* and James Cameron's *The Terminator* spearheaded the re-emergence of the nuclear tension movie. These films are less about the holocaust itself than the pressures upon those who could destroy or save the human race in an era which might seem to be the last days of man on Earth. Set in a modern world that encompasses Cronenberg's emotionally wintry Canadian wilderness and Cameron's punk *noir* city of neon and pain, the films conjure up the Apocalypse through fantastical plot devices: Christopher Walken's psychic vision of future President Martin Sheen pushing the button with a whispered 'hallelujah' in *The Dead Zone*, President Eddie Albert's *Dreamscape* nightmares about the radioactive ruins he might one day be forced to create, and time-traveller Michael Biehn's flash-forwards to the uptime holocaust situation in the devastated LA of *The Terminator*. The movies are thrillers, bristling with chases and conspiracies, but visions of nuclear doom permeate them, inflating the heroes' struggle with conventional villains into a desperate attempt to prevent the nightmares from coming true.

For the most part, the plots are resolved with guarded optimism. Walken's attempt to kill Sheen fails, but the 'dangerous turkey' loses his political future when a picture of him shielding himself from an assassin's bullets with a little boy appears on the cover of *Time*. Sheen commits suicide but Walken uses himself up, and the future, after their deaths, remains an undetermined 'dead zone'. In *Dreamscape*, psychic Dennis Quaid is projected into the President's nightmare in order to save him from the dream-hopping psycho hit man (David Patrick Kelly) assigned to prevent Albert from implementing his disarmament policies by paranoid CIA supremo Christopher Plummer. The good guys defeat the bad guys, but there is no guarantee that Plummer isn't right in thinking Albert's rash diplomatic initiative will increase the chances of nuclear devastation. *The Terminator*, the most successfully realised action thriller in the group, is also the bleakest in its attitude to holocaust. After a relentless pursuit, the loss of her ally/lover from the future and a hard-won victory over the lethal android (Arnold Schwarzenegger) sent from the twenty-first century to kill her, heroine Linda Hamilton, a fast food waitress pregnant with the child who will grow up to haul mankind off the radioactive scrapheap, heads into the desert. The far future may be saved, but the war between man and his ambitious machines is inevitable. A gas station attendant thinks there's a storm heading this way, and Hamilton resignedly agrees.

These films provide flashes of an avoidable holocaust to remind us of the danger. They lack the specific political angles of superficially similar seventies movies like Joseph M. Sargent's *Colossus: The Forbin Project*, which uses the same plot hook as *The Terminator* (sentient machines are given control of the world's nuclear arsenals and subjugate humanity) but thinks in terms of totalitarianism rather than extermination, and Robert Aldrich's *Twilight's Last Gleaming*, a nuclear blackmail film in which renegade General Burt Lancaster takes over a missile silo and threatens to start World War Three unless President Charles Durning tells the American people the truth about Vietnam. However, sixties, seventies and eighties films all agree in favouring an accidental Armageddon, triggered by a lone madman or malevolently malfunctioning machines, over the deliberate use of nuclear weapons in a shooting war. Even Michael Anderson's mini-series of Ray Bradbury's *The Martian Chronicles* (1980), in which a cataclysmic war writes Earth out of the plot, is vague about how it happens and leaves you to assume hubris is being punished rather than strategy pursued. All of this despite the fact that television films, from *The War Game* to *The Day After* and *Threads*, remind us that the possible first strike use of battlefield nuclear weapons is a policy of the NATO alliance.

John Badham's *WarGames* is less an atomic scare story than a cautionary lesson for a computer-literate society. In a surprise test, the orders come down through SAC to start the Big Hot One, and twenty-two per cent of the men refuse to turn the keys. 'Screw the procedure,' shouts one missile man, 'I want someone on the goddamn phone before I kill twenty million people!' Because of this shortfall, presidential adviser Dabney Coleman is allowed to 'take the men out of the loop' and install a computer, the War Operations Plan Response (WOPR). Meanwhile Matthew Broderick, high school underachiever and megabyte whizzkid, is trying to tap into a toy company in the hope of poaching their latest line in computer games. He accidentally plugs into the WOPR and decides to play a fun-sounding arcade game, Global Thermo-Nuclear War.

While the computer/missile link-ups in *Colossus* and *The Terminator* lead to disaster because megalomaniac machines attain a level of self-awareness that encourages them to execute self-aggrandising schemes of world conquest, the WOPR is dangerous because it is no more able than the adolescent time waster to distinguish between a game and reality. A happy ending is provided because the computer's dinosaur-loving inventor (John Wood) has instilled it with the capacity to learn from its mistakes. *WarGames* opens like *Dr. Strangelove*, then turns Disneyish as the WOPR and Broderick mature out of the games-playing phase to emerge as Responsible Adults. In the exciting climax, the computer tries to launch a real life retaliatory strike against an imagined Russian offensive, and the nervous teenager steps up to the terminal after all the NORAD experts have failed. Broderick teaches the WOPR to play noughts and crosses, a game which is pointless because there can be no winner, and the machine applies the lesson. After a lot of flashing lights and animated target maps, the WOPR comes to a conclusion — Global Thermo-Nuclear War is 'a curious game. The only winning move is not to play.'

WarGames is well-intentioned, but the punchline is misleading. The film's visual appeal depends entirely on NORAD hardware, and so it turns into a hymn to sleek consoles, giant light-up maps, flickering VDU screens, cavernous underground installations, blinking, beeping gadgets, and push button devices. Like Badham's *Blue Thunder* (1983) and *Short Circuit* (1986), the movie is informed by blinkered technophilia. Its conclusion is less radical than it seems, an argument not for disarmament but deterrence. If Broderick had chosen to play Limited Thermo-Nuclear War (ie one side has the missiles, but the other hasn't), then WOPR would logically and sensibly have concluded that the nuclear game is easily winnable and seen no objection to launching an attack on New Zealand or Liecht-

enstein. The film works best as an emotional rather than an intellectual argument, with Broderick and his chaste girlfriend Ally Sheedy ('I'm only seventeen years old, I don't want to die') persuading the crusty and disillusioned Wood ('nature knows when to give up') that it's all worth it. A similarly desperate optimism is inherent in the redeeming, indeed world saving, relationship of Hamilton and Biehn in *The Terminator*, a film whose fascination with the apparatus of destruction is much darker than Badham's simplistic sense of wonder. In Schwarzenegger's brutal, unstoppable automaton, the film presents a chilling picture of unreasonable, mechanised, impersonal violence.

WarGames is a mainstream Hollywood liberal effort — it even inspired a rip-off in Jonathan Kaplan's *Project X* (1987), where Matthew Broderick frees chimps who have been experimentally irradiated by the American air force — while *The Terminator* is gutsy, low budget and radical, but both tap successfully into the tensions of the eighties. Even more extreme is the contrast between John Milius's *Red Dawn* (1984), a slice of right-wing romanticism, and Alex Cox's *Repo Man* (1984), an exercise in politicised punk. Curiously, both films cast Harry Dean Stanton as an emblematic American, but Milius has him as a resolute, steadfast patriarch passing the torch of liberty on to his sons, while Cox depicts him as a seedy, sleazy car repossessor with a bleary eye for the fast buck. Milius unusually conceives a mostly non-nuclear World War Three, where the Russians take out the American silo chain with pinpoint missiles, but the conflict is mainly conventional. The shock arrival of Soviet paratroops in middle America and the subsequent Russianisation of the populace is less an Awful Warning of what complacency could lead to than a paranoid excuse for Milius's heroes to go into the wilderness, hunt deer and become cowboy guerrillas. A sympathetic Cuban commander (Ron O'Neal) laments that, in the past, he has always fought with the rebels rather than the oppressors. In *Red Dawn*, Milius gives an America cringing under criticism of its policies in Central America and the Middle East the chance to follow its natural inclination and side with the rebels again.

Obviously the idea was appealing at the time, for Joseph Zito has superman Chuck Norris follow it with a new version of *Invasion USA* (1985), with a smaller Soviet force taking a flame-thrower to the neighbourhood Christmas tree, and there was even a TV imitation, Donald Wrye's miniseries *Amerika* (1987). The survivalist side of Milius's war is taken up in David Hemmings' *Comes the Day* (1985), a *Panic in Year Zero!* for the eighties with Peter Fonda and his kids taking to the hills and blasting anyone who threatens their happy home. Throughout the early years of the Cold War, a trickle of Russian invasion novels had emerged from Britain (Constantine FitzGibbon's *When the Kissing Had to Stop* [1960]; D.G. Barron's *The Zilov Bombs* [1962]; and, later, Kingsley Amis's *Russian Hide and Seek* [1980]) and America (Theodora Dubois's *Solution T-25* [1951]; Robert Shafer's *The Conquered Place* [1954]; C.M. Kornbluth's *Not This August* [1955]; Samuel B. Southwell's *If All the Rebels Die* [1968]; Oliver Lange's *Vandenberg* [1971]). This was renewed as a minor flood in the eighties and nineties, with several competing series of pulp paperbacks (Jerry Ahern's *The Survivalist* [1981-93]; Ryder Stacy's *Doomsday Warrior* [1984-91]) along with no less patriotic one-offs, including Douglas C. Terman's *Free Flight* (1980), Pauline Glen Winslow's *I, Martha Adams* (1982), G.C. Edmonson and C.M. Kotlan's *The Takeover* (1984). It is probably not comforting that many of these fictions read a lot like Andrew MacDonald's *The Turner Diaries* (1978), the notorious Bible of America's neo-Nazi militias, in which heroic rebels are opposed to the domination of America by ethnic minorities and gun control advocates. Unsurprisingly, *Red Dawn* is a favourite film for the militia types who rate *The Turner Diaries* as their favourite book.

Repo Man is a less cut-and-dried tract than *Red Dawn*, blending punk with SF, and resurrecting the fear symbols of the fifties in a cool Californian milieu. A crazed nuclear scientist (Fox Harris) drives a battered '64 Chevrolet Malibu with a $20,000 price on its hood. In the trunk, he has some dead aliens who give off enough high intensity radiation to burn a traffic cop out of his shoes in true *Kiss Me Deadly* fashion. Otto (Emilio Estevez), a punk recruited by Harry Dean Stanton into the repo business, learns of the bounty on the Chevvy, and competes for the prize with mad scientists, Mohawk shoplifters, Hispanic Grand Theft Auto experts, hippie mystics and government clones. *Repo Man* is one of the few films to turn eighties nuclear anxieties into the stuff of genuine comedy, and as such was perhaps a precursor of a new how-to-live-with-the-Bomb movement. The strain of it-could-all-end nihilism displayed in Penelope Spheeris's *Suburbia* (1983), Tim Hunter's *River's Edge* (1986) and David Byrne's *True Stories* (1986), in which powerless Americans shrug at the prospect of oblivion and already cultivate an emotional deadness suitable for post-Apocalypse life, informs Otto's behaviour, but Cox is a punk with a streak of commitment and optimism.

Otto is unmoved by the weird philosophies he is subjected to, from Stanton's Repo Code ('the ordinary person avoids tense situations; Repo Man spends his life getting into tense situations') to the peace and love Gandalf-isms mouthed by the last of the flower children. Contemplating love, war, money and ambition with an offhand 'fuck that', Otto climbs into the glowing green radioactive car. As in Chris Windsor's *Big Meat Eater* (1980), the atomic car escapes the confines of everyday misery by taking to the skies. Left behind are the teenagers of John Duigan's Australian *One Night Stand* (1984) and Ray Boseley's *Smoke 'Em if You Got 'Em* (1989), and musician Anthony Edwards in Steve DeJarnatt's *Miracle Mile* (1988), who react to the imminent nuclear holocaust not with attempts to survive but by getting their romantic and partying affairs in order.

DeJarnatt, who also made *Cherry 2000*, rushes his plot into a few hours after Edwards, who has just met his ideal woman (Mare Winningham), answers a ringing pay-phone and is connected with a soldier in a silo who is trying to get the news out that war has started. As the story spreads and the citizens of Los Angeles panic, Edwards and Winningham commit to each other and, in a strangely positive climax, wind up sinking into the LaBrea tar pits to become fossils together.

In this era, schemes to survive came to seem increasingly loopy, to the extent that John Prescott's Australian *Bootleg* (1985) makes a band of self-styled survivalists, who are in training for a holocaust they obviously anticipate with glee, into villains as absurd as they are dangerous. John Milius and Rambo aside, the cinema has had little sympathy with survivalists, whose philosophy seems to date back to Wells's nasty little artilleryman in *The War of the Worlds*. Whether the comic stereotypes played by Bob Gunton in Mark Romanek's *Static* (1985) or Michael Gross in Ron Underwood's *Tremors* (1990), or the neo-fascists of Costa-Gavras's *Betrayed* (1988), survivalists have always been shown up as the sort of people more likely to cause World War Three than to preserve civilisation in its aftermath.

International angles on a post-nuke future were provided throughout the eighties, as the whole world got more worried. From France, Christian de Salonge's *Malevil* (1981), based on Robert Merle's 1972 novel, has a group of rural petty bourgeoisie holed up in a picturesque chateau at the time of the holocaust and grubbing along afterwards with a shrug and a sense of strained ennui that feels familiar from many a French film not set after a nuclear war. The most unsettling aspect is its concentration on the reformation of power, as fascist Jean-Louis Trintignant comes to the fore in the crisis and an ominously buzzing helicopter symbolises the return of a confining 'civilisation'. From the Soviet Union, Konstantin Lopushansky's *Pisma Myortvoi Chelovyeka* (1986, *Letters From a Dead Man*) is the grimmest possible vision of a functioning post-holocaust society, set in a dingily orange-lit and leaky underground complex where bureaucracy still rules.

There were also fairly serious-minded post-nuke dramas from the Philippines (Eligio Herrero's *Human Animals* [1983]), Wales (Tom Huckabee and Kent Smith's *Taking Tiger Mountain* [1983]), West Germany

(Rainer Erler's *Plutonium* [1978]; Volker Schlöndorff and Heinrich Böll's *Krieg und Frieden* [1983]), Poland (Piotr Szulkin's *O-Bi, O-Ba — Koniec Cywilizacji* [1985, *The End of Civilization*]) and Czechoslovakia (Milos Zàbransky's *Masseba* [1989]), with less respectful efforts from Belgium (Picha's dire cartoon *Le big bang* [1987]) and Poland (Julius Machulski's satire *Seksmisja* [1984, *Sex Mission*]). Meanwhile, states who felt themselves likely to be caught between the superpowers in any major shoot-out contributed edgy little paranoia pictures like the British *Defence of the Realm* and *The Whistle Blower* (1986) and Ola Solum's Norwegian *Orion's Belt* (1985), in which innocents blunder into the way of governments who are merely preparing for a possible war or covering up the ineptitude with which they handle their thermo-nuclear weapons, and are ruthlessly removed from the picture. Peter Watkins struck back from Sweden with *The Journey* (1987), a *fourteen-and-a-half-hour* documentary-drama film covering the arms race and resistance to it in ten countries.

Even before the end of the Cold War, there was a feeling that the nuclear holocaust was getting tired. Though the apocalypse movie was still thriving, the atomic angle was taking centre stage less often. Thom Eberhardt's *Night of the Comet* and Geoffrey Murphy's New Zealand-made *The Quiet Earth* (1985), from Craig Harrison's 1981 novel, revive the 'deserted world' sub-genre of *Target Earth* and *The Day of the Triffids*. These films rely on cosmic phenomena, with *Comet* varying the *Triffids* sky-at-night spectacle to powderise rather than blind most of humankind, while *The Quiet Earth* uses a mysterious global energy grid that malfunctions, wiping out all humankind except three New Zealanders who happen to be on the point of death at the precise moment of the effect (an idea borrowed from *Target Earth*). The business of these films is playing in the ruins, and as usual the same old mistakes are made again. The *Comet* girls, who see the end of the world as an excuse to go shopping, are forming middle-class families by the fade-out, while the survivors of *The Quiet Earth* enjoy an ironic distance from the old emotional tangles that crop up as soon as they meet in an emptied Auckland.

'There Ain't
No Sedalia!'

The most striking irony with regard to the depiction of the future in works of science fiction is that in my opinion the planet Earth does not have a future. Even the bleakest portrayals of postnuclear worlds have some people in them. By my lights (which are dim) even the most banged-up specimens of humans represent unwarranted optimism on the parts of film-makers. We'll be lucky if a dozen or so of us end up as mutants. I understand that filmmakers, attempting to depict the future, are forced to include people — without them the stories would be considerably duller. Maybe that's the truly unacceptable price of nuclear devastation: eternal nothingness equals eternal boredom for today's audiences... At the present rate, it seems clear to me that the human race will have succeeded in utterly annihilating itself, probably before the turn of the century. This, of course, will play hell with ticket sales.

Nicholas Meyer, *Omni's Screen Flights/Screen Fantasies*

Opposite:
The Day After

Perhaps the only adequate television treatment of nuclear war would be two hours of a totally blank screen in prime time. But who would sponsor it?

Paul Boyer, *By the Bomb's Early Light*

In the 1980s, during the last major spike of nuclear war paranoia to date, the cinema was increasingly irrelevant. Television had long since replaced the theatrical film as the principal source of effective fictions. As a mass medium, television combines the visual appeal of the movies in their hey-day, the immediacy of newspapers and the potential informational content of printed books. Serious-minded eighties successors to *On the Beach* and *Dr. Strangelove* came from the small screen.

The War Game was, of course, originally supposed to be a TV programme. British television also offered such nuclear-minded pieces as *The Burning Glass* (1956, 1960), J.B. Priestley's *Doomsday for Dyson* (1958), *Underground* (1958), the mock-documentary *Before the Sun Goes Down* (1959), Marghanita Laski's *The Offshore Island* (1959), *The Poisoned Earth* (1961), *Danger Zone* (1961), Nigel Kneale's unsettling pre-holocaust ghost story *The Road* (1963) and Aldous Huxley's *Ape and Essence* (1966). In America in 1956 and 1960, *Playhouse 90* mounted adaptations of Pat Frank's nuclear-related novels, the brink-of-doom *Forbidden Area* (1956) and the post-holocaust *Alas, Babylon* (1960), while Judith Merril's thoughtful *Shadow on the Hearth* (1953) became *Atomic Attack* (1954). *The Twilight Zone* offered 'Time Enough at Last' (1959), 'Elegy' (1960), 'Third From the Sun' (1960), 'The Shelter' (1961), 'Two' (1961) and 'The Old Man in the Cave' (1963) — grim, moody episodes, dependent on cheaply imaginative settings and twist endings (bibliophile Burgess Meredith, left alone in a library, breaks his glasses; a survivalist is so prepared for war that he is locked in his own fantasy of devastation) to express downbeat horror, but also unfussily direct in depicting the complete shattering of the American way of life ('Two' plays an Adam and Eve game with the last American and Russian soldier survivors, while 'The Old Man in the Cave' is about who or what governs the surviving communities — a computer or fascist soldier James Coburn). Effectively, this activity provided television footnotes to the cinema's full-scale holocausts. In the eighties, the box was the source of more lavish nuclear nightmares.

'We see them moving, moving, moving, towards a war they believe will never happen,' says Robert Joseph, author of the teleplay for *World War III* (1982), a two-part NBC mini-series, 'two civilised countries going through this *danse macabre*, this jingoism, never wanting war, saying it can't happen... then provoking each other to greater and greater excesses.' In its concentration on the diplomatic and military engagements that lead to a non-accidental nuclear exchange, *World War III* is unique. In the winter of 1987, Russia suffers famine because American President Rock Hudson (a glamourpuss running mate elevated to the Oval Office upon the death of the elected man) has imposed a grain embargo in retaliation for a

Soviet invasion of Poland. Unbeknown to humanitarian Premier Brian Keith, renegade KGB head Robert Prosky has sent a detachment of crack troops into Alaska with orders to mine the oil pipeline so he can blackmail the Americans into shipping Russia 'a million megatons of wheat.'

The first part of the movie suffers from director David Greene's concentration on the banal private lives of the main characters — Hudson flirts with political journalist Katherine Helmond, Keith tries to relate to his polo-necked teenage son and the depressed colonel (David Soul) in charge of the Arctic defence forces rekindles an old flame (Cathy Lee Crosby). However, once the politicians get on the hot lines the tension is remarkably sustained. The invaders' casual assassination of a family of innocent trappers and a lost National Guard unit, and the murderous activities of a Soviet double agent inside the Distant Early Warning (DEW) line are chilling examples of purposeful violence. The last minute bluff-calling session between Hudson and Prosky, after Keith has been murdered out of the plot, goes horribly wrong in a genuinely disturbing manner — with the missiles in the air, Prosky murmurs 'he thought I'd go that far... I wouldn't have.' While the film ends with a weak borrowing from *Fail Safe* — shots of ordinary people and happy children acting unaware while the roar of the approaching rockets gets louder on the soundtrack — the real climax is a bit of wishful thinking on the battlefield as Soul confronts his Soviet opposite number (Jeroen Krabbe) and they make a personal peace. Needless to say, the sneaky KGB man on Krabbe's team breaks up the idyll with a grenade and precipitates the final conflict.

London Weekend Television produced its own road to ruin, Andrew Marshall and David Renwick's six-part comedy series *Whoops! Apocalypse* (1982), in which the deposed Shah of Iran's clumsy brother, a religious fanatic White House aide and the Devil (John Cleese) bring about the end of the world by fooling around with the deadly Quark Bomb. The series flirts with the idea of turning a nuclear crisis into a comedic situation but suffers from a fatal anything-for-a-laugh approach that prevents it from achieving the concentrated terror-through-humour of *Dr. Strangelove.* However, Barry Morse as ex-actor President Johnny Cyclops ('anybody who tries to give me a lobotomy gets a piece of my mind') and Peter Jones as left-wing British Prime Minister Kevin Pork, who believes that he is secretly Superman, provide an unsettling mix of knockabout and satire.

Right:
Whoops!
Apocalypse,
Richard
Griffiths

The series finally cops out by attributing its war, not to the muddled political leaders of *World War III*, but to a vague conspiracy of unknown manipulators and a supernatural entity. The property was even less effective when filmed by Tom Bussmann in 1986, with Loretta Swit as President and Peter Cook as Prime Minister. By depicting world leaders and militarists as comic bungling idiots, *Whoops! Apocalypse* highlights what is in retrospect a truly chilling aspect of *Dr. Strangelove*, that all Kubrick's warmakers are frighteningly good at their jobs.

World War III and *Whoops! Apocalypse*, like Fred Barzyk's cable TV movie *Countdown to Looking Glass* (1984), deal with insiders — politicians, generals, diplomats, soldiers. Audiences could worry about the fact that their lives were in the hands of people no more competent or wise than they were, but it was difficult to feel personally involved. Ordinary people don't appear in the scenarios until it's too late. Nicholas Meyer's *The Day After*, a prestigious ABC production, takes exactly the opposite approach. 'The film is simply about you and me,' explained writer Edward Hume. 'It shows what would happen to ordinary Americans after a nuclear war.' In an apparently irrelevant scene near the beginning, a minor character talks about Chinese landscape painting, an art form designed expressly to make the spectator feel a part of what is being looked at. When *The Day After* was shown on British television, it was widely criticised for its adoption of soap opera stratagems in its depiction of people like us. Set in Lawrence, Kansas, geographically almost the centre of the USA, *The Day After* is a specifically American grass roots view of the nuclear holocaust, and hence off-putting for those unable to take American television seriously.

The film opens with an Airborne Command plane making a routine flight, allowing for a series of attractive aerial views under the credits. Accompanied by an Aaron Copeland-ish score, this is a vision of America the beautiful, unaware of mounting international tension. The most obviously soppy aspect of the pre-holocaust scenes of *The Day After* is the preoccupation with sex — Denise Dahlberg (Lori Lethin) tries to get out of the house to spend the night with her fiancé (Jeff East), a couple who live next to a silo make love while their children stare in bewilderment at crisis news bulletins. Dr Russell Oakes (Jason Robards) reminisces, 'My God, it's just like 1962 again... and we were in New York, in bed, just like this.' But, he says, 'it didn't happen then, and it's not gonna happen now... people are crazy, but not that crazy.' While the film, and the audience, is concentrating on soon-to-be-dead issues like Denise's troubled relationship with her grim father (John Cullum), Oakes's daughter's wish to move to Boston to be with her boyfriend and black airman McCoy's (William Allen Young) attempts to avoid extra duty at the base so he can be with his wife, news broadcasts and background chat suggest the deterioration of East/West relations. For *The Day After*, the holocaust is a giant *coitus interruptus*.

The higher-ups were keen to stress the apolitical message of the film. ABC president Brandon Stoddard said, 'I don't think audiences will be able to find a political statement. It does not say there should be less nuclear

bombs or more nuclear bombs. We do not deal in great detail with the causes.' And vice-president Stu Samuels stressed, 'we are not a news division. We
do not have the franchise to editorialise. This is not a docudrama because,
thank God, it didn't happen.' However, director Nicholas Meyer saw the
enterprise in a different light — 'ABC gave us millions of dollars to go on
prime time TV and call Ronald Reagan a liar.' Buried in the background are
several criticisms of current American nuclear deployment. '*The Day After*',
wrote Julian Petley in the *Monthly Film Bulletin*, 'demonstrates the dangers
of NATO's policy of "flexible response", which includes "first use" of nuclear
weapons... global nuclear war is sparked off by NATO's forces using battle-

field tactical weapons in Europe against a Warsaw Pact advance using conventional weapons, which leads rapidly to a strategic nuclear exchange. (The film originally included a fragment of a radio broadcast in which a Soviet official stated that it was the co-ordinated movement of Pershing 2 launchers which provoked the original attack, but because Pershing 2 deployment is a specific policy of the Reagan administration, this was cut.)'

After the war, the film's mood changes. For a start, no advertisers were willing to buy space after the Bomb drops, so on its first broadcasts *The Day After* proceeded through its post-holocaust section with no commercial breaks. The kissing has to stop — Oakes's wife and daughter, Denise's fiancé and McCoy's wife simply disappear and are barely mourned. They were in Kansas City, epicentre of the local missile attack. We see extras instantly turned into skeletons, firestorms raging in the cities, electro-magnetic pulse (EMP) wiping out all micro-electric circuits and crippling the power system. Then the characters try to cope. The Dahlbergs cower in their fruit cellar, fighting hysteria but following government instructions. McCoy joins a shabby column of indigents. Oakes tries to cope with the massive influx of wounded into the unlit, dirty halls of the University of Kansas campus hospital. And Joe Huxley (John Lithgow), a leftie academic, digs out an old valve radio, tuning in to whatever is left. The mood is summed up by Alison (Amy Madigan), an expectant mother explaining why she is overdue, 'if you were *in utero* and you had a choice in the matter, would you want to be born into a world like this?'

For a while, *The Day After* struggles to be optimistic. The university doctors may be under incredible stress, but they keep on with their job; the Dahlbergs humanely take in a stray pre-med student (Steve Guttenberg) and form a post-nuclear family; and McCoy joins up with a shuffling derelict whom he takes under his ragged blanket. The unwashed, unshaven and unwell survivors stagger through blasted, dead-cow-littered fields. The post-holocaust world looks a lot like Woodstock the day after the festival ended. Huxley tunes into the President, who proudly announces, 'there is at the present time a cease-fire in the Soviet Union... During this hour of sorrow, I wish to assure you that America has survived this terrible tribulation. There has been no surrender, no retreat from the principles of liberty and democracy for which the free world looks to us for leadership. We remain undaunted.'

As the politician speaks, the camera tracks through vistas of complete devastation, providing a silent 'what do you mean "we"?' to the uplifting speech. Despite official reassurances, chaos spreads throughout the state. 'You know what Einstein said about World War Three,' says Huxley. 'He said he didn't know how they were going to fight World War Three, but he knew how they'd fight World War Four... with sticks and stones.' Denise begins to menstruate uncontrollably during a pitiful church service held by the preacher who is barely recognisable as the man who was supposed to officiate at her wedding. Dahlberg attends a rowdy meeting where the National Emergency Reconstruction Administration hands out impractical advice, and is shot dead (and eaten?) by the sullen squatters who have moved onto his land. The handsome actors and pretty actresses, familiar from a hundred TV series, lose their blow-dried hair in ragged clumps and get their perfect faces covered with scabby keloids. Oakes abandons the hospital and staggers back to the pile of radioactive bricks where he used to live, hopelessly embracing the dying man he finds crouched in his former home.

The film ends with a quote from Orson Welles's Mercury Theatre of the Air version of *The War of the Worlds*, which is ironically mentioned earlier in the teleplay to counterpoint an unbelievable news bulletin (Meyer is the author of *The Night That Panicked America*, a 1975 TV movie about Welles's 1938 Hallowe'en hoax). The screen fades to black, and we hear Huxley's voice on the air, asking 'is anybody there... anybody at all?' And what's more, in place of the There Must Be a New Beginning end titles of many post-holocaust films, there is a horribly expressive *envoi*: 'The catastrophic events you have just witnessed are, in all likelihood, less severe than the destruction that would actually occur in the event of a full nuclear attack against the United States. It is hoped that the images of this film will inspire the nations of the Earth, their peoples and leaders, to find means to avert the fateful day.'

Threads, produced and directed by Mick Jackson from a teleplay by Barry Hines, was the BBC's answer to *The Day After*. In Britain, said Hines, 'a lot of people saw *The Day After*, but were able to dissociate from it because it portrayed an American experience.' The film has many parallels with Meyer's movie — the first half deals with the ordinary people of Sheffield, too wrapped up in their personal problems to care about a Russo-American war breaking out in the Middle East; and the second half shows

what kind of life survivors could expect to lead in the thirteen years following an all-out nuclear attack. *Threads* does its best to counter the misleading post-war scenarios of films like *On the Beach*. 'The apocalyptic
vision is very neat,' said Jackson in the *Radio Times*. 'An almost painless way
to go. There's nothing apocalyptic about nuclear war. If the evidence is correct, more people would survive than die. But survive into what? A living
hell decimated by disaster and disease and moral breakdown. In dramatic
terms we could have tied up *Threads* with a neat apocalyptic end, it resolves things for the audience. I think the way we've done it, with a slow
wind-down, leaves the audience more thoughtful.'

Jackson was highly critical of *The Day After*: 'A lot of potential viewers were put off... "the most shocking film juniors will ever watch", "make
sure you have the phone number of a counsellor beside you". Whilst at the
same time people who expected *Driller Killer* horror were disappointed,
and the people you wanted to watch switched over. I'm appalled by this
level of sensationalism. Nuclear war is not entertainment. But it is important to think about the unthinkable. People have become addicted to a diet
of horror and destruction, but at the same time most people's thinking
about nuclear war is truncated by the fact that they can't imagine what a
devastated nuclear wasteland would look like.' To British eyes, the human
drama of *Threads* seems more convincing, since it is rooted in the vein of
working class realism mined by *Saturday Night and Sunday Morning*
(1960), *A Kind of Loving* (1962) and Hines's *Kes* (1969), whereas *The Day
After* bears the stigma of American television's talking haircut characters
and an emotional crisis before every commercial break. The central character is Ruth (Karen Meagher), a young woman who finds herself unex-
pectedly pregnant. 'Don't worry,' she tells her boyfriend, 'it's not the end of
the world.' As in *The Day After*, marriage plans and imminent motherhood
are prominent before the war and irrelevant after.

Unlike *The Day After*, but similar to *The War Game*, *Threads* is a
drama/documentary. Whereas Meyer and Hume have informed characters
like Huxley to explain what EMP and rad levels are, and give useful lectures
('you can't burn wood that's been contaminated... it just puts radiation
back in the air'), Jackson and Hines punctuate their fiction with teletype
captions that editorialise ('the entire peacetime resources of the British
health service, even if they survived, would be unable to cope with the

effects of the single bomb that has hit Sheffield'), provide facts and statistics ('Likely epidemics: cholera, dysentery, typhoid') or add bleak ironies (in a direct reference to *The War Game*, one depressing tableau is underlined with the date 'Sunday, December 25th'). This approach counteracts the tendency to hysteria found in the American film, and establishes that the events are more important than individuals.

Opposite:
Threads,
Rita May,
David Brierley

Threads is far more blatant in its anti-government stance than any other nuclear war film, taking digs at media bias, civil defence inadequacy and official irresponsibility. A news account of the international crisis includes a sideswipe at the peace protesters who are trying to stave off World War Three. Ruth is seen at a 'Jobs not Bombs' demo, shakily aligning the film with CND and (at that time) Labour Party policy. We see county councillors in their bunker beneath the town hall, failing to keep the city running and finally dying of radiation poisoning. Meanwhile, the police are supplemented by the military and any other available uniform, but still can't handle the bombed-out population. Food stocks are controlled by what is left of central government and looters are summarily executed. One victim shouts, 'I'm not fucking going to be shot by a traffic warden!'

Though less expansive than *The Day After*, *Threads* is more convincing. The unfamiliarity of the actors (including many non-professionals) and the grubbiness of the ruins (there are no howlers like Jason Robards's pristine white shirt) make for a persuasive aftermath. The actual bombing is shown through telling details — melting milk bottles, fried cats, a couple trying to build a shelter in their council house. But, after the Bomb has dropped, *Threads* becomes bearable. While the build-up is terrifying, the post-holocaust scenes, depressing as they are, lack the overwhelming despair of the dying fall of *The Day After*. Perhaps too many films have shown the radioactive riots, the rat-eating survivors and the crucified cities. The images are in danger of losing their potency. *The Day After* and Lynne Littman's *Testament*, which are scientifically inaccurate but present involving characters, are more affecting than *Threads*.

Though relentlessly grim, *Threads* does try to imagine a survivor society. 'There would be some survivors of course,' said Hines. 'But many would have hideous, untreated injuries, and then there would be widespread radiation sickness and leukaemia. There would be a sort of Third World-cum-medieval peasant agriculture. There could be barter, a re-learning of old manual skills, a new language among kids because there wouldn't be the standardising influence of schools, newspapers and television. And I can't imagine loving parents. As soon as kids were big enough, they would have to work and fend for themselves. The generation which would follow us would be brutal, stunted both physically, emotionally...' '...and mentally,' added Jackson. 'There has been a rather optimistic belief maintained by officials in Europe and America that after the first few weeks survivors are going to come out of their shelter, gung-ho like the Seven Dwarfs with picks over their shoulders, and set off to work on the reconstruction of Britain. But even after the bombs on Hiroshima and Nagasaki, when the Allies poured in money to rebuild the cities, there was no psychological improvement for the survivors. So you can imagine what it would be like in a global nuclear war when there would be no outside forces to provide assistance. We must expect profound and prolonged psychological damage.'

Threads depicts a believable years-after world, in which Ruth's daughter grows up as a scavenger, but the invented argot and scarred geriatrics watching flickering videos of forgotten children's television take it all too near Mad Max's stretch of the wasteland. Hines and Jackson, therefore, have to come up with the most horrible, depressing ending imaginable. Ruth's grandchild is stillborn, and the frame freezes on the screaming face of the twelve year-old mother as she sees what her dead baby looks like. Few images in the atomic cinema are as shattering.

Though *Threads* was the BBC's major contribution to the 1980s nuclear debate, the corporation made many other programmes — including documentaries like *QED: A Guide to Armageddon* (1982) and *The Survivalists* (1982) — dealing with the momentarily hot issue, from the satirical *Plays for Tomorrow: The Nuclear Family* (1982), in which the long-term unemployed take holidays working on a missile submarine and a teenage girl is asked to press a button and kill a rabbit to determine her suitability to life in the navy, to a revival of the theme in the *Doctor Who* serial 'Warriors of the Deep' (1984), which cocks up a despairing script with a pantomime horse monster. Otherwise, the BBC mounted careful literary adaptations, including Anthony Garner's film of Robert O'Brien's 1974 novel *Z for Zachariah* (1984), and Stuart Burge's serial *The Old Men at the Zoo* (1982), from Angus Wilson's 1961 novel. *Z for Zachariah*, borrowing from *The Day the World Ended*, is a post-nuke pastoral set in a Welsh valley with its own climate, protected from unseen wastelands beyond. In an allegory that works in the novel but seems forced in the faithful dramatisation, sensible but glum surviving farm girl Pippa Hinchley has to cope with incipiently warlike scientist Anthony Andrews, who shows up in a decontamination suit and repays her nursing of him by trying to molest and enslave her.

Scripted by Troy Kennedy Martin, *The Old Men at the Zoo* is another allegory, a state-of-the-nation address that concentrates on the farcical workings of the National Zoo during the build-up to war with an Arab state, which has become a nuclear power thanks to weapons Britain has sold a prince whose English wife leaves him and takes the children. 'I must say I think the Foreign Office has made a frightful mess of it this time,' muses a civil servant as the missiles are incoming. In accordance with Home Office regulations, as soon as war is inevitable, 'the dangerous species' are destroyed. Four episodes of office politics, dotty zoologists too wrapped up in their specialities to pay attention and cynicism about the manipulative but blundering Lord Godmanchester (Robert Morley) set up the shattered London of the final hour, in which a fascist government takes power and a resistance movement adopts a stuffed Yeti as the symbol of rebellion. Well-meaning protagonist Simon Carter (Stuart Wilson) descends from struggling secretary of the zoo to a blindfolded and caged inmate demeaningly nick-named 'Tigger', abused by the reckless guard he has learned to mistrust. Like Wilson's novel, the serial has a sudden up-beat liberation at the climax, but Kennedy Martin — warming up for *Edge of Darkness*— suggests yet another administration is liable to make the same old mistakes.

> Some fundamental change happened to my relationship with the world after I had a baby. I think all mothers experience a feeling that boils down to 'we're not giving life in order to watch our children die'. Men seem to think about this issue in completely different terms than women, who simply insist, 'this simply cannot be allowed to happen', while men seem to get involved in debating the logistics of nuclear warfare.
>
> **Lynne Littman**

Motherhood, an important theme in *The Day After* and *Threads*, is central to Lynne Littman's *Testament*. Adapted from Carol Amen's story 'The Last Testament' (1980), Littman's film was made for the American Public Broadcasting Service and then bought by Paramount for theatrical distribution. Ironically, it is an intimate, televisual film that, unlike *The Day After* and *Threads*, never seems to be straining for widescreen effects. It is also less concerned with scientific actualities — sparing us the details of radiation poisoning except a few hairs in the sink — but it is the most emotionally and intellectually powerful of the three movies. The film never leaves the small town of Hamlin in northern California, where the nuclear war is at first seen only as an interruption of the television schedules. We don't even get the shadow of a mushroom cloud or glowing fall-out flakes. The central character is Carol Wetherby (Jane Alexander), wife of commuter Tom (William Devane) and mother of three. Tom works in San Francisco and vanishes in the surprise attack. Carol tries to hold her family together but invisible death comes to town and she soon realises there is no hope. Watching her formerly troublesome son Brad (Ross Harris) dashing about on a bicycle, doing errands and being a credit to the dying community, Carol reflects proudly on 'the man he's become', then corrects herself, 'the man he'll not live to be.' Later, she tries to explain to Mary (Roxana Zal), her barely adolescent daughter, what making love is like and the child comments 'not for me.' Soon, Carol is sewing Mary into a makeshift shroud.

Testament is simply about loss. Loss of family, of comfort, of company, of community, of country, of the world, of hope. Not all of its characters are dead by the fade-out, but the title makes it clear that human life is coming to an end. By staying away from the fiery holocaust and radioactive ruins, the film zeroes in unmercifully on the sheer emotional impact of such large-scale tragedy. Jane Alexander's Oscar-nominated performance combines extraordinary tact with anguished sensitivity; for perhaps the first time, a performer *has* created a convincing simulation of appropriate behaviour for a confrontation with the inconceivable.

The other narrow-focus nuclear war TV drama is Jimmy T. Murakami's *When the Wind Blows* (1986), an animated feature based on Raymond Briggs's 1982 graphic novel, which was backed by Britain's Channel 4 but given a theatrical release. Retired couple Jim and Hilda Bloggs live in a cottage in remote Sussex and do their best to muddle through after a nuclear incident, following the (often contradictory) advice given in (all-too-real) government pamphlets about building a shelter. Before scripting the story as a film, Briggs turned his book into a radio play, and the wordiness unfortunately carries over in the unending chatter of the Bloggses, caricatured simple folk voiced by Sir John Mills and Dame Peggy Ashcroft with many a malapropism. The images are extremely effective, however — the cottage is vividly realised through then-innovative three-dimensional animation and its destruction in the firestorm has the most impact of all the TV depictions of an actual nuclear war.

The film is unusual in assuming its audience knows more about nuclear war than its characters. While other dramas use intermediary characters or captions to fill in details, Briggs takes it for granted that we know all about fall-out, the inadequacies of civil defence, the symptoms of radiation poisoning and the concept of nuclear winter. To our horror, the Bloggses, whose idea of war is rooted in fantasies of World War Two, do everything fatally wrong: leaving the shelter too early, drinking contaminated rainwater, expecting the utilities to be switched back on. For them, World War Three means no milk deliveries, the flush toilet being out of action and all the curtains being burned. There is an edge of smugness, reinforced by the whining sentiments of David Bowie and Roger Waters on the soundtrack, suggesting that the more 'aware' elements of society are entitled to a few 'I told you sos' in the event of World War Three. In the end, the film seemed less useful than the other TV dramas because, unlike *The Day After*, *Threads* or *Testament,* for all their flaws, it was not made for people like Jim and Hilda but for radical yuppies who took their kids to CND marches and needed to convince them that nuclear weaponry was an uncomplicated, as opposed to a complex, Bad Thing.

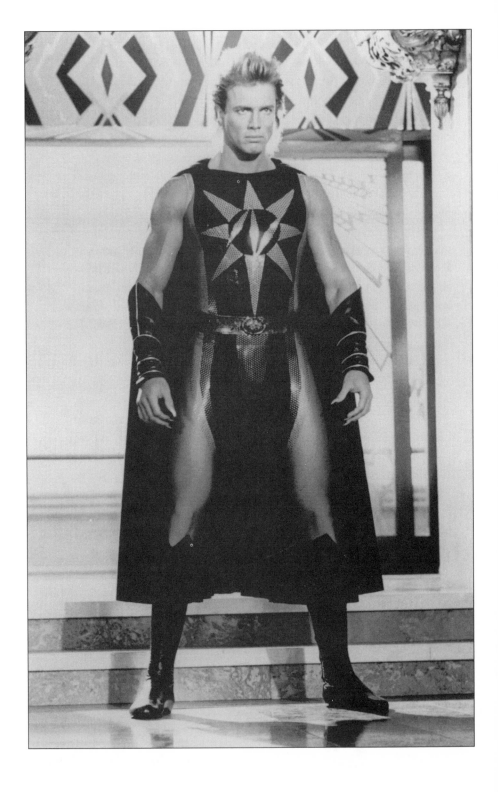

No Nukes?

Opposite:
Superman IV,
Mark Pillow

Miracle Mile, the last significant nuclear movie of the Cold War, is a turning point. As in so many apocalyptic visions, street-level characters are powerless to affect one way or another the course of world events decided by politicians and generals whom we never even see. In Steve DeJarnatt's film, there isn't even any public awareness of the international crisis that leads to war — which intrudes as rudely as the conflicts of Evelyn Waugh's novel *Vile Bodies* or Andrzej Zulawski's *Possession* (1982) and blots out the personal concerns of its ordinary characters. However, the effect of the countdown to doomsday on *Miracle Mile* is not only to stir people into a panicky and futile attempt to survive, but to force the hero and heroine to concentrate on what is really important to them, their love. The film isn't a counsel of despair, and it finds ultimate comfort in the persistence of life. Even as fossils, humanity is preserved.

In the 1980s, the spectre of nuclear holocaust seemed so vivid that everybody, from CND to Ronald Reagan, was looking for ways to avoid an end earlier doomsayers had accepted as inevitable. In the second half of the decade, a remarkable number of films from an amazing variety of sources seemed to apply themselves to the project of George Orr in *The Lathe of Heaven*, making the threat of nuclear apocalypse go away through sheer force of will. In Andrei Tarkovsky's fable *Offret* (1986, *The Sacrifice*), a Bergmanesque academic (Erland Josephson) seems to live through a world-ending war, while characters drift from window to window in a perfect interior as missiles pass overhead, but is able to pray it away on the condition that he make a supreme sacrifice, burning down his own home in order that the world and his son's life be restored. Further miracles occur in Vincent Ward's *The Navigator: A Medieval Odyssey* (1988), in which peasants from Cumbria in 1438 tunnel to the contemporary Antipodes to erect a cross on a spire to ward off the Black Death and tangle with a variety of potential world-killers from AIDS to a nuclear submarine.

There is a real sense that humanity needs to, or ought to, have out-grown its childish commitment to nuclear fission. The smug whale-saving twenty-fifth century time travellers of Leonard Nimoy's *Star Trek IV: The Voyage Home* (1986) are astounded at the twentieth century's reliance on unstable atomic power (all very well if your civilisation is based on non-exis-tent energy sources like dilithium crystals), and fail to realise that a shakily Russian-accented Chekov (Walter Koenig) turning up in an American naval dockyard and asking to see the 'nuclear wessels' will be treated with suspi-cion. The idea that we will look ridiculous to our descendants is hardly unprecedented in science fiction, but *Star Trek IV* is part of a franchise that at least insists we will have descendants. An aged Akira Kurosawa, always haunted by visions of the Apocalypse, contributed the crotchety *Konna Yume Wo Mita* (1990, *Dreams*), featuring Godzilla-influenced episodes in which Japan is blighted by nuclear reactor malfunction and (another) nuclear attack, and concludes, more or less, that none of this would have happened if young urban types hadn't insisted on indoor plumbing and electric lights. More literal but in the same spirit are the averted-at-the-last Biblical holo-causts of Graham Baker's *The Final Conflict* (1981), Ivan Reitman's

Ghostbusters (1984), Carl Schultz's *The Seventh Sign* (1988), Anthony Hickox's *Waxwork* (1988) and Gregory Widen's *The Prophecy* (1995).

The mood of these times, treated with some subtlety and conviction by novels like Marty Asher's *Shelter* (1986) and James Morrow's *This is the Way the World Ends* (1986), is especially well caught by films which seemed embarrassments at the time and have not worn well since. In Sidney J. Furie's *Superman IV: The Quest for Peace* (1987), from a script 'co-devised' by star Christopher Reeve, a schoolboy writes to the superhero asking him to do something about nuclear weapons, and the Man of Steel makes a rare intervention in international politics by scooping up the world's arsenals and depositing them into the sun. In a plot twist that goes back as far as Spencer Bennet's *Atom Man vs Superman*, Lex Luthor (Gene Hackman) retaliates by creating an atomic-powered evil Superman clone thuddingly named Nuclear Man (Mark Pillow), whose defeat signals the end of an era. Another grass-roots protest features in Mike Newell's *Amazing Grace and Chuck* (1987, *Silent Voice*) in which a trip to a nuclear silo prompts twelve year-old Chuck (Joshua Zuehlke) to a gesture as significant and symbolic as any Tarkovsky sacrifice, refusing to play Little League baseball until the world disarms. Other athletes join the protest and neither the kindly President (Gregory Peck) nor a scheming armaments millionaire (Lee Richardson) can dissuade Chuck, who even takes a vow of silence when his basketball player ally Amazing Grace (Alex English) is killed. A worldwide sports strike forces the USA and the Soviet Union to negotiate a complete programme of nuclear disarmament. In these films, pro-nuclear factions are depicted much like the wicked armaments manufacturers who appeared in post-World War One pacifists' efforts like *The Man Who Reclaimed His Head* (1934).

All attempts at achieving military superiority over the USSR are futile. The Soviet Union will never let that happen. It will never be caught defenceless by any threat, let there be no mistake about this in Washington. It is time they stopped devising one option after another in the search for the best ways of unleashing nuclear war in the hope of winning it. Engaging in this is not just irresponsible. It is insane.

Yuri Andropov, 1983, in *Cold War: For 45 Years the World Held Its Breath*

The Reagan administration's first serious attempt to break the dead-lock was to side-step the premise of Mutually Assured Destruction with the Strategic Defence Initiative, a science fictional programme of orbiting anti-nuclear laser weapons that, it has been argued by Michael Rogin, Reagan modelled on the MacGuffin of his forgotten vehicle *Murder in the Air* (1940). With its 'Star Wars' nickname poached from an un-amused George Lucas and precedents in far-fetched movies from *Diamonds Are Forever* (1971) to *Meteor*, the SDI was widely-criticised as unworkable and a money pit. Strieber and Kunetka's novel *Warday*, inspired by a 1960s panic over deployment of a *Russian* anti-ballistic missile system which threatened to upset the balance of terror, uses the deployment of such a high-tech shield as the trigger of World War Three, speculating on a fatal combination of arrogant American fantasies of a technological upper hand and paranoid Soviet visions of encirclement. In the cinema, the SDI was invariably represented as a sick joke: the psycho villain of John Murlowski's slasher movie *Return of the Family Man* (1989) is an ex-Star Wars boffin, while there are comically catastrophic malfunctions of satellite weaponry in John Landis's *Spies Like Us* (1985) and Paul Verhoeven's *Robo-Cop* (1986), and an unscrupulous armaments manufacturer drags out the process of developing unworkable SDI weaponry in Guy Hamilton's *Remo Williams: The Adventure Begins* (1985, *Remo: Unarmed and Dangerous*). SDI boosters like science fiction writers Larry Niven and Jerry Pournelle now like to claim that the programme was a confidence trick, designed to bring down 'the Evil Empire' by forcing the Soviet Union into bankrupting itself while trying to match American defence spending.

This change of attitudes to Armageddon is most obvious in *Terminator 2: Judgment Day* (1991), which revisits the most despairing of the eighties doomsday scenarios and teases out several strands of hope. The implacable killing machine (Arnold Schwarzenegger) is humanised into a father figure programmed only to wound, the scientist (Joe Morton) whose foolhardy commitment to pure research would lead to the creation of humanity's artificially intelligent mortal enemy is dissuaded from his programme, and — almost disappointingly — Linda Hamilton's dream of a world-engulfing holocaust is cancelled out by a vision of happy children as the course of history is altered by James Cameron's second-thoughts plotting. The sequel,

Above:
Terminator 2:
Judgment Day,
*Edward Furlong,
Arnold Schwarz-
enegger*

with its more spectacular effects and shape-changing metal villain (Robert Patrick), is more in love with technology than the original, for after all this is a film made possible by enormous research expenditure and the resources of major corporations. In rehabilitating Schwarzenegger as a cool, comical gadget, the film manages not only to love the Bomb but also morph it into a ploughshare. The fatalism of the first film is replaced by a hard-won hope, and tearaway kid John Connor (Edward Furlong) won't have to grow up to be a guerrilla leader. As in *Offret*, *Superman IV* and *Amazing Grace and Chuck*, a child has saved the world.

The Cold War could not be wound up, however, without one last revision. If *Terminator 2* merely addresses itself to its prequel, Jack Sholder's *By Dawn's Early Light* (1990), from William Prochnau's novel *Trinity's Child* (1983), is a return to and an argument with *Dr. Strangelove*. Soviet dissidents detonate a nuclear device and its origins are misinterpreted, prompting the Russians to launch a strike against the West. With Martin Landau's President and Rip Torn's General Fargo evoking memories of Peter Sellers and George C. Scott, the film unusually makes a hero of its Slim Pickens character, B-52 Captain Cassidy (Powers Boothe). The tensions of the plot are wound up in attempts to back-pedal out of World War Three, and the crisis is eventually averted because the chain of command contains human links like James Earl Jones, a survivor of *Dr. Strangelove*, and Rebecca DeMornay. The most hawkish character on view is a politician, the Secretary of the Interior (Darren McGavin) promoted to power when the President is thought dead ('you don't kill the enemy's leaders,' he is advised, 'somebody's got to be there to turn it off'), while all the soldiers in the film work desperately to avoid going to war. The message is 'let us not allow human error and the technology of the Cold War to destroy our hopes, and our world'. The TV film works hard to be as convincing in its depiction of a crisis resolved as earlier versions were of the brink of doom.

The end of the Cold War, which enabled a certain kind of nostalgia for the Cuban missile crisis in Joe Dante's *Matinee*, has not meant an unproblematic end to the threat of nuclear war. Indeed, it might be argued that the removal of the superpower face-off at the centre of the world war games map has made 'brushfire' nuclear conflicts — between Pakistan and India, Israel and whoever — more likely. Roman Polanski's *Frantic* (1988), which is about an unnamed Arab nation trying to obtain nuclear detonators on the black market, and Sidney J. Furie's *Iron Eagle II* (1988), in which American and Soviet jet pilots get together to destroy the weapons-making capabilities of another unnamed Middle East tyranny, are both examples of the 'let's keep the Doomsday Club exclusive' philosophy. James Cameron's *True Lies* and Mimi Leder's *The Peacemaker* are among many thrillers that address the worry of how states of the former Soviet Union might dispose of their Cold War surplus arsenals, with Aziz (*True Lies'* Art Malik) as the incarnation of the mid-nineties nightmare, a fanatical Islamic terrorist (from the 'Crimson Jihad') armed with Russian nuclear weapons.

Andy Davis's *The Package* (1989) is about a plot to destabilise a disarmament conference — presumably along the lines of the Reagan-Gorbachev summit dramatised for TV by Ronald Harwood as *Breakthrough at Reykjavik* (1987) — as renegade hawks on both sides of the Iron Curtain collaborate in an evil scheme to keep the Cold War going so they can maintain their hold on military power. Mick Jackson's TV series *A Very British Coup* (1988) hinges on a left-wing British Prime Minister (Ray McAnally) whose attempt at unilateral disarmament is thwarted by sinister Civil Servants and, finally, an American invasion. This theme, presented via fantastic conspiracies or more convincing crack-ups, recurs in a number of films in which suddenly redundant Cold Warriors decide to threaten the world one last time. In Larry Elikan's *Disaster at Silo Seven* (1988), the technology is at fault as a fuel leak in a Texas missile base nearly triggers a warhead ('I think the people round here are more frightened of the Titans than the Russians'), but most films on the theme assume that the real problem lies with the mindsets of men who have been trained to destroy the world and are on the point of redundancy. Jonathan Mostow's *Flight of Black Angel* (1991) offers William O'Leary as an air force pilot who finds a sense of mission in a conviction that God wants him to drop a nuclear weapon on Las Vegas, while John Woo's *Broken Arrow* has John Travolta as a more cynical rogue bomber jock who merely steals his payload for a spot of extortion.

In Tony Scott's *Crimson Tide* (1995), a reprise of *The Bedford Incident* in a submarine, Gene Hackman is the Queeg-like skipper who insists, while cut off from all communications, on preparing for a war no one else wants to wage. Divorced from the Cold War tensions of earlier nuclear sub movies, the film becomes a clash of wills between the megalomaniac Captain and sensitive junior Denzel Washington, in which the global consequences are given less dramatic weight than the sweaty one-on-one glowering match between the macho stars. Similar incidents are dramatised in Larry Peerce's *The Fifth Missile* (1986), with Robert Conrad cracking up during a war game and threatening to fire a hot shot, and David Drury's docudrama *Hostile Waters* (1997), with Soviet skipper Rutger Hauer manoeuvring to prevent an explosion that 'will make Chernobyl look like a backyard barbecue' after an underwater collision off the coast of Bermuda. The point is that all these missile-brandishers are hold-outs, and the true spirit of the age is represented by Captain Raimius (Sean Connery) in John McTiernan's *The Hunt for Red October* (1990), from the 1984 novel by Tom Clancy. Raimius is a Russian skipper who defies his own people and suspicious Americans to defect, symbolically gifting America with the latest Soviet sub.

> Perhaps the most common attitude which people hold toward nuclear war is that such a conflict would simply be the end of the world in some sense or other. The fascination of secular apocalyptic literature, much of it drawing on traditional reli-

gious imagery of Armageddon and the Last Judgement, has been widespread in our century since long before 1945. It is no surprise, then, that works depicting nuclear war should be written from the same perspective. Consider some titles: *Doomsday Eve, Doomsday Clock, Doomsday Wing, After Doomsday, The Day After Doomsday, The Last Day, The Last Days, On the Last Day, The Seventh Day, Deus Irae, Alas, Babylon, A Small Armageddon, The Dark Millennium.* The fact that in none of these works does the world end in any sense comparable to that depicted in the Book of Revelation underlines the symbolic nature of this fascination with the apocalyptic theme. Yet, since most of us in our modern secular culture no longer believe in the Last Judgement, and the solar nova which will one day engulf the Earth is too far distant to capture most people's imaginations, nuclear war is the nearest thing we have to Armageddon, if not to the end of the world proper.

Paul Brians, *Nuclear Holocausts: Atomic War in Fiction, 1895-1984*

If, in the late 1990s, the Cold War is over and the threat of all-out superpower nuclear conflict has receded, the culture is still in the grip of a millenarian fever understandably a few degrees hotter than that of the 1890s. If worlds devastated by nuclear war are limited to the likes of Danny Cannon's *Judge Dredd* (1995), based on a comic strip begun in 1977 in a publication whose very title suggested a sell-by date of *2000 AD*, then other apocalypses have stepped in to take their place. The nineties have offered futures blighted by genocidal plagues (Mick Garris's *The Stand*; Terry Gilliam's *Twelve Monkeys*), the melting of the polar ice caps (Kevin Reynolds's *Waterworld*), drought (Rachel Talalay's *Tank Girl*), massive alien invasion (Roland Emmerich's *Independence Day*; Tim Burton's *Mars Attacks!*; Paul Verhoeven's *Starship Troopers*), out-of-control street technology (Robert Longo's *Johnny Mnemonic* [1995]; Brett Leonard's *Virtuosity* [1995]; Kathryn Bigelow's *Strange Days* [1995]), weather-control devices that lock cities in instant ice ages (Joel Schumacher's *Batman & Robin*; Jeremiah Chechik's *The Avengers* [1998]), wars whipped up to boost the ratings of cable news shows (Roger Spottiswoode's *Tomorrow Never Dies*

[1997]), the imminent arrival of chunks of killer space rock like the one which wiped out the dinosaurs (Mimi Leder's *Deep Impact*; Michael Bay's *Armageddon*), and general ecological-economical collapse of the United States of America (*The Fire Next Time* [1993]; Kevin Costner's *The Postman*). As early as A.J. Prowse's negligible *Driving Force* (1989), it was possible to show a future America going to barbarous hell through a simple decline of the standard of living. Perhaps the most resonant of all film apocalypses is the VUE ('Violent Unknown Event') that has affected all the subjects of Peter Greenaway's *The Falls* (1980). At 182 minutes, Greenaway, with typical perversion, offers not an epic but a collation of ninety-two mini-biographies, all of people whose unlikely names have the prefix 'Fall' (Falla to Fallwaste, via Fallacie, Fallanx, Fallbute, etc), which allow for the sort of obsessive cross-referencing and intertwining that would come into its own with electronic publishing of novels like Geoff Ryman's *253* (1997). A great deal of information about a great many things is conveyed, if only in dissection diagrams and lists — as to the nature of the catastrophe, we are of course no wiser after three hours and change, which is presumably part of the point. By contrast, the causes of the societal (and narrative) collapse of Derek Jarman's *The Last of England* (1987), which extends its bomb site imagery to a lengthy sequence of a shivering naked man trying to eat a raw cauliflower, are all too apparent, though it represents the finale of an entropic fading for the United Kingdom that Jarman had been charting as early as the pre-Thatcher *Jubilee* (1978).

Wim Wenders's *Bis ans Ende der Welt* (1991, *Until the End of the World*) sets out to be the ultimate road movie, straggling on across four continents before anything like a plot comes along — a plot, indeed, something very like that of Douglas Trumbull's *Brainstorm* (1983), albeit with Max von Sydow hauled in to replay his role from Bertrand Tavernier's *Le Mort en direct* (1979, *Death Watch*). In 1999, with the Earth endangered by another out-of-control Star Wars satellite, various characters — enigmatic wanderer Solveig Dommartin (who co-wrote the original story with Wenders), mystery criminal William Hurt, Dommartin's ex-lover (Sam Neill), a private eye (Rudiger Vogler), some bank robbers, Hurt's parents (Jeanne Moreau, von Sydow) — traipse from Venice to France to Berlin to Lisbon to Tokyo to San Francisco to the Australian outback, revolving around each other and such MacGuffins as stolen money, various prices on Hurt's head, sundered relationships, computerised person-trackers and, finally, a camera device invented by von Sydow which can help the blind see and also transmit images from one brain to another. This invention has driven von Sydow into retreat, since he has a paranoia movie fear of American government intervention: 'it can take visual information straight from the brain. Once they can do that, they can suck out your dreams and look at them like television.' Hurt, gradually going blind, comes to depend on von Sydow's device which, when the explosion of the satellite convinces him the world has ended, opens the way into Aboriginal dream worlds. Wenders builds the film on references to his earlier works ('Weren't you the angel in Lisbon?'), which sometimes come close to self-plagiarism. His grab-bag of ideas are not drawn together by the arbitrary device of the coming of the Millennium or half-hearted attempts to mimic the generic forms of the international conspiracy thriller or the apocalyptic science fiction film. In its international version, it is stuck with tin-ear narration from Sam Neill and scads of trendy music samplings, while an earnest

Left: Twelve Monkeys, *Bruce Willis*

group of excellent actors struggle to make something of amazingly thin characterisations. Nevertheless, it has a real agenda-setting feel, and its ideas have fed back into the mainstream, recurring in many subsequent stabs at millennial filmmaking, especially the segue from scientific and social concerns to mystic matters.

Twelve Monkeys, an expanded remake of Chris Marker's hallucinatory short *La Jetée,* is the Hollywood version of the kind of apocalypse imagined by visionaries like Greenaway, Jarman and Wenders, layering nineties fears of a genocidal supervirus into the calculated surrealism of a snow-wracked city where zoo animals have overtaken the streets. As in many earlier films, the end of the world has driven what is left of civilisation underground and turned everyone into caricatures of bureaucratic totalitarianism, with sneering civil servants treating shaven-headed convicts as experimental subjects in vast, clanking, Heath Robinson-style machines. Gilliam finds cause for hope in a redemptive last flare of love rather than Marker's actual escape in time, though the passion that springs up between reluctant time traveller Bruce Willis and contemporary theorist Madeleine Stowe is also, at least indirectly, as responsible as any other plot device for the spread of the bio-engineered plague. The final scene, as another time traveller sits next to plague-spreader David Morse on an aeroplane — presumably to contract an early strain of the disease which she can transport back to the future in her own body — affords a slim chance that an antidote can be developed and the wintry, wild surface world reclaimed.

Kevin Costner's *The Postman*, adapted from David Brin's 1985 novel, achieved the distinction of failing commercially on an even grander scale than *Tank Girl*, a would-be funky comic strip movie that has Lori Petty's sneer to recommend it but otherwise seems to be a remake of some early eighties Italian warrior of the wasteland epic with unworkable musical numbers and kangaroo mutant jokes thrown in. Costner was critically and commercially slaughtered for daring to take the fall and rise of America as seriously as he did the destruction of the Indian nations in *Dances With Wolves* (1990). Despite the not-inappropriate but embarrassingly pompous stiffness of Costner's persona as director and performer, the film is genuinely complex and thought-through, and even contains trace elements of irony, as Costner is forced to invent a resurgent United States (under the presidency of Richard Starkey) which then gradually coalesces around something as simple as a postal delivery service. Set in 2013, after a war and a plague and whatever other catastrophes were necessary, the film resets North America to a pre-union state of scattered communities at the mercy of roving survivalist armies. Not since *On the Beach* has anyone dared to take the end of the world as important enough for an epic motion picture (the more 'science fiction' elements of the book, like cyborg villains, are dropped) and this movie perhaps makes more sense compared with Westerns than other post-apocalypse adventures.

With remarkable thematic consistency, *The Postman* keeps returning to literacy, culture and communication in the opposition of the nameless hero (Costner), a Shakespearean actor who poses as a mailman and is forced to make the fantasy real, and General Bethlehem (Will Patton), a photocopier salesman who finds his survivalist philosophy in a self-help manual and does his personal best to prevent communication (cutting out tongues, burning books, destroying post offices). It's a truly loony movie, which mangles real-world ideologies to pass as a Hollywood picture (Patton is clued-in enough to the symbolism to be a flag-burner, while his real-life equivalents forget what the Stars and Stripes stand for and appropriate the flag as their own emblem), and Costner's would-be monolithic presence is as unhelpful here as in Lawrence Kasdan's *Wyatt Earp* (1994). But strokes of audacity, mostly grown out of its obsession with the popular culture of lost America, single it out from much play-it-safe cinema: Tom Petty's bizarre cameo as himself in the future, becoming mayor of a post-holocaust dam community; the stoning of a projectionist who has dared to thread up Roland Emmerich's *Universal Soldier* (1992) instead of Robert Wise's *The Sound of Music* (1965); a jarring, cheeky, thought-provoking cut from John Wayne leading the Cavalry in John Ford's *She Wore a Yellow Ribbon* (1949) to a line of horsemen reconquering the same Western landscapes.

Various forms of totalitarianism loom in near-future visions, represented by the apparatus of the surveillance industry (Wim Wenders's *The End of Violence* [1997]; Tony Scott's *Enemy of the State* [1998]), the cynical news-doctoring of the Clinton-Blair political era (Barry Levinson's *Wag the Dog* [1998]; Mike Nichols's *Primary Colors* [1998]) and the paranoid imposition of martial law (Edward Zwick's *The Siege* [1998]), while a few years down the line we can look forward to rule by exploitative television networks that reduce real life to a soap opera complete with commercial plugs (Peter Weir's *The Truman Show* [1998]) or a world of genetically engineered supermen where regular people are persecuted as second-class citizens (Andrew Niccol's *Gattaca* [1997]). Alongside all this activity, which notably hops around the *zeitgeist* by containing some of the biggest hits (*Independence Day*) and the biggest flops (*The Postman*) of the era, many smaller apocalypses localise the special effects destruction to those affected by dinosaurs (Steven Spielberg's *Jurassic Park*; Adam

Simon's *Carnosaur* [1993]), bombs (Jan De Bont's *Speed* [1994]; Stephen Hopkins's *Blown Away* [1994]), tornadoes (De Bont's *Twister* [1996]), volcanoes (Roger Donaldson's *Dante's Peak* [1997]; Mick Jackson's *Volcano* [1997]), a collapsing tunnel (Rob Cohen's *Daylight* [1997]), a forest fire (Dean Semler's *Firestorm* [1998]) or the D-Day landings (Spielberg's *Saving Private Ryan* [1998]). Though man's hubris plays a great part in the problems of most of these pictures, the general thrust of all these movies is to shift the responsibility away, as Peter Biskind noted of fifties pictures, onto nature run amok.

A persistent thread in apocalypse fictions, from the concerted animal attacks of Arthur Machen's 'The Terror: A Fantasy' (1917) through the massed avians of Alfred Hitchcock's *The Birds* (1963) and the black poison flowers of *Edge of Darkness* to the elements out of control in nineties disaster movies, is that if man causes too much trouble — by waging world wars, jumping naked into fountains or devising nuclear weapons — then the world will have to do something about him by unleashing a natural cleansing process that will simply wipe us all away. Perhaps related to this is the irrational millennialist panic best exemplified by Don McKellar's *Last Night* (1998), an odd drama influenced by *Miracle Mile*, in which a diverse group of characters familiar from Canadian art cinema — including David Cronenberg, Geneviève Bujold and Sarah Polley — are informed on New Year's Eve that the world will mysteriously end at the stroke of midnight on 31 December 1999, and they then variously rush about, coping with this knowledge.

In a way, this train of thought is even more pessimistic than the Cold War era certainty of atomic Armageddon, in that humanity is not only no longer capable of averting the end of the world but can't even claim to have brought it about. As the millennium looms, there have even been a few extinction-level threats from supernatural forces, like the Cthulhoid shadow that employs Gary Oldman in Luc Besson's *The Fifth Element* (1997) or the demon who reads the Book of Genesis backwards in an attempt to 'undo Creation' in Jamie Dixon's *ShadowBuilder* (1998). Michael Tolkin's *The Rapture* (1991) is one of the most classical film apocalypses, presenting at its finish a literal vision of the Biblical Judgement Day with prison bars falling as the last trump sounds and the Four Horsemen of the Apocalypse galloping over the landscape. In a highly unusual move, Tolkin uses the premise that all those fundamentalists were exactly right to question the Creator's right to wind up the experiment, suggesting His treatment of the desperately-seeking heroine (Mimi Rogers) in granting her faith and tribulations before letting everyone else into Heaven is at best incomprehensible and at worst utterly sadistic.

It is notable that among the perceived box-office losers of the late nineties wave of apocalypse movies are those which dare to imagine a credible end of civilisation (*The Postman*), be the most cynical about the American way of life (*Mars Attacks!*), confront a future that will be here by the time the film gets its second network television run (*Strange Days*) or even touch on a nuclear angle (*Godzilla*). The hits in the group imagine the most fantastical threats (an alien armada, meteorites, the Devil, genegineered velociraptors) and then have these paper tigers blown away by traditional American movie heroism and know-how. In *The Stand*, a militarily-engineered plague sends the world (or, as usual, at least America) literally to Hell, but the cleansing fire that wipes out Las Vegas and the Devil himself, preparing the way for the return of civilised values and the Stars and Stripes forever, comes from a left-over thermo-nuclear weapon set off apparently by the Hand of God. The jury-rigged atom bombs of both *Deep Impact* and *Armageddon* are also employed to *save* the world, and are thus tamed, domesticated and added to the usable arsenal of big, dirty, macho tools.

> During the week I drafted this column, there were two starkly contrasting news events. First, NASA revealed that it was hard at work devising procedures for informing the world about impending asteroid collisions — an activity that seems just as vital as drafting protocols for meetings with alien visitors... Second, India exploded three atomic bombs as part of an accelerated programme to build a nuclear arsenal, which inspired its neighbour Pakistan to announce its own plans for atomic weapons. So, for the first time in history, two nations which hate each other, share a common border, and have fought three wars will both be armed with nuclear weapons... A possible nuclear war worries me much more than the slim prospect of an asteroid hitting the Earth.
>
> **Gary Westfahl, 'The Sky is Appalling' (*InterZone*, August 1998)**

Nuclear weapons are still out there. In his article on the flurry of speculation about the possibilities of the Earth being struck by a giant meteorite, fuelled more by the publicity campaigns for a couple of giant movies than anything like scientific likeliness, Westfahl homes in on the way the immediately pre-millennial sense of doom shifts and changes according to whatever is fashionable, or the subject of a current major motion picture. The most likely causes of catastrophe are again too terrible to address.

Afterword

'Stay away from that lever, you'll blow us to atoms!' cautions Dr Pretorius (Ernest Thesiger) in a Chekhovian set-up line half-way through James Whale's *Bride of Frankenstein* (1935). Of course, in the finale, the Monster (Boris Karloff) disregards the warning, concludes 'we belong dead', and pulls the lever. The resulting explosion turns the watchtower-cum-laboratory where Pretorius and Frankenstein (Colin Clive) have been working into a pile of flaming rubble, and buries the Monster, the madder scientist and the new-born female creation (Elsa Lanchester) under it all — at least until Rowland V. Lee's *Son of Frankenstein* (1939). Why any laboratory, no matter how insane its master, should come equipped with such a lever is a question that cannot be answered logically, any more than the similar question of why the space ship Nostromo in Ridley Scott's *Alien* (1979), a glorified cargo freighter, should have an inbuilt self-destruct device. In real life, laboratories and ships are not built around bombs — though, as this study has demonstrated, human civilisation is, which is perhaps all the justification that the writers who incorporate such devices into their scripts really need for their convenient existence.

The only function served by the explosive triggers of *Bride of Frankenstein* and *Alien* is to set up a literal and metaphorical big bang of a climax. Even before the cinema, let alone the H-bomb, the cataclysmic finale was a staple of fiction: think of Poe's House of Usher (which is also America) tumbling into the tarn, or Lord Lytton's Pompeii (which is also Britain) ossifying under a rain of lava. While thinking about this book, I've found it impossible not to see even the smallest-scale last-reel conflagration as symbolic of some larger, more devastating inferno. Is it too much to think of the somewhat mushroom-shaped column of black smoke that rises from the furnaces of Xanadu as 'Rosebud' burns at the end of Orson Welles's *Citizen Kane* (1941) as an intimation of an American holocaust to come? It is certainly impossible to watch Cody Jarrett (James Cagney) pumping bullet after bullet into a giant gas holder at the climax of *White Heat* (1949), bowing out with an exultant 'made it, Ma, top of the world!', without thinking of Hiroshima.

Since Cody went up in flames, movie explosions have had to mushroom to retain their visual and aural impact: the multi-angle, overlapping-take, slow-motion destruction of a luxury desert house at the end of Michelangelo Antonioni's *Zabriskie Point* remains an unsurpassable, eroticised vision of the End of All Things, but there's also an undeniable, *ne plus ultra* effect to the burning of the film in the gate that shuts off Monte Hellman's *Two-Lane Blacktop* (1971). Those two triumphs of the apocalypse, visions parallel with the novels of J.G. Ballard and Kurt Vonnegut Jr, came from an era when art cinema was at the cutting edge, a phase which had its last flare of genius with the napalm-candle jungle vistas of Francis Ford Coppola's *Apocalypse Now* (1979), a work whose ambition is signalled by the name of its elusive central character, Walter E. Kurtz (Marlon Brando), half Joseph Conrad, half (Walter Elias) Disney. Already, with George Lucas's *Star Wars*, mainstream movies had gone beyond nihilism into a vacuum whereby an explosion that involves the deaths of millions and perhaps the destruction of an entire planet could take place on screen and remain utterly meaningless.

There are unforgettable explosions in eighties and nineties cinema — the flame curtains that rise up around Rambo (Sylvester Stallone) in George Pan Cosmatos's *Rambo: First Blood Part 2* (1985), the exploding plane that tosses Bruce Willis high in Renny Harlin's *Die Hard 2* (1990), the arson holocausts that pepper Ron Howard's *Backdraft* (1991), the destruction of an entire office block that opens Richard Donner's *Lethal Weapon 3* (1992), the Oklahoma City-style bombings of Rob Bowman's *The X Files* (1998) and Mark Pellington's *Arlington Road* (1998) — but they are stripped of metaphor, reduced to simple plot functions, rarely even given the dignity of serving as a given film's actual climax. Though movies like Jan De Bont's *Speed*, Michael Bay's *Armageddon* and Edward Zwick's *The Siege* are structured around minor explosions, their plots depend on the build-up to a true apocalypse which is averted through American heroism and screenwriters' logic. Action movies in the nineties use walls of flame as pretty backdrops, and one of the most pernicious clichés of the age — easily on a par with the suggestion in fifties films that ducking behind a rock a hundred yards from Ground Zero is protection enough from an A-bomb blast — is that all explosions can be outrun by Nicolas Cage or Tom Cruise pumping away in slow motion with carefully-controlled special effects or even CGI flames at their heels, or that certain he-men, most notably Bruce Willis and Arnold Schwarzenegger, can simply stroll out of an inferno with a touch of blacking on their cheeks and get on with beating the bad guys.

Fire has almost become devalued as a danger — the most successful disaster of the turn of this century is James Cameron's *Titanic* (1997), which uses water as its primal element and whips up its most upsetting moments in the cold, as life-jacketed survivors become a Sargasso of frozen corpses in the wake of the sinking. Others have retold the story of the *Titanic* as if it meant something, the end of 1912's social order, soon to be swept away by the First World War, but Cameron isn't really interested in addressing the past — his disaster is backdrop for a Hollywood love story, and while Roy Ward Baker's *A Night to Remember* (1958) is about how to die, Cameron is obsessed with the survivor type, yet again requiring a skilled hero to pass on his knowledge to a woman plucked apparently at random so that she can be the mother of the future. *Titanic* is an enormously impressive, enormously effective film, but it is equal parts historical trivia, theme park ride and B picture romance. After the first hour, Leonardo DiCaprio and Kate Winslet are on their own, as the director pours a million gallons of water onto his stars and slowly wrecks his lavishly detailed sets. The image of filmmaker as Trickster God of Destruction is common, most memorably perhaps in the person of Peter O'Toole in Richard Rush's *The Stunt Man* (1980), but it has never seemed more apt than now.

The simple fact is that stories need endings, and often the most satisfying ending is to wipe the board. A last-minute explosion need not mean anything more than that it's time to get your coat and go home, but film is a twentieth century art form and the twentieth century is — was, perhaps, by the time you read this — the era when the destruction not only of civilisation but of all life on Earth became not merely a fantastical, far-future inevitability but a Sword of Damocles hanging over the heads of every man, woman and child on the planet. Our culture is permeated with a sense of the possibility of imminent doom, and that infiltrates every movie made since 1945 and a great many from before that date. Every death on screen is the death of us all and every explosion is the end of the world.

And every end of the world is the end of cinema, something Nathanael West realised when imagining 'The Burning of Los Angeles' as a centrepiece of his 1939 story *The Day of the Locust* and which the Coen brothers evoked with the Hollywood hotel fire that teaches a life lesson at the finale of *Barton Fink* (1991). That the medium, and humanity, can survive so much fictional carnage suggests something about the indomitability of our spirits, or the callousness it has been necessary to cultivate in order to make it through the millennium.

> This is the way the world ends,
> Not with a bang, but a credits crawl, listing a thousand CGI technicians...
> or:
> ...what rough beast slouches towards Hollywood to be born?

The most profound ending the cinema has yet conceived of must be the regular sign-off of the Looney Tunes and Merrie Melodies Warner Brothers cartoons. After seven minutes of anarchic carnage, often featuring fizzing sticks of dynamite that fill the screen with a jagged primary colour blast and wreak untold havoc on Daffy Duck or Wile E. Coyote but leave them alive enough to blink in fury, the only possible ending has to be the stutter of Porky Pig, at once hesitant and rapid-fire, 'th-th-th-that's all, folks!'

Bibliography

Lisa Alther, *Kinflicks* (Chatto and Windus 1976)

Brian Ash, *The Visual Encyclopedia of Science Fiction* (Pan 1977)

Marc Ian Barasch, *The Little Black Book of Atomic War* (Angus & Robertson 1983)

John Baxter, *Science Fiction in the Cinema* (Zwemmer/Barnes 1970)

John Baxter, *Stanley Kubrick: A Biography* (HarperCollins 1997)

Cedric Belfrage, *The American Inquisition 1945-1960: A Profile of the 'McCarthy Era'* (Bobbs-Merrill 1973)

Michael Benson, *Vintage Science Fiction Films 1896-1949* (McFarland 1985)

Peter Biskind, *Seeing is Believing: How Hollywood Taught Us to Stop Worrying and Love the Fifties* (Pluto 1983)

Paul Boyer, *By the Bomb's Early Light: American Thought and Culture at the Dawn of the Atomic Age* (Pantheon Books 1985)

Paul Brians, *Nuclear Holocausts: Atomic War in Fiction 1895-1984* (Kent State University Press 1987)

Mick Broderick, *Nuclear Movies: A Critical Analysis and Filmography of International Feature-Length Films Dealing with Experimentation, Aliens, Terrorism, Holocaust and Other Disaster Scenarios 1914-1989* (Post-Modern Publishing 1988; revised McFarland 1991)

John Brosnan, *Future Tense: The Cinema of Science Fiction* (MacDonald & Jane's 1978; revised as *The Primal Screen*, Orbit 1991)

Kevin Brownlow, *The Parade's Gone By...* (Secker & Warburg 1968)

Mark C. Carnes (ed), *Past Imperfect: History According to the Movies* (Cassell 1995)

Tom Charity, *BFI Modern Classics: The Right Stuff* (BFI 1997)

Carlos Clarens, *An Illustrated History of the Horror Film* (Capricorn Books 1970)

I.F. Clarke, *Voices Prophesying War: Future Wars 1763-1984* (Oxford University Press 1966; revised as *Voices Prophesying War: Future Wars 1763-3749*, Oxford University Press 1992)

John Clute & Peter Nicholls (ed), *The Encyclopedia of Science Fiction* (Granada 1981; revised Orbit 1993)

Richard Combs (ed), *Robert Aldrich* (BFI 1978)

Martin Connors & Jim Craddock (ed), *VideoHound's Golden Movie Retriever 1998* (Visible Ink 1998)

Roger Corman, *How I Made a Hundred Movies in Hollywood and Never Lost a Dime* (Random House 1990)

Jonathan Lake Crane, *Terror and Everyday Life: Singular Moments in the History of the Horror Film* (Sage Publications 1994)

J. Philip DiFranco (ed), *The Movie World of Roger Corman* (Chelsea House 1979)

William K. Everson, *The Bad Guys* (Citadel Press 1964)

Alan Frank, *The Films of Roger Corman: 'Shooting My Way Out of Trouble'* (Batsford 1998)

Christopher Frayling, *BFI Film Classics: Things to Come* (BFI 1995)

Sean French, *BFI Modern Classics: The Terminator* (BFI 1996)

Otto Friedrich, *City of Nets: A Portrait of Hollywood in the 1940s* (Headline 1987)

Roger Fulton, *The Encyclopedia of TV Science Fiction* (Boxtree 1990; revised 1997)

Stuart Galbraith IV, *Japanese Science Fiction, Fantasy and Horror Films* (McFarland 1994)

Stuart Galbraith IV, *Monsters Are Attacking Tokyo!: The Incredible World of Japanese Fantasy Films* (Feral House 1998)

Joseph A. Gomez, *Peter Watkins* (Twayne 1979)

General Sir John Hackett & Others, *The Third World War: August 1985* (Sidgwick and Jackson 1978)
Phil Hardy, *Samuel Fuller* (Studio Vista 1970)
Phil Hardy (ed), *The Aurum Film Encyclopedia: Science Fiction* (Aurum Press 1995)
Robert Heinlein, *Farnham's Freehold* (Corgi 1967)
Margot A. Henriksen, *Dr. Strangelove's America* (University of California Press 1997)
David Howe & Stephen James Walker, *Doctor Who: The Television Companion* (BBC Books 1998)
Jeremy Isaacs & Taylor Downing, *Cold War: For 45 Years the World Held Its Breath* (Bantam Press 1998)
Mark Jancovich, *Rational Fears: American Horror in the 1950s* (Manchester University Press 1996)
David Kalat, *A Critical History and Filmography of Toho's Godzilla Series* (McFarland 1997)
Ephraim Katz, *The International Film Encyclopedia* (Macmillan 1980; revised 1994)
Stephen King, *Danse Macabre* (Macdonald 1981)
Andy Lane & Paul Simpson, *The Bond Files* (Virgin 1998)
Walt Lee, *Reference Guide to Fantastic Films* (Chelsea-Lee 1972-74)
Patrick Lucanio, *Them or Us: Archetypal Interpretations of Fifties Alien Invasion Films* (Indiana University Press 1987)
Norman & Jeanne Mackenzie, *The Time Traveller: The Life of H.G. Wells* (Weidenfeld & Nicolson 1973; revised The Hogarth Press 1987)
Peter Malone, *Nuclear Films* (Spectrum 1985)
Leonard Maltin (ed), *1998 Movie & Video Guide* (Penguin 1997)
William Manchester, *The Glory and the Dream: A Narrative History of America 1932-1972* (Little Brown 1974)
Gerald Mast & Marshall Cohen (ed), *Film Theory and Criticism* (Oxford University Press 1979)
Helen McCarthy, *The Anime Movie Guide* (Titan Books 1996)
Todd McCarthy & Charles Flynn (ed), *Kings of the Bs* (Dutton 1975)
Frank McConnell, *The Science Fiction of H.G. Wells* (Oxford University Press 1981)
Harry Medved, Michael Medved & Randy Dreyfuss, *The Fifty Worst Movies of All Time* (Angus & Robertson 1978)
Douglas T. Miller & Marion Nowak, *The Fifties: The Way We Really Were* (Doubleday 1977)
James Monaco, *How to Read a Film* (Oxford University Press 1977)
Alan Morton, *The Complete Directory to Science Fiction, Fantasy and Horror Television Series* (Other Worlds 1997)
Ed Naha, *The Films of Roger Corman: Brilliance on a Budget* (Arco 1982)
Kim Newman, *Nightmare Movies* (Proteus 1985; revised Bloomsbury 1988)
Kim Newman (ed), *The BFI Companion to Horror* (Cassell 1996)
John E. O'Connor & Martin A. Jackson, *American History/American Film: Interpreting the Hollywood Image* (Ungar 1980)
James Robert Parish & Michael R. Pitts, *The Great Spy Pictures* (Scarecrow 1976)
James Robert Parish & Michael R. Pitts, *The Great Science Fiction Pictures* (Scarecrow 1977)
Danny Peary, *Cult Movies* (Vermilion 1981)
Danny Peary, *Cult Movies 2* (Vermilion 1983)
Danny Peary (ed), *Omni's Screen Flights/Screen Fantasies* (Dolphin 1984)
Danny Peary, *Guide for the Film Fanatic* (Simon & Schuster 1986)
Danny Peary, *Cult Movies 3* (Fireside Books 1988)
Stephen Pendo, *Aviation in the Cinema* (Scarecrow 1985)

Mark Phillips & Frank Garcia, *Science Fiction Television Series* (McFarland 1996)

David Pirie, *A Heritage of Horror* (Gordon Fraser 1973)

Frederik Pohl & Frederik Pohl IV, *Science Fiction Studies in Film* (Ace 1981)

Thomas C. Renzi, *H.G. Wells: Six Scientific Romances Adapted For Film* (Scarecrow 1992)

Ray Richmond & Antonia Coffman, *The Simpsons: A Complete Guide to Our Favorite Family* (HarperCollins 1997)

Michael Rogin, *Ronald Reagan the Movie, and Other Episodes in Political Demonology* (University of California Press 1987)

Michael Rogin, *BFI Modern Classics: Independence Day* (BFI 1998)

Nora Sayre, *Running Time: The Films of the Cold War* (The Dial Press 1982)

David J. Schow & Jeffrey Frentzen, *The Outer Limits: The Official Companion* (Ace 1986)

Bryan Senn & John Johnson, *Fantastic Cinema Subject Guide* (McFarland 1992)

Jack G. Shaheen (ed), *Nuclear War Films* (Southern Illinois University Press 1978)

Alain Silver & Elizabeth Ward (ed), *Film Noir* (Secker & Warburg 1979)

David J. Skal, *Screams of Reason: Mad Science and Modern Culture* (Norton 1998)

Julian Smith, *Looking Away: Hollywood and Vietnam* (Scribner's 1975)

Vivian Carol Sobchack, *The Limits of Infinity: The American Science Fiction Film* (Barnes 1980)

Brian Stableford, *Scientific Romance in Britain 1890-1950* (Fourth Estate 1985)

Chris Steinbrunner & Burt Goldblatt, *Cinema of the Fantastic* (Saturday Review Press 1972)

Philip Strick, *Science Fiction Movies* (Octopus 1976)

A.W. Strickland & Forrest J Ackerman, *A Reference Guide to American Science Fiction Films* (Volume 1, TIS Publications 1981)

Lawrence H. Suid, *Guts and Glory: Great American War Movies* (Addison-Wesley 1978)

David Thomson, *A Biographical Fictionary of the Cinema* (Secker & Warburg 1980)

François Truffaut, *Hitchcock* (Secker & Warburg 1968)

George E. Turner & Michael H. Price, *Forgotten Horrors: Early Talkie Chillers From Poverty Row* (A.S. Barnes 1979)

Bill Warren, *Keep Watching the Skies! American Science Fiction Movies of the Fifties Volume 1: 1950-1957* (McFarland 1983)

Bill Warren, *Keep Watching the Skies! American Science Fiction Movies of the Fifties Volume 2: 1958-1962* (McFarland 1986)

Peter Watkins, *The War Game* (Andre Deutsch 1967)

Thomas Weisser & Yuko Mihara Weisser, *Japanese Cinema: The Essential Handbook* (Vital Books 1996)

Michael Weldon, *The Psychotronic Encyclopedia of Film* (Ballantine 1983)

Michael Weldon, *The Psychotronic Video Guide* (St Martin's Griffin 1996)

H.G. Wells, *The World Set Free* (Corgi 1976)

H.G. Wells, *The Time Machine* (Pan 1978)

James White, *Star Surgeon* (Ballantine 1963)

David Will & Paul Willeman, *Roger Corman: The Millennic Vision* (Edinburgh Film Festival 1970)

Donald Willis, *Horror and Science Fiction Films: A Checklist* (Scarecrow 1972)

Donald Willis, *Horror and Science Fiction Films II* (Scarecrow 1982)

Donald Willis, *Horror and Science Fiction Films III* (Scarecrow 1984)

Donald Willis (ed), *Variety's Complete Science Fiction Reviews* (Garland 1985)

Donald Willis, *Horror and Science Fiction Films IV* (Scarecrow 1997)

Marc Scott Zicree, *The Twilight Zone Companion* (Bantam 1982)

Index